THE NEW BULL TERRIER

I made it!

Hannah McHanna 56

THE NEW

Bull Terrier

Compiled by

JOHN H. REMER, JR.

First Edition

HOWELL
BOOK HOUSE
New York

Macmillan General Reference
A Simon & Schuster Macmillan Company
1633 Broadway
New York, NY 10019-6785

Library of Congress Cataloging-in-Publication Data

The New bull terrier.

    1. Bull terrier.   I. Remer, John H.   II. Title.
SF429.B8N48   1989   636.7'55   88-34822
ISBN 0-87605-096-8

10   9   8   7   6   5   4

Printed in the United States of America

Contents

An Appreciation

IN preparing the update and revision of this book, I came to realize that much has been written in the last fifteen years by a number of breed experts which clearly expresses many thoughts about various aspects of the breed previously unpublished in book form. Thanks to the total cooperation of many of these authors, I have managed to compile what I consider to be a useful and informative compendium of ideas which will benefit the novice and expert alike. To call it complete is not appropriate. Most of the important information is included and that which is included is correct. I have not omitted anything purposely within the context of these pages, but I know some material is lacking. I have every confidence that this will be brought to my attention before the next update and can be included then.

My most sincere thanks goes to all of the many breeders around the world who supplied photographs, written materials, general concepts and personal insights. My wife, Mary, has been a great help and support especially in the area involving training and conditioning. Without generous contributions by Cynthia Morse, Alan Vargo, Winkie Mackay-Smith and Kate Less, the book would be sadly lacking in crucial information. Margaret Sweeten, Ralph Bowles and George Schreiber have lent me numerous photographs which help to complete the picture. All the breeders who so kindly shared their personal stories and photographs were unanimously generous with their time and their insights.

Bull Terriers have enriched my life significantly. I have learned many things about life and communication through the dogs. I hope that through these pages, all Bull Terriers will derive some small benefit as thanks for the enormous richness they have provided to me.

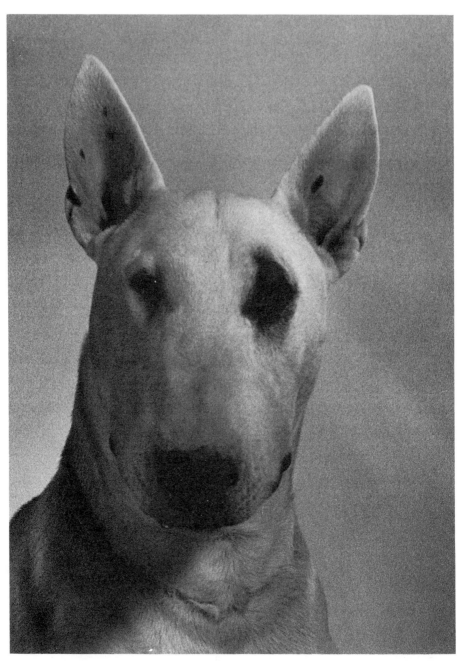

Special care given in the first year can provide a firm foundation for a happy, healthy life as shown by Ch. Tareyton of Woodland Hills.

THE NEW BULL TERRIER

Jumping for water sprayed from a hose amuses this young bitch on a hot afternoon.

1

Introduction to the Bull Terrier

(Originally written by W.E. Mackay-Smith and published by the Bull Terrier Club of Philadelphia. Now distributed by the Bull Terrier Club of America.)

THE character of the Bull Terrier is probably the most outstanding feature which draws prospective owners to the breed. A typical Bull Terrier is active, interested, playful and clownish. It is also extremely attached to its owners or family. These all sound like attributes of the perfect dog, however there are drawbacks to these characteristics which do not suit every prospective owner or every situation.

Bull Terrier Character

Bull Terriers are unique individuals. The combination of courage, intelligence, sensitivity . . . coupled with a peculiar sense of humor, sets the breed apart from all others. Life with a Bull Terrier is sometimes trying, often chaotic, but NEVER dull! They seem to take great pleasure in stirring up a little excitement wherever they go. You may not always find this trait amusing. If your ego demands a dog that will always be flattering to you,

11

you ought to look elsewhere! Deeply perceptive of human character, they invariably seek out the only dog-hater around to torment! Their antics will entertain you, sometimes even embarrass you, but you can always count on a Bull Terrier to make you smile when everything else in the world seems to be going wrong.

Your Bull Terrier will need firm, intelligent discipline if he is to mature into a well-mannered representative of his breed. If you are not confident in your ability to make corrections when needed, you probably should not get a Bull Terrier. They are energetic, outgoing dogs that can also be obnoxious when not trained properly. They have a stubborn streak a mile wide, but never mistake this for stupidity! A Bull Terrier will be quick to pick up on your weaknesses and take advantage if you don't establish yourself as the boss. Once he has you pegged as a pushover, the battle is lost. It is your duty to train the dog properly from puppyhood. The breeder provides you with a blank canvas with which you can either make a "work of art". . . or a DISASTER! It's up to you. If you haven't got the time or inclination to make an honest effort to raise the dog properly, please get a hamster or goldfish instead.

If you put time and effort into training your dog correctly, you will probably never want any other breed. Bull Terriers are addicting! However, before buying one, study the breed and other breeds as well. If, by comparison, you still feel the Bull Terrier is the breed for you, then you are probably made for each other!

Activity is a characteristic which is present in nearly every young Bull Terrier. The young Bull Terrier is in fact almost indistinguishable from a three-year-old child in a dog suit. All puppies are extremely "busy" and many Bull Terriers continue to be active and playful until well into middle age (5-6 years). Bull Terriers like to be *doing something*. For this reason they fit very well into active families where they receive a great deal of companionship and supervision. They also adapt well to quieter situations such as homes of elderly (but active) retired persons who have a great deal of time to spend with their dog. Bull Terriers do not do well in situations where they are expected to remain alone in the home or yard for long periods of time or where their physical activity is very restricted. In these situations, very much like a three-year-old child, Bull Terriers become bored and destructive. They will often chew and destroy, are difficult or impossible to housebreak, and develop incessant barking, tail chasing and peculiar personality quirks. It would make just as much sense to leave a little boy alone in an apartment for eight or nine hours as to do this with a Bull Terrier.

Bull Terriers become very attached to their owners and their families. This usually makes them very good natural guard dogs, but care must be

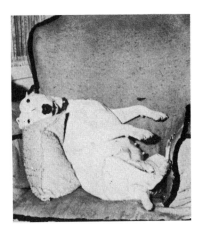

Bull Terriers like to make themselves
comfortable, and often are as relaxed
as a cat.

Between scenes during the filming of "Patton," star George C. Scott and featured
players Paul Stevens and Bill Hickman relax with Abraxas Aran, who portrayed
"Willie." Actually there were two dogs used for the filming. From photographs of the
real Willie, the filmmakers had to duplicate the General's "aide" twice because of
quarantine regulations. One Willie had to be found for location shooting in Spain, and
another later for filming in England.

Courtesy, Twentieth Century-Fox Film Corporation

Exhibiting the Bull Terrier's adaptability with other pets is Bodger, one of the stars of the movie *The Incredible Journey*. His companion is the Siamese cat, Tao. *Disney Productions*

Davy Crockett of Ernicor types out the news following his Best of Breed at Westminster 1956, at only nine months of age.

taken that they are not encouraged to become possessive and jealous. While this would seem a desirable attribute for someone who wants a dog to protect the family, it can be a nuisance if the dog does not distinguish between acceptable strangers and malevolent ones. Bull Terriers can also become involved in the presence of violent physical activity such as children's fist fights or exceptionally rough play activity where they see no reason not to join in, either to play roughly (which, with Bull Terriers, often includes nipping and knocking) or to guard the family against the physical assaults of outsiders.

Bull Terriers like to join family activity and for this reason require constant and firm discipline. They can be wonderful with children if handled with common sense, both by the adults and the children. Bull Terriers will tolerate a large range of children's behavior but they will not tolerate being teased and can be rough if constantly provoked. In their formative years, as do children, Bull Terriers require large amounts of supervision. They are tireless playmates and will chase balls, follow the children and watch their games for hours on end.

Many Bull Terriers can and do enjoy the company of other dogs, with certain exceptions. Male Bull Terriers who have not been altered do not, as a rule, get along indefinitely with other male dogs. There comes a time when one male must dominate, and there is inevitably an unpleasant fight after which the two must live entirely separately for life. A male and a female Bull Terrier can live together quite happily, and two females can often share the same house. Again, care must be taken that jealousies do not arise. It is not fair to expect an older Bull Terrier who has enjoyed the full attentions of the family to want to share with another dog. Again, this is very similar to a young child who suddenly finds himself confronted with a baby sibling—some care must be taken to assure the older one that the youngster belongs to the whole family.

Bull Terriers as a breed are quite fortunate in being generally free of disabling genetic diseases. A puppy should be checked for deafness, as this does occasionally occur and is difficult for the breeder to notice especially in a relatively young puppy. One problem common to many Bull Terriers is a propensity to skin allergies. Certain insect bites, such as fleas, and sometimes mosquitoes and mites, produce a generalized allergic response of hives, rash and itching. This can be controlled by keeping the dog free of contact with these insects, but this is definitely a consideration in climates or circumstances where exposure to these insects is inevitable.

Puppies up to a year of age are also susceptible to sudden and severe lameness. This is due to a combination of the weight and density of the muscle, rapid growth rate and the active character of the breed. Great leaps, sudden changes of direction or sudden stops at high speeds produce a great deal of strain on the immature joints and ligaments of this very muscular breed. The joints are simply not "set" enough to resist the torque applied by the weight and musculature of the young dog. For this reason young dogs should not be encouraged in this type of activity until they are fully mature.

Bull Terriers shed their coats twice a year. The loose hair can be removed by a daily rubdown with a special rubber glove. The hair does shed during these periods and the white hairs are more noticeable than the colored ones on furniture and clothes.

Old age brings on the usual battery of infirmities to which Bull Terriers are not immune. A Bull Terrier may well live an active and healthy life until he is eleven or twelve, which is about the normal life span of this breed.

Males and females vary only slightly in temperament. The unaltered males tend not to tolerate prolonged association with other unaltered males as previously noted. Undesirable tendencies produced by the sex drive can be remarkably reduced by spaying and neutering females as well as males. There can be more difference in the temperament of Bull Terrier families than in general between the sexes. Some families tend to be more possessive and less tolerant of other dogs and some families have a tendency to some shyness and apprehension with strangers and in strange places. Some families are very bright and innovative (which can be a mixed blessing) and some are less intellectual and more placid.

A Bull Terrier which is acquired with future breeding in mind should be selected for qualities of conformation and temperament which will produce top quality puppies. The responsibilities of breeding a litter of Bull Terriers must be assumed by the owner of the mother and it is very important that they be adhered to faithfully if the breed is to continue as temperamentally and physically sound as it is today.

The breeder of the litter should select a mate for his bitch which has excellent physical properties as well as a good temperament. The puppies must be placed in homes suitable to the special needs and requirements of this breed. This often means keeping puppies for months until suitable homes are found. Puppy buyers should be encouraged to have their animals assessed by an authority before they breed them and all which are not up to breeding quality should be kept as pets and not bred. Rather, they should be neutered. Breeders should also be prepared to either take dogs back which they have sold to homes which don't work out, or help the owners of their Bull Terriers place them in another suitable home.

Bull Terriers are unique in the spectrum of dogs. They have been carefully selected and bred largely by responsible and caring people who understand the legacy of their chosen breed. They can give tremendous joy or wreak havoc, depending on the time and effort spent by their owners to control and develop their special character.

16

2

The Bull Terrier
and His Times

by Ernest Eberhard

LIKE most breeds, the Bull Terrier has a sporting past which developed from the needs and fashions of days gone by. Badger and bull fighting were common amusements in the days when humans made a holiday of executions, when cruelty not only to animals but also to other human beings was the natural thing.

The Bull Terrier was developed from a variety of breeds into a dog with great virtues that were prostituted by the baser instincts of those who bred and owned him. His courage was proverbial, endurance and resistance to pain unbelievable, and intelligence almost uncanny. These virtues, which we admire in both humans and animals, made him a great fighter, so much so that he is remembered as a fighter rather than for his other sterling qualities.

There were two other attributes which the Bull Terrier possessed above all rivals, which not only added to his value as a fighting dog, but also remain today to make him an ideal family dog. One of these was the ability to solve new problems and to think for himself in case of emergency. Once in the pit, the dog that could not solve a new attack died. The other quality

17

was that under pain and excitement the Bull Terrier would not lose his head and bite his master when being separated from another dog in the pit. Added to these attributes is a craving for human companionship, a friendly love for all people, especially his own particular family. These qualities make him not only unusually reliable with children, but also a companion and protector who can be depended upon in any emergency.

The Bull Terrier of today has retained the great physical and mental qualities of his redoubtable ancestors, but he has largely lost the instinctive combativeness of early days. It is the other dog who is generally most willing to start a fight, but it is the Bull Terrier who is least willing to quit. I have owned Bull Terriers for over sixty years, yet I have never had one of my dogs seriously hurt another dog or kill a cat.

Birth of the Breed

It was in the early part of the nineteenth century that the breeding of the basic Bull Terrier was started. At that time, an improvement in Terriers generally was being sought and new types were being developed. For fighting purposes, a cross between the Bulldog and various types of Terriers proved to be outstanding. The cross generally retained the courage and dogged determination of the Bulldog but added the speed, agility, and quick thinking of the Terrier. On the whole, these old-time dogs were a blocky-headed, ill favored looking lot and were to be found in all colors including white. They came to be known as the Bull and Terrier.

As time went on the Terrier characteristics became more noticeable. Heads were sharpened and legs were lengthened. White as a breed color became more frequent and was much admired. When James Hinks, a dealer of Birmingham, England, introduced his pure white strain at a show in 1862, the colored dog fell into disrepute.

There is no doubt that we are indebted to James Hinks for the more elegant dog who graced the latter part of the century. Robert Leighton, in Cassel's *Book of the Dog,* 1907 edition, states:

These Birmingham dogs showed a refinement and grace, and an absence of the crooked legs and colored patches, which betrayed that Hinks had been using an outcross with a White English Terrier. . . . Many persons objected that with the introduction of new blood he had eliminated the pugnacity that had been one of the most valuable attributes of the breed. But the charge was not justified, and to prove that his strain had lost none of its cherished quality of belligerence, Hinks matched his forty pound bitch, Puss, against one of the old Bull faced type (a sixty pound bitch) for a five pound note and a case of champagne. The fight took place at Tuffers in Longacre and in half an hour Puss had killed her opponent. Her own injuries were so slight that she was able to appear the next morning at a dog show and take a prize for her good looks and condition.

We find that some illuminating comments on the birth of the Bull Terrier were published in the now extinct American magazine *Dogdom.* These were written by James Hinks, son of the James Hinks previously mentioned. Mr. Hinks wrote:

> The forbears of my father's dog presented a comical appearance with their short thick heads, blunt muzzles showing a certain amount of Bulldog layback, bow legs, thick-set bodies and overhanging lips, whilst in colour they varied between black and tan, brindle, red, fallow, etc. They were known as Bull and Terriers, owing to their being a cross between the Bull Dog and a Terrier, the latter being chiefly the large Black and Tan Terrier, and any Terrier which showed gameness and a nose for rats was used in the crossing. They were queer looking dogs, being neither Bull Dogs nor Terrier; however, they served the purpose they were bred for, i.e., fighting, ratting, badger and bull baiting. . . . The cross was ideal, as the strength of the Bull Dog was united with the quickness and intelligence of the Terrier.
>
> Around the end of the fifties a great change came about. My father, who had previously owned some of the gamest of the old stock with which he had been experimenting and crossing with the White English Terrier and Dalmatian, bred a strain of all white dogs, which he called Bull Terriers, by which name they became duly recognized.
>
> These dogs were refined and their Bull Dog appearance being still further bred out, they were longer and cleaner in head, stronger in foreface, free from lippiness and throatiness and necks were longer; they became more active; in short they became the old fighting dog civilized, with all his rough edges smoothed down without being softened; alert, active, plucky, muscular and a real gentleman. . . .
>
> The Bull Terrier, although classified as a Terrier, should not be judged on Terrier lines, but by the Bull Terrier Standard correctly interpreted. In comparing dogs of the past with those of the present, the latter have a more uniform type of head, but there is a tendency to get the dog too leggy, and they do not stand so firm on the ground as did the oldsters.

Carleton Hinks, grandson of the original James Hinks, adds a bit on how the breeding was done (*Annual,* Bull Terrier Club of England, 1955). He states, "After many trials and disappointments he took to very close breeding, father to daughter, mother to son, the cry being to save the puppy with the most white."

In those early days pedigrees were a most mixed up affair. It is impossible to tell exactly what breeds were mixed together to form the Bull Terrier. However, it is quite well established that the old-fashioned Bull Dog (a much leggier type than we have today), the White English Terrier, and the Dalmatian furnished the basic crosses used by Hinks, as testified to by his son. It is quite probable that the Greyhound, Spanish Pointer, and Foxhound were also used. We do know that even in the 1930s, a Bull

The Bull Terrier Ch. Tarquin, imported to the United States in 1880. With him is the Dalmatian "Captain."

Eng. Ch. Bloomsbury King, whelped 1898, cropped after winning his championship. Bred and owned by H. E. Monk. King's type was pretty much the ideal in the United States until the 1930s.

Terrier with a typical Hound ear would occasionally be whelped. There is some slight evidence that perhaps either the Borzoi or a smooth-coated Collie was used to help get length of head and a greater arc to the profile, for occasionally a Bull Terrier will be whelped whose head has a long, narrow muzzle that suggests a cross. (In England, crossbreds can be registered and in four generations are classed as purebreds.)

As an example of the difficulty of tracing any of the early pedigrees with any degree of accuracy, in the Kennel Club *Stud Book* for 1874 there are no less than a dozen Bull Terriers with the name of Hinks' famous sire, Madman.

In these very early days, classes were generally divided above or below 16 pounds and some of the early Standards go as low as five pounds. Sometime in the 1880s, a middle-weight class was established, so that the division became: under 20 lbs., 20 lbs. to 30 lbs., and over 30 lbs. Of this division, Vero Shaw wrote in *The Illustrated Book of the Dog* (1890):

> The institution of a class for middle-weights by the Committee of the Kennel Club has practically destroyed the old Bull Terrier. At the time the innovation was suggested we remonstrated most strongly with the perpetual president of the club—Mr. Shirley, himself a Bull Terrier breeder—against the scheme. We pointed out to him that if persisted in, the change would degrade the breed, by rendering it too easy to breed a good dog, as the main difficulties were to get first-rate heavy weights and first-rate little ones. . . . The appeal was ineffectual, the result being that now a good dog of 45 lbs. is indeed a *rara avis* and the 16 pounder is extinct.

Bull Terrier Clubs

Various attempts were made in England to start a Bull Terrier Club, but it was not until 1888 that efforts were successful and The Bull Terrier Club was formed. The Colored Bull Terrier Club was formed in 1937.

In the United States, the Bull Terrier Club of America made application for active membership in the American Kennel Club on July 19, 1895. The name was submitted and approved at the American Kennel Club meeting November 12, 1895, making it the forty-seventh Club to be admitted to active membership. (There were also a number of associate members of the AKC at that time.)

This date of 1895 conflicts with the erroneous date of 1897 generally used in the Club's records. Frank F. Dole was the first president of the Bull Terrier Club of America, J.P.D. Brereton the first secretary, and Arthur Thomson was the first delegate.

A dog became a champion during that era when he had won three prizes in a challenge class, and the *Gazette* listed all living champions in each issue. (At the time the Bull Terrier Club of America joined the American Kennel Club, 1895, there were twelve living Bull Terrier champions.) The challenge class was confined to dogs that had won four first prizes in the open class at recognized shows, one of which shows had to offer at least $1,750 in cash prizes.

Two of the top dogs of the time were Ch. Streatham Monarch and Ch. Carney. These two dogs met for the first time in Chicago at the four-day Mascoutah Kennel Club Show. The judge, Harvey L. Goodman, stated in his critique that "The open class for dogs over 30 lbs. was the sensation of the show, as it was here that Streatham Monarch and Carney met for the first time on this side of the water.. . . Ultimately I placed them equal first. In doing so I well recognized Monarch's grand head, strong, powerful jaw, well-set eye and expression, also his great bone and good feet. But aside from these points, Carney excels. He beat his rival in color of eye, cleanness of neck, compactness of body, coat and carriage of stern."

The English ban on cropping, 1895, set the breed back considerably. It came about as the result of a letter that King Edward VII wrote to the Kennel Club, as its patron, in which he strongly expressed his opinion that cropping must stop. It was equivalent to a royal command, and so cropping was stopped.

At first, any type of erect or semi-erect ear was permissible. Gradually, the present type ear developed, but even now the exact shape and placing of the ear on the head is by no means standardized. Some modern ears are small and narrow with little lobe, and are placed near the top of the head. Others are large and wide with ample lobe, and placed on the side of the head. Dogs with the latter type ear tend to be or to grow coarse and are not to be favored.

In the United States, no official action was taken against the cropped ear until late 1956, when the new Standard specified an erect ear. Cropped ears had been called for by the Standard until the early thirties, but the Standard was then changed to permit either a cropped or an uncropped ear.

When back in 1896 the American Kennel Club proposed a rule to prohibit cropping, Bull Terrier fanciers waxed so hot over the subject that the Bull Terrier Club of America was first suspended and later expelled from membership in the AKC. The Bull Terrier Club of America was dropped from the list of clubs in the May 18, 1897, issue of the *American Kennel Gazette.*

Apparently there was then a considerable reorganization of the Club because an application for reinstatement was received on July 20th and Arthur Thomson (the delegate of the exiled Club) was elected delegate and approved by the American Kennel Club in December 1897.

The AKC never did take any action against cropping. It was not until 1928 that an uncropped Bull Terrier—Blodwen of Woenwood—became a champion.

Regional Clubs

There was a sound reason for the growth of the regional clubs during the thirties, an influence which resulted in eighty Bull Terriers being benched at Westminster in 1930 and continual talk of a goal of one hundred. This was discussed by the late Enno Meyer, then treasurer of the Bull Terrier Club of Ohio, who wrote in the Bull Terrier column in the *American Kennel Gazette:*

> I think it is a good plan for each section of the country to develop the prevailing families in each district, and then breed to those that are similarly line-bred in other sections. This is what the Bull Terrier Club of Ohio has in mind. At a recent meeting, Willard Bitzer presiding, we compared pedigrees and agreed to exchange services and help one another in every way. In fact, you might say that we are pooling our dogs with the intention of producing something outstanding. It does not matter who may own the dog, we will all feel that we have had a part in its production and will all be as pleased as if each one was the fortunate owner.

This desire to progress as a breed, rather than as a collection of individuals each going his own way, brought about a desire to investigate and learn, as indicated in an article by Benno Stein in the *Gazette.* He states,

> All specialty clubs should seriously consider changing their Standards so as to prohibit ear cropping. But before this step is undertaken much educational work would have to be done. Such work cannot be done in two months. It would take several years perhaps.
>
> In September, 1931, the American Kennel Club ruling only prohibited the showing of dogs with cropped ears in the United States where any cropping laws were on the books, but did not change Standards of the breed affected.
>
> It should be remembered that in order to breed a certain type of ear, possibly it will be necessary to make other changes in the dog. For instance, after years of breeding, fanciers may find out that they can get a certain type of ear only by changing the whole head of the dog.
>
> To my knowledge very little research work of any kind has been made as to what kind of ears would be desired in the breeds affected by the proposed law. Take Great Danes and Doberman Pinschers as examples. It hardly seems possible that fanciers of these breeds would decide on ears carried erect, as it would take too many years before it would be possible to breed erect ears on these breeds. However, it is to be feared that all breeds where a standing ear is out of the question may decide on the next best thing in that direction; that is, a small ear. I said it is to be feared because the popular trend seems to be to breed full ears without seriously considering other qualifications.

23

The first Specialty show held by the Bull Terrier Club of America of which I have been able to find record was held in Philadelphia on November 26 and 27, 1908. There were fifty-six entries with eight absentees. The judge was W. Freeland Kendrick, later mayor of Philadelphia. Devil's Deputy, owned by Martin and Green, was the Winners' Dog and Merry Widow, same owners, was Winners' Bitch.

In 1926 came one of only two dog shows ever put on by the American Kennel Club itself—at the Philadelphia Sesqui-Centennial Exposition. This was a three-day show with 2,153 dogs in 2,899 entries; 1,767 dogs were actually benched.

The Exposition itself offered a solid gold medal for the best of each breed; on one side was a replica of the Liberty Bell and on the other side was a facsimile of the head of the Bull Terrier Ch. Queensbury Boswain. The AKC offered a solid gold medal for Winners' Dog and Winners' Bitch, and a sterling silver medal for the reserves. There were, of course, other notable prizes and over $20,000 was paid out in prize money. Even the English Kennel Club came across with an antique silver cup for Best in Show.

Alfred Delmont judged the Bull Terriers, 42 dogs with 59 entries. Winners' Dog and Best of Breed was Coolridge Prince (by Ch. Coolridge Grit of Blighty out of Coolridge Ladybird), owned by E. Koons and bred by Wyatt T. Mayer. Winners' Bitch was Newcoin Creation (by Ch. Newcoin Regret out of Newcoin Sally), owned by Frank P. Leach and bred by I. Smith. Prize money was $20 for first, $10 for second, and $5 for third in all classes. William L. Kendrick, active today as an all-rounder, offered a silver trophy for the Best American-bred bitch, champions barred, and there were other trophies and cash prizes. Indeed, it was quite a show.

The Terrier Group was judged by Alfred Delmont, Russell H. Johnson, Jr., and Theodore Offerman. The cash prizes in each Group were $50 for first, $30 for second, and $20 for third, plus other cash prizes and trophies. In the Terrier Group, Hon. W. Freeland Kendrick, mayor of Philadelphia and a prominent Bull Terrier breeder, offered a silver trophy for first.

The leadership of the Bull Terrier Club of England seems to have been most progressive and to have been working for the benefit of the breed as a whole. Two interesting pledges appeared in the application for membership in this club. For some time the club's constitution had forbidden the exhibiting of deaf dogs. Now it became a condition of membership that no deaf dog be bred from, that it not be exhibited, and that the applicant cooperate with the club in preventing others from so doing.

The other pledge, adopted later, was: "All members do solemnly pledge not to allow their photographs of Bull Terriers to be touched up by the photographers." However, we still see back lines and profiles, in particular, "improved."

Acceptance of the Colored

The "big battle" of this period, after Standards were set, was fought over the Colored Bull Terrier and especially over the Color Bred White. In England, the Coloreds had been making considerable progress. In 1919, Bing Boy, a brindle and white dog bred by R. S. Sievier, was the first to win a certificate. (He was by Ch. Oaksford Gladiator, out of a brindle and white bitch Stoat, pedigree unknown.) Immediately the award was challenged, but the Kennel Club upheld the judge, Major Count V. C. Hollender. In 1931 came the first Colored champion, Lady Winifred (Typical Jim—Princess Ida), bred by W. Dockerill. In 1935 came the first Colored male to win its championship, Boko's Brock (Boko's Double—Expectation) bred by Miss P. K. Timins. These first two champions were brindle and white.

The increasing success of the Coloreds caused a growing feeling on the part of the breeders of the White stock that these Colored dogs, if interbred with the Whites and their progeny then used for further breeding of White strains, would cause the White strain to degenerate by bringing in faults that it had taken years to reduce in the White strain. So fearful were the breeders of the Whites that the Bull Terrier Club put on its application for membership the following pledge, "They do also undertake not to breed from brindle-bred Whites as a foundation for a White strain, and breeders and owners of Colored Bull Terriers shall, upon selling 'brindle-bred Whites,' point out the disadvantage of having 'Colored blood' in a 'White strain.'" (After the Club agreed in 1950 to recognize the Colored dog, this was changed to: "They do undertake on selling a White dog who has a Colored ancestor within three generations that they shall reveal this circumstance to the purchaser.") The Bull Terrier Club in 1935 assumed a sort of limited jurisdiction over the Colored dogs.

In the United States, much the same pattern as developed in England followed the introduction of the Colored Variety in 1934. In that year, R. Wallace Mollison imported the first two Coloreds, Tismans Tango, a black bitch, and Brigadier of Blighty, a brindle male. These were bred together to give the first Colored litter bred in the United States, and a black-brindle from this litter was Ch. Darkfleet's Brandywine, bought by Herbert H. Stewart. Both these breeders were among the top experts of their time. Mr. Mollison had imported Int. Ch. Faultless of Blighty (later sold to the screen star Dolores Del Rio for a reported $5,000). Mr. Stewart had bred Ch. Buccaneer, three times Best of Breed at Westminster. These two men were active in securing recognition of the Colored variety by the American Kennel Club.

The Colored Variety immediately ran head on into a storm of criticism. Forecasts had come of how much the Colored dog was going to contribute to the welfare of the White dog and how it was going to cure all

Eng./Am. Ch. Rebel of Blighty

First Colored male champion, Boko's Brock (Boko's Double ex Expectation), finished in 1935. Bred by Miss P. K. Timins.

the ills of the breed: no longer would there be deafness, ticked coats, blue eyes or a host of other faults. These statements immediately antagonized the breeders of the White dogs, especially when they got their first look at the highly touted imported Colored dogs which on the whole left much to be desired. (I myself saw first generation Coloreds who were deaf, ticked, or blue-eyed.) The idea that these were the dogs which it was proposed to breed with the Whites to improve the Whites made no sense to the average American breeder, who felt that such assertions insulted his intelligence. It was probably the overselling of the Colored dogs more than anything else that so incensed American breeders against the Colored.

These Colored were first exhibited in 1936 at the Westminster Kennel Club in New York City, where they were shown in the same classes as the Whites. At the next Westminster show (1937), separate classes were provided. Few American breeders could see any virtue in the Coloreds that made their debut at this show.

The Bull Terrier Club of America immediately revised its Standard to disqualify any Bull Terrier with color behind the set-on of head, a device that had been tried in England with no success. Any judge who put up a Colored over a White was immediately boycotted on the basis that he had put up a disqualified dog. Indignation was great when Herbert H. Stewart put the Colored dog Ch. Wickselme's Brock's Double to Best of Breed at the 1939 Morris and Essex show. Although at that time separate classes were provided, the two colors met for Best of Breed.

In the meantime, the Color-bred White, Rebel of Blighty, in 1936 started a terrific storm that was to involve both sides of the Atlantic. Rebel became the first Color-bred White English champion.

So stirred up were the breeders of the White Variety in England that an "Extraordinary General Meeting" of the Bull Terrier Club was called to consider barring the Color-bred White from all competition for the Club's prizes, including the Regent Trophy for which Rebel had been invited to compete. The problem was left unsolved at this meeting and before the judging for the Regent Trophy brought about a further crisis, Rebel sailed for the United States, having been bought by L. Cabot Briggs.

In 1937 the Bull Terrier Club in England decided to bar all Club trophies to the Color-bred White, and this ban stood until 1950.

Also in 1937, the Bull Terrier Club inaugurated the *White Bred Stud Book* in order to protect the purity of the White strain. All dogs registered in this *Stud Book* had no Colored blood subsequent to the early matings of James Hinks and others of that day. When peace was finally signed in 1950 between the warring factions, the definition of a purebred White for the *White Bred Stud Book* was that laid down by the Kennel Club—three generations of White dogs in back of the dog to be registered.

When Rebel of Blighty came to the United States, he immediately became a storm center, just as he had been in England. The sea air was hardly out of his lungs before he appeared at the 1937 Westminster Kennel Club Show in New York, where he went Winners' Dog, Best of Winners, and then battled it out with the imported Pantigon of Enderly, an American champion, for top honors. Pantigon won—on his hind action, as the judge, T. W. Hogarth, later stated. I well remember the impression Rebel made on me, for he had by far the best expression I had ever seen—his slanting eyes and wicked look were something to be remembered in those days when a really good expression was a rarity.

American breeders felt, as had English breeders, that a top-flight Color-bred White like Rebel could cause untold harm to the breed by introducing the grave faults felt to be inherent at that time in the Colored strain. However, Mr. Briggs did not allow the dog to be used at stud with any Whites. At that stage of the development of the Colored, which needed to keep on tapping the White strain in order to breed true, this feeling probably had much basis in fact.

In 1939 the Canadian Kennel Club recognized the Colored Bull Terrier as a separate breed, which meant that litters from White and Colored parents could not be registered. This action of the Canadian Kennel Club fanned anew the hopes of the agitating members of the Bull Terrier Club of America, which immediately passed motions intended to bar registration and exhibition of Colored Bull Terriers and Color-bred Whites. The American Kennel Club gave no cooperation and so this part of the battle was quickly lost. Some years later Canada decided to handle the two varieties separately as was done in the United States, but still later combined them, thus following the lead of England.

In this same year, 1939, a clause was inserted in the Constitution of the Bull Terrier Club of America stating that "It shall be deemed prejudicial to the best interests of the Club if a member breeds a Colored and White Bull Terrier or the progeny of such a union." This provided grounds for the expulsion of any member conducting such a breeding.

Wallace Mollison, one of the two sponsors of the Colored Variety in the States, and his wife immediately resigned. Other resignations followed, for some of the most canny breeders had become interested in the Coloreds.

In England, prior to 1950, the Bull Terrier Club several times had found itself in an uncomfortable position due to its having banned Color-bred Whites from competition for club trophies. Color-bred Whites were qualifying for club trophies, and second-place dogs were being awarded them. The skill of some of the breeders of Coloreds had produced several outstanding Color-bred Whites. It came to be recognized that these breeders were going to outstrip the breeders of Whites as they were able to tap the fruits of White progress, whereas the breeders of Whites were unable to take advantage of the progress which the Coloreds were obviously making. The situation had changed decidedly from the thirties. Raymond Oppenheimer, the leading breeder of the day, announced that if he found a Color-bred White that would help the breed progress, he would have no hesitancy in breeding to it—and he later did exactly that with his famous, undefeated Ch. Ormandy Dancing Time.

In 1950 the hatchet was buried and the battle in England was over. Mr. Douglas Lindsay and Mrs. G. M. Adlam took the lead in a movement to put both the White and the Colored on an equal basis in all respects. All barriers on interbreeding were removed, and all club trophies became open to all. Where trophies had been restricted by their donors to the purebred White, it was voted to accept the Kennel Club definition of a purebred dog, e.g., one whose parents, grandparents and great-grandparents were all White (even though the great-grandparent might have Colored brothers or sisters).

This decision of the Bull Terrier Club was a milestone in the progress of the breed. Almost immediately there was an improvement in the quality of the White dogs, especially in their head qualities. Now the White breeders could tap such a great source of heads and bone as Ch. Romany Reliance.

Today there is hardly a really top dog whose excellence does not owe something to the qualities developed in the Colored strain which is part of his background. In fact, the February 1956 Open Show of the Bull Terrier Club was in itself a testimonial to the truth of the above statement, for nearly every dog or bitch competing for the Jugs and the Regent Trophy was either the child or the grandchild of Eng. Ch. Ormandy's Limpsfield Winston, the white brother of the red Eng. Ch. Romany Rhinegold.

In the United States, in 1942, the American Kennel Club very sensibly settled the "battle of the colors" by making the Colored a separate Variety. The Colored and White varieties then were only to compete with each other in the Terrier Group.

With no further controversies to keep animosities alive, feeling towards the Colored gradually died down. In 1948, on motion of Herbert H. Stewart, the Bull Terrier Club of America voted to recognize the Colored Variety and to provide classes for them at its 1949 Specialty Show held in New York City in conjunction with the Associated Terrier Club. Four Coloreds were benched at this first show, although nine had been entered.

For the first time since 1942, Colored and White competed together again at the 1953 Specialty Show of the Bull Terrier Club of America, when the Jug offered by the Bull Terrier Club of England was offered on a hastily

Ch. Ormandy Dancing Time

Eng./Am. Ch. Dulac Heathland's Commander, whelped 1954, Best in Show all-breeds the first time shown in America. Commander achieved 8 Bests in Show and in 1957 became the first Colored to win over the Whites at the Specialty. He won the Isis Vabo Trophy for 1957. Owned by Dr. E. S. Montgomery.

drawn motion which provided for the winning White and the winning Colored to compete for the Jug. The White, Am. Ch. Taverner of Tartary, imported and owned by Mrs. S. G. Yearsley, placed over the Colored, Mysterio Charmain (who later became a champion), bred and owned by Helen A. Boland.

In 1954, the American Kennel Club ruled that at any Specialty Show not held in conjunction with an all-breed show, the White and Colored varieties would have to meet for a Best of Breed. (At all-breed shows, the two varieties compete against each other only in the Terrier Group). Therefore at the Specialty Show held in conjunction with the Associated Terriers in February, 1957, the Colored and the White again competed against each other for a Best of Breed, under the new American Kennel Club ruling and the Colored dog, Int. Ch. Dulac Heathland's Commander, went to the top.

As may be inferred from the foregoing, the Colored variety had a rugged time of it in the United States, as it did in England. The first Colored champion whelped in the United States was Beltona Brindigal, a daughter of Boko's Beltona, who had been imported by W. J. McCortney while in whelp.

Ch. Slam of Blighty was imported by Mr. Stewart in the late thirties. After that, I recall no Colored importations of any importance until after 1950, when several good ones were brought over—Int. Ch. Romany Remarkable, by Percy R. Davis, and Int. Ch. Kentigern Baronswood Firefly, by Colonel James K. Marr, both of California; Ch. Baronswood Herald of Westmeath and Ch. Brendon Burntwood of Westmeath, by Mrs. Florence Gogarty; Ch. Abraxas Oldtrinity Spaniard and Ch. Romany Ritual (four times Best in Show, all breeds), by Dr. E. S. Montgomery. In 1956, Dr. Montgomery imported Eng. Ch. Dulac Heathland's Commander, who went Best in Show, all breeds, the first time shown in the States, and then again won the Terrier Group the next day.

Since 1967, the entire fancy has dramatically changed. There are now over 600 members of the Bull Terrier Club of America. Two specialty shows are held each year, one in conjunction with the Silverwood Trophy Competition and the other floating around the country. There are twenty regional clubs which also hold supported and specialty shows. So great has been the increase in showing both varieties of Bull Terriers, that I have included a list of only those dogs gaining their Recognition of Merit status at the end of the book.

With the increased popularity comes increased responsibility on the part of the Parent Club and of individual breeders. This is important due to legislation proposed throughout the United States against Pit Bulls. Unfortunately, due to public ignorance, the breed of Bull Terriers is lumped in with other Bull breeds. Thanks to the efforts of the American Dog Owners Association and the public relations committee, headed by Cynthia Morse, we are winning.

The most efficient way to get more information that is up to date on current affairs in the Bull Terrier world is to contact the American Kennel Club. They will provide the name of the current secretary of the local Bull Terrier club in your area who will provide you with all pertinent information. The Parent Club publishes a quarterly magazine, "BARKS," as well as an annual "Record." These are award-winning publications and have done more to advance information and goodwill than any other single element. The Board of the Bull Terrier Club of America has done a remarkable job over the years of maintaining high standards.

Official seal of the Bull Terrier Club of America.
The headstudy is of Ch. Queensbury Boswain.

32

3

How to Buy a Good
Bull Terrier Puppy

ANYTHING worth having is worth waiting for, especially when it concerns the next ten to fifteen years of your life! We are always amazed at the number of inquiries we get from people who simply must have a puppy, NOW! They approach the acquisition of a Bull Terrier puppy as they would the purchase of a new pair of shoes. Unlike shoes, a Bull Terrier is a living, feeling creature that will need a great deal of work to raise properly. Surely something that important merits more than a little consideration and time.

The prospective purchaser should make an effort to look at several litters and talk to a variety of breeders before selecting a puppy. Because Bull Terriers are an uncommon breed, litters may be few and far between. Proximity alone should not be a determining factor. By talking to different breeders, the newcomer can get an idea of the type and personality of dogs produced by various kennels. Where distance is prohibitive, the buyer should select a breeder in whom he has confidence . . . that means one who will answer all questions honestly and who will stand behind the dogs he sells. The buyer can then leave selection of a suitable puppy to the breeder and be assured that the breeder will try to pick the best puppy for the buyer's situation.

When talking to breeders, try to get an idea of how the puppies from their litters will mature. Don't be hesitant to ask direct questions. Consider the size and temperament of the parents. Bull Terriers can be a wonderfully diverse breed. Mature dogs can be quite petite (30 lbs.) or rather large (65-70 lbs.). Adult size should be taken into consideration, especially when the buyer's living area is limited (as in an apartment) or when there are small children or elderly persons who might be easily bowled over by a 65 lb. dog.

Bull Terriers also vary somewhat in temperament. Some lines are more mellow than others. Some tend to be aggressive towards other animals. Some are always busy, busy, busy! Most Bull Terriers are quite ornery when young and some never outgrow it. If your personality cannot cope with a dog that is always on the go, you might find this type of dog irritating. If you don't think you can keep up with a puppy, perhaps you should consider getting an adult instead. Breeders frequently have older dogs, usually retired breeding or show stock, that they would like to place in homes where they can get more individual attention than the breeder can provide. Too many prospective buyers refuse to consider anything over a year old, often forgetting that an older dog is probably already house-trained, it may be spayed or neutered, and has probably outgrown the bratty stage most puppies go through.

The Bull Terrier Club of America and most regional clubs operate placement services for dogs that, for reasons often beyond their control, are in need of new homes. Bull Terriers sometimes find themselves "out in the cold" when divorce, death or other problems disrupt the lives of their owners. Often these dogs are housed by volunteer club members until suitable homes can be found. Most of these dogs are perfectly lovable pets that can give many years of companionship and affection to the right owner. For more information about adopting a Bull Terrier through the placement program, contact the Bull Terrier Club of America or your nearest regional club.

The Big Step

Once you have found a puppy or adult that interests you, be sure that you understand all of the conditions of its purchase. Some breeders will require that all pet quality puppies, both male and female, be neutered by a specific age. Sometimes a breeder will sell an especially good puppy only with the understanding that it is to be shown and/or bred according to the provisions of the purchase contract. Any conditions must be understood clearly from the outset to avoid misunderstandings and bad feelings later on. Try to establish a good relationship with the breeder. If you have any doubts about any part of an agreement, don't hesitate to say so. Never go

34

along with an agreement that you do not feel you can fulfill. It is better to have everything out in the open. Once you and the breeder have come to an understanding, make sure everything is down on paper. This can eliminate many problems in the future.

Ask what guarantees come with the puppy. Most breeders will guarantee temperament and health for a specific period of time. Do not expect a breeder to guarantee show quality on a young puppy. No Bull Terrier breeder in his right mind would guarantee an immature puppy to be show quality. If you want to show your dog, look for an older puppy or young adult. Breeders can only give an "educated guess" as to the show potential of an immature animal. As far as health and temperament go, however, be wary of any breeder who seems reluctant to stand behind his stock. No reputable breeder harbors a "sell 'em and forget 'em" philosophy. A good breeder feels responsible for the puppies he has bred throughout their entire lives.

Within the first week after buying your puppy, take it to a veterinarian for a health check-up. If you find that the puppy has a serious defect, such as deafness, contact the breeder immediately. You are entitled to a refund or replacement. Minor defects, such as undershot bites, flat feet or cow-hocks are commonly found in what is termed "pet quality" puppies. Such superficial faults do not affect the pup's ability to be a happy, healthy pet, and therefore do not justify return of the puppy. Do not wait longer than a week to have your puppy vet-checked. This is for the protection of the breeder as much as it is for the buyer. You cannot neglect the puppy's diet, wormings and regular vaccinations and expect to get a refund or replacement when the puppy becomes ill! The breeder will sell you a healthy puppy. It is your responsibility to keep it that way!

In addition to a health guarantee, many breeders also guarantee temperament. This means that if your puppy is extremely shy or is aggressive toward people, you might be entitled to a refund or replacement. Most puppies will be a little unsure of themselves in strange surroundings, but should soon rally around. If the puppy just never seems to adjust normally, or is shy to the point of being a fear-biter, the puppy should be returned. You should be able to evaluate the pup's temperament fairly accurately within a week of purchase. Likewise, if the puppy snaps and snarls when you remove his food or toys, or if he resents any sort of discipline to the point of going after you, you should contact the breeder right away. Many pups will "test" you at some point in their adolescence. This is natural in puppies with a very dominant attitude. You must establish yourself as THE BOSS with no ifs, ands, or buts about it! If a puppy EVER growls or snaps at you in anything other than a playful manner, you must immediately seize him firmly by the scruff of the neck,

Berryborn Harvester, above as a 6- weeks puppy, and left as an adult, but before being shown.

Ch. Madame Pompadour of Ernicor, seen (at left) at 11 weeks, and (right) at six months of age.

shake him till his eyes rattle and scold him in your most businesslike voice. If he shows resentment by growling during this reprimand, you must be more forceful. A good slap is not out of line. We normally do not advocate striking animals, but a Bull Terrier is too strong and too powerful an animal to be allowed to display any sort of nasty behavior towards humans. A puppy who does not back down after a few such corrections may represent a real problem later . . . when he weighs 65 lbs. and is biting you or your kids! Consult the breeder right away!

Aggression toward other animals is not quite the same thing as aggression toward people. While a feisty dog may be a headache to own, he cannot be said to have a bad temperament, per se. You must remember that Bull Terriers are TERRIERS . . . members of a family of dogs bred for courage and fire. Your Bull Terrier may not be any more scrappy than the Wirehaired Fox Terrier or Scotty down the street, but you can bet that, because of his size and power, if he gets into trouble, it will be BIG trouble! For this reason, supervision of your Bull Terrier is mandatory, especially if he is inclined to be feisty. This desire to fight may be more or less evident in individual dogs. Some are real pacifists! However, scrappiness is simply a trait of the terrier breeds and should be taken into consideration before you buy a Bull Terrier. If you don't feel that you can live with a dog that might be inclined to scrap (or at least attempt to), then perhaps you should consider another breed. Even aggressive dogs can be taught to behave themselves, but may never be entirely trustworthy around other dogs. No dog should be permitted to become a total maniac, however. Early neutering or spaying can help mellow out many dogs and should be considered ESSENTIAL for any Bull Terrier kept strictly as a housepet.

At the time of purchase, the breeder will provide you with a copy of your dog's pedigree, health record and registration papers. Some breeders routinely complete registration of each individual puppy before it is sold, rather than give the buyer the blue slip (application for registration). If this is the case, it is possible that the registration process will not have been completed by the time you pick up your pup. If you are dealing with a reputable breeder, you should not worry . . . you will undoubtedly receive your pup's papers within a week or two. Some breeders register each puppy themselves to insure that it will be registered with their kennel name. You should not be concerned about this . . . it is his or her "trademark" and identifies that puppy as being from his line. If you buy a well-bred dog, you can be proud that it carries a good name! Aside from identification purposes, the registered name of a dog helps the breeder and others to associate your pup with a given litter. For example, some breeders will register all of the pups in a litter with similar names. If the kennel name, for instance, is "BARKLEIGH," then the puppies in the litter might have names like Barkleigh Daisy, Barkleigh Rose, Barkleigh Dandelion, etc. By registering the individual puppies himself, the breeder is assured that the names will remain as he wishes. If the breeder elects to give you the blue slip instead, please do not tamper with the name he has chosen. (You can CALL it anything you wish!) If there is no name written in the space provided, you can assume the breeder is leaving the name choice up to you. Give careful thought to your choice of names . . . once registered with the AKC, a name can never be changed.

If the breeder does give you the blue slip, this must be filled out and returned to the AKC with the appropriate fee. In a few weeks you will receive a white certificate of registration listing you as the dog's owner. If the breeder has already individually registered the puppy, he will give you a white registration certificate which lists the breeder as the owner. Both breeder and owner must complete the transfer of ownership section on the back of the slip. Mail this to the AKC with the transfer fee and in a few weeks you will receive a revised copy listing you as the new owner.

The Buyer's Responsibility

So far, the breeder has made a lot of promises and guarantees concerning the puppy. You, as buyer, have some responsibilities to the relationship as well. You will be expected to make every effort to assure the dog will be properly cared for and protect it from accident or theft. In addition, you are expected to represent yourself honestly. Don't tell the breeder you have a fenced yard if you don't. If you own other pets, don't "forget" to inform the breeder of this fact. Don't tell him you "just want a pet" then immediately proceed to breed it. Much of the breeder/buyer relationship is based on mutual trust. You will only hurt yourself by undermining it with falsehoods and half-truths. Ownership of other pets or lack of a fenced yard may not necessarily mean the breeder won't sell you a dog . . . he may ask about such things only to determine whether or not a specific puppy or dog is suitable for your situation.

You will be expected to keep in touch with the breeder and give occasional "progress reports." Photos of the puppy in various stages of growth are very much appreciated. Don't hesitate to call the breeder with problems or questions. That's what they are there for. Most breeders also REQUIRE (sometimes in writing) that the purchaser agree to contact the breeder FIRST if for any reason the buyer is unable to keep the dog. If the breeders cannot buy the dog back, they will have the know-how and contacts to find a suitable buyer for it. The inexperienced pet owner trying to sell a dog through common channels could easily sell it into the wrong hands. If you care about the dog at all, let the breeder help you.

38

4

Grooming and Showing

T HE ideal Bull Terrier coat is harsh, almost like a wire coated terrier. This coat texture does not hold dirt like softer coats do. Therefore, regular brushing is far preferable to frequent bathing for a Bull Terrier. Some Bull Terriers will not have the desired coat texture and may require a bath now and then, but in most cases a vigorous brushing will remove most dirt and will stimulate the skin as well. Many Bull Terriers enjoy being "brushed" with a natural bristle grooming mitt, sometimes called a "hound glove." This indispensable grooming tool fits over your hand like a mitten, enabling you to easily massage all parts of the dog's body. Regular attention to your dog's coat will result in a nice shine, even on a white coated dog. Your dog will begin to look forward to his daily "rub down!"

Grease can easily be removed from the coat by the application of a little bit of waterless hand cleaner . . . the type used by mechanics. This will also remove the gray marks left on a white coat by a metal choke chain or dog tags. Just rub it in and towel it off.

For a general "all over" cleaning, short of a tub bath, you can use one of the dog shampoos on the market that requires no rinsing. These are handy to take along to shows or for touch-ups while traveling with your dog.

For actual bathing, it is better to use a whitening shampoo for white dogs and a conditioning or color-enhancing shampoo for coloreds. Avoid continual use of human shampoos. The PH level in human shampoos is not suited to dogs and may result in skin irritation or flaking. Whatever you use, MAKE SURE YOU RINSE WELL and keep the dog in a warm, draftless area until he dries thoroughly. Tub baths should only be needed if the dog gets very dirty or finds something disgusting to roll on. Of course, a white dog that is being shown will require frequent baths too.

Bull Terriers, fortunately, are not prone to ear problems. You should, however, remove accumulated wax from time to time by gently swabbing out the ear with a cotton ball dipped in slightly warm mineral oil. If your Bull Terrier likes to swim, he will have to be checked frequently for signs of inner ear infection. Head shaking, tenderness or pawing at the ears will indicate a developing problem. Let your vet have a look.

Nail trimming is probably the most dreaded and most neglected part of the grooming process. Most Bull Terriers are not terribly fond of having their nails trimmed, but will grudgingly tolerate it if accustomed to the process while still young. If you wait until the nails are long and hooked before you tend to them, you can count on having problems. It is much wiser to trim a little on a regular weekly schedule than to let the matter get out of hand. Care must be taken to avoid cutting into the quick, for this is painful and will surely result in dogs who hate having their feet touched. Cut off only the hooked part that is white. Never cut into the pink area. On coloreds, the nails may be brown or black, making it difficult to see where the quick begins. In this case, you will notice that the nail is grooved out underneath, near the tip. You can safely cut this part off. When in doubt, proceed cautiously, removing just a little at a time. If you do nick the quick, apply a little bit of styptic powder or monsel solution (available at the drugstore). If nothing else, apply an ice cube or cold compress to the tip of the nail and hold in place until the bleeding stops. A nicked quick always bleeds like crazy, but don't worry, it's not as bad as it looks!

If you just don't think you're up to cutting the nails, you can file them with a flat "bastard" rasp. Most hardware stores should be able to provide you with a suitable type. Filing takes longer than trimming, but there is little risk of cutting into the quick and there is an added benefit in that, by filing, the nails are left nicely rounded and less "scratchy".

* * * * * * * *

It is important that a sincere effort be made to accustom your puppy to all sorts of experiences as a youngster so he will not acquire fears that will hinder his development into a socially well-adjusted companion. Take him for rides in the car frequently, even if only for a short jaunt. In our dog grooming shop, we see many, many dogs whose only exposure to the automobile is either to go to the vet, or to come to us for a clip and a bath. . . . These dogs are almost always "antsy" in the car, even to the point of carsickness and hysteria. Is it any wonder? They have come to associate the

40

Ch. Ormandy's Westward Ho, twice Best in Show and dam of four champions in her first litter. She was sired by Ormandy Souperlative Bar Sinister ex Ch. Ormandy Duncannon Double Two, bred by Raymond Oppenheimer and owned by Alex T. Shaner.

Ch. Radar of Monty-Ayr, whelped 1957, established an all-time record of 333 Best of Variety wins, 6 Bests in Show, 45 Group Firsts and 171 Group placements, as well as the Isis Vabo Trophy for 1961, 1962 and 1963. Bred by Dr. E. S. Montgomery, owned by Dr. Howard R. Doble.

Ch. Wilton's Orion, son of Ch. Harper's Huntsman, winner of 3 Groups in the 1960s. Owner, Lt. Col. and Mrs. W. R. Barnes.

Ch. Westmeath's Reliance, California Specialty winner of the 1950s.

Ch. Carlings Solitaire, Best White White at Bull Terrier Club of America Specialty 1969. Bred and owned by Mr. and Mrs. Carl Ackerman.

vehicle with less-than-happy experiences. Keep this in mind and try to make car outings fun for your dog. For his health and safety, do not allow him to ride loose in the car . . . take his crate along and confine him to it. A dog taught to ride quietly in a crate is much safer than one left loose to bound about. An unconfined dog could cause an accident or be thrown off the seat and injured should you have to slam on the brakes. Also, if he is crated, you can leave the windows down without worrying about him jumping out. Most Bull Terriers love to ride in the car and will respond enthusiastically when you say, "Let's go for a ride!"

* * * * * * *

It should not need saying, but I'll do so anyway . . . NEVER LEAVE YOUR DOG IN A CAR IN THE SUN! Not even for ten minutes! The temperature inside a car, even with the windows down a few inches, can rise quickly enough to kill a dog in a very short time. Don't leave the car parked in the shade, thinking he'll be all right for a few hours . . . in that time the sun's position could change and leave your dog in a veritable oven. If you will be unable to take him out of the car where you are going, leave him at home. He'll be much safer.

Showing Your Bull Terrier

People who are interested in exhibiting their dogs in conformation and/or obedience would do well to seek the expertise of an experienced Bull Terrier breeder who also exhibits.

Bull Terriers are shown differently than most other breeds in that they stand free and are not stacked. There is a definite art to teaching handler and dog how to best accomplish this.

Before entering competition, the owner should train the dog to obey simple basic commands, so that the dog may be readily controlled in the ring as well as at home. The Bull Terrier has six characteristics that must be taken into consideration when one starts to train for home obedience or for the show ring. Remember that the Bull Terrier:

> is highly intelligent,
> is anxious to please,
> is unusually sensitive,
> is very determined,
> craves human companionship and attention, and
> thrives on praise.

The whole theory of training a Bull Terrier successfully, so that they enjoy training and the fruits thereof, is simply this: One must understand what the dog is expected to do and how to explain it to the dog, with patience enough to overcome the dog's determination not to do what is wanted. An encouraging kindness never fails regardless of the provocation.

To keep Bull Terriers showing well, they have to have fun. If the dog is expected to "show" all the time, the routine could become very tedious very quickly. Always keep one eye on the judge and when he or she isn't looking at your dog, let the dog relax, chew on a toy or a biscuit.

Eng. Ch. Romany Robin Goodfellow made history by going Best in Show all-breeds at Windsor. 1957 Ormandy Jug winner. Breeders, Miss Montague Johnstone and Miss N. Williams.

5

Obedience and
the Bull Terrier

by Kate Less
with Mary Remer and Jeanine Dunn-Harmon

"COME on. That's a Bull Terrier. They'll never be that obedient. Besides, that's a show dog and obedience ruins show dogs; it makes them into robots and breaks their spirit."

I cannot believe these notions as my Bull Terrier is as obedient as any Bull Terrier can be. "Toby" finished his championship, earned his Recognition of Merit from the Bull Terrier Club of America, was a Silverwood Trophy Competition finalist in 1983 and received his Companion Dog obedience degree all during the same period of time. In the breed ring he is always full of fire (sometimes too much so), yet this same dog would sit quietly between two big male dogs in his obedience class without a peep.

There are no excuses and there are far too many Bull Terriers who would do well to have a little obedience work. In today's world of bad reputations and prejudice against breeds with "pit bull" origins, obedience is a need. Civil obedience is a plus for any dog. Any who does not have such manners is showing the owner's laziness and lack of responsibility.

45

Let us take a look at what obedience in its most basic form can do for you. First, your dog knows who is boss. You may not be the pack leader in your house, but you do rank over your Bull Terrier. Read a few books on wolf and dog behavior and it may shed some light on problems you may have with your dog.

Obedience training teaches the owner the art of communication. At first glance obedience training appears to be exercises in control which have little practical application. However, the exercises are very relevant to daily life. For example, brushing, bathing, toweling, and vet examinations are much more easily and rapidly accomplished with a dog that has been taught to STAND/STAY. A dog that will SIT or DOWN/STAY is a welcome guest in most situations. Certainly a brisk city or country walk will be more pleasurable if your shoulders are still attached to your torso at the end of the outing.

After that, obedience is being able to live with your Bull Terrier. They learn that the punishment for the crime, even if it is merely your displeasure, is far worse than the reward for being an angel. We all know for a Bull Terrier it is very hard to "be good," but they will try. Bull Terriers are people oriented dogs and even though they do not show the same desire to please as some breeds, they do have a desire not to be bad. If they are bad, you won't talk to them, or give them cookies or play with them. It is much more fun to be a good dog. That is obedience in its most basic form.

Dogs have a language, body language, and the language of dogs is universal. All dogs understand each other regardless of breed. If we can come to understand, trust, and respect the canine system of communication our relationships with dogs will become possible when relationships are truly balanced. A good obedience class will help to open the channels of communication with your Bull Terrier and in turn enhance and enrich the relationship.

Your Bull Terrier may not know any commands, but if the laws and rules of the house are known, that is obedience. Your Bull Terrier will then be a good citizen.

Take obedience a step further and it serves many useful purposes. In the breed ring, it will help your dog catch the eye of the judge. Your dog will stand still on a loose lead and show his or her heart out or gait on a loose lead and show that true Bully swagger. Your hand will not have blood blisters after five minutes of showing the beast. The judge will appreciate being able to examine the dog's teeth without a ten-minute struggle. The dog will enjoy the show and so will you. You can do all this by teaching your dog to heel, stand *and* stay. It takes about fifteen minutes per day and can be done right in your kitchen. (If you can't spare fifteen, perhaps you should consider replacing your dog with a cat.)

The straight recall, as in the
Novice Class. *Less*

Retrieve on the flat, an **Open**
exercise. *Less*

47

A good return following the Retrieve. *Less*

The retrieve over the high jump in **Open** work. *Less*

48

Diamond Jim Brady of Ernicor, CDX, pictured earning a 200 in Open—first perfect score ever for a Bull Terrier. Owner, Frank Neff. Judge, Mrs. Alva McColl.

An enthusiastic performer sails over the broad jump.   *Less*

I don't care if your Bull Terrier is a stunner with a real whacked-over profile; if he or she can't stand still or gallops when gaited, the judge won't be able to evaluate the dog properly.

Now you think you'd like to take the challenge and show your Bull Terrier in obedience. Brave soul! This is when you will be tested to the limit; not by the judge, but by the little gargoyle you thought was your best friend. What you need to train and show a Bull Terrier in obedience is a truckload of patience, a tough constitution and a belief in magic. What you must always keep in mind is that your Bull Terrier is not, I repeat, not a Golden Retriever, a Sheltie or a German Shepherd. This is a Bull Terrier. They will not do anything for you without your asking. They will always ask why. Why jump when it is easier to go around? Why? You must show them how it can be fun when they do what they are asked. Fun, fun, fun. Bribe them with biscuits. They will soon learn that they are much happier doing what is asked, than disobeying. You must be as creative, energetic and stubborn as your Bull Terrier.

For instance, it is the Bull Terrier's "great sense of self" and independence that makes teaching OFF LEAD HEELING a difficult proposition at best. The Bull Terrier's memory, similar to an elephant, makes learning anything through excessive repetition a TOTAL DRAG. One must be very careful of exactly what is learned as the information is rapidly processed from short to long term memory.

Understanding the influence breed characteristics have on the method of teaching various exercises will help you succeed with your dog. Keep in mind that Helen Whitehouse-Walker developed obedience exercises for her breed (Poodle) to prove their intelligence. These exercises became the basis of today's obedience exercises, so remember, the design was for Poodles. If a Newfoundland breeder had developed the exercises, we would all be teaching our dogs water sports. Imagine what we'd be doing if a Bull Terrier breeder had developed these exercises!

Beware of classes and instructors trying to mold all dogs into Goldens or Dobermans. They do not understand the terrier temperament, especially the Bull Terrier outlook on life and obedience. You are better off avoiding such trainers. Bull Terriers cannot be drilled; they get bored and so will you. Drill them and they will refuse to do anything. You will have ruined them for obedience.

If you cannot find an enthusiastic and creative trainer, buy a few books and start from there. Find a method that works for you. Dare to be different. Bull Terriers need it. Do not nag your Bull Terrier while training. Make training fun. Be swift with punishment and lavish with praise.

Know how to read your dog. When the dog does not do something, you must know whether it was because what you wanted was not understood or what you asked was physically very difficult to do, or maybe your Bull Terrier was being truly rebellious. If you punish the dog for being confused, he will hate obedience. Wouldn't you?

Now it is time for your first show or match. Don't be intimidated. You will attract a lot of attention. Bask in it. Use it to promote a good image for the breed. Even if your Bull Terrier plays dumb in the ring, you will have done more than many other handlers. And maybe, just maybe, your beloved gargoyle will blow away all those smiling retrievers. They can when they want to. The thrill is worth three Bests in Show. It took talent and brains (yours and the dog's) to get a score and no personal opinion came into play. You worked against no one but the scoresheet and you beat the odds.

The adventures you have and the people you meet are some good things that come out of the show ring. You may never show above the Novice level, but once you are hooked, you're hooked for life. After Novice comes Open, with jumping and retrieving and then Utility, with hand signals, scent discrimination, directed jumping and directed retrieving. Bull Terriers are smart enough to do all this, but you, as the handler, must persevere. Nothing ventured, nothing gained.

Tracking is another aspect of the sport that Bull Terriers can and do enjoy. If you like early morning walks through parks, woods and fields, then try tracking. If a Bull Terrier has a nose, the dog can track.

Maybe you try showing and just never make it. Nothing was lost but so much was gained. You can walk your well-behaved dog with pride. You can take your dog out under the critical public eye and his or her good manners win friends. Your Bull Terrier stays put and will ignore other dogs. Yet this is still a Bull Terrier who may occasionally swear at another dog, dash after a cat, bounce a tennis ball all over the house and dig holes in the rose garden, after which the ears lie flat, the tail wags and you see a grin while you chastise severely. A Bull Terrier will try so very hard to be good.

But remember, this is a Bull Terrier and the halo sits a mite crooked on the head.

Obedience Title Winners 1970 - 1986

1970
Dreadnought's Krackton Kwick CD
Lavender's Sir Michael CD
Key-Ken's Amanda of Montague CD
El Dorado's Soldier of Fortune CD

1971
No titles earned

1972
No titles earned

1973
Ardine Tigger of Crestmere CD
Key-Ken's Lady Macbeth CD
Belle Terre's King Porter CD

Winsted's Bedford Belle,
UDT, the first Bull Terrier to
attain a Utility Dog degree.
Owned by Dr. Harry L. Otis.

Ch. Duncan Willie
of Camaloch, CDX.

Ch. Romany Righteous Wrath, CD, VG, an outstanding English show and
Obedience star of the mid-50's, pictured clearing a 9-ft. jump. He had to his credit a
phenomenal jump of 15 feet. Bred by Miss Montague Johnstone and Miss M.
Williams.

"Wildfire" receiving the 1955 Annual Patsy Award (Picture Animal Star of the Year) for his work in the MGM movie, "It's A Dog's Life." Accepting the award from B. Dean Clanton, president of the American Humane Association, is Wildfire's co-star, Jarma Lewis, with Dr. W.W. Young, Western regional AHA director, looking on. In real life "Wildfire" was Cadence Glacier, CD, bred and owned by Lillian Koehler.

Graduation Day, 1954, for what is believed to be the largest number of Bull Terriers ever entered in one Obedience class. Trainer, William R. Koehler. Back row, l. to r.: Jack Reddick's Serenade's Casey Jones, Marilyn Reddick's Serenade's Song of Songs and Lillian Ritchell's Serenade's Button and Bows. Front row, Katy Ickis' Glorycady's Star of Even and Jill Bradshaw's Cadence Clown.

53

1974
Highland's Lady Abberlien CD
Tarlow's Cleopatra CD
Bill Sike's Bullseye CD

1975
Samson CD

1976
Banbury Brass Tack of Maldon CD
Chimera Carte Blanche CD

1977
Casino's Lady Baccara CD
Tarlow Lighty Moses CD

1978
Argona's Sassy Sally B Goode CD
Docker's Derehit CD

1979
Arteclair CD
Ch. Banbury Bralph CD
Battlestar Centurion CD
Hotspur's Firedrill CD
Bejobos Kaslrock Whyt Elefant CD
Brown Bomber of Ocotillo CD
Flow's Rough Row Rocky CD
Greystoke's Shogun CD
Griffwood's Lady Jane CD
Lothlorien Sting CD
Miner's Mountain Chapparral CD
Nippy's Ebony Eyes CD
Raider CD
Carnelian's Nero of Bulrun TD

1980
Windrush Belle Annie CD
Bejobos Kaslrok Whyt Elefant CDX

1981
Glynwood's Snow Magic CD
Nippy's Brindle Gripper CD
Sir Gee of Montara CD
Windrush Belle Annie CDX
Wright's Baron of Terry Town CDX

1982
Wright's Baron of Terry Town UD

1983
Sleepy Ethne CD
Ch. Westbrook White Hot CD

1984
Benson Aces Are Wild CD
Bt's Madman Across the Water CD
Cadence Halleluiah CD
Mulligan Strong of Piranha CD
Ch. North Star's Blue Horizon CD
Rapparee Musashi CD
Unaka's Jennifer Moonbeam CD

1985
Benson Aces Are Wild CDX
Rapparee Musashi CDX
Ch. Bonney's Bane Tarroo CD
Brocaire's Carrie B CD
Ch. Brummagem Angel Fire CD
Hoku's Hey Misbehavin' CD

1986
Deva Rebel of Richman CD
Sarah of Wendigo CD
Kimberley's Gwyn CD
Ch. Maggeroo's Storm Dancer CD
Ch. Bonney's Bane Tarroo CDX

6

The Show Winners

THE first Bull Terrier on record to go Best in Show all-breeds in the United States was the Canadian-bred Ch. Haymarket Faultless, when he topped the Westminster entry in 1918. At that time, Best in Show was judged by two men, with a third being ready to be called in as referee if necessary. Vinton Breese held out for the Bull Terrier, Charles G. Hopton held out for the Pekingese, and neither would give an inch. So George P. Thomas, the referee, was brought in and agreed with Mr. Breese that the Bull Terrier was the better dog.

I have heard that a California dog, Ch. Sound End Sombrero, went Best in Show several times before 1918, and such research as I have been able to make seems to bear this out. However, writing to the descendants of the family that owned him has brought no answer and so we will have to put this dog's wins down as a probability, but not a verified certainty.

The following is a listing of the Bull Terriers that have gone Best in Show all-breeds in the United States through the end of 1970. The parenthesized figures represent the total Bests in Show won by the dog. The d or b following the dog's name identifies whether it was a dog or bitch, and the W or Col identifies its Variety—White or Colored.

Ch. Haymarket Faultless, d-W (1)
Ch. Cloudland White Mits, b-W (1)
Ch. Cylva Barbara, b-W (2 or 3)
Int. Ch. Faultless of Blighty, b-W (2)
Ch. Ferdinand of Ormandy, d-W (1)

Ch. Forecast of Monty-Ayr, left, Best White, and Ch. Madame Pompadour of Ernicor, right, Best Opposite at the 1949 Westminster. Forecast, an all-breed Best in Show winner, won the Isis Vabo Trophy for 1947, and "Pompy" for 1949.

Ch. Heir Apparent to Monty-Ayr, whelped 1942, first American-bred Bull Terrier to go Best in Show all-breeds. Isis Vabo Trophy winner for 1944, 1945, and 1946.

Int. Ch. Faultless of Blighty (by Rubislaw ex Broncroft Bridget), whelped 1932. Pictured are some of her trophies including the painting of her by Herbert H. Stewart. Faultless, winner of two Bests in Show, was imported by F. Wallace Mollison and later sold for a reported $5,000 to Dolores Del Rio, the movie star.

Ch. Heir-Apparent to Monty-Ayr, d-W (1)
Ch. Forecast of Monty-Ayr, d-W (1)
Ch. Argent Arrogance, d-W (1)
Ch. Tap Dancer of Tartary, b-W (1)
Int. Ch. Braxentra Balechin, d-W (2)
Ch. Marko of Monty-Ayr, d-W (1)
Ch. Romany Ritual, b-Col (4)
Int. Ch. Kashdowd's White Rock of Coolyn Hill, d-W (10)
Int. Ch. Dulac Heathland's Commander, d-Col (8)
Ch. Dancing Master of Monty-Ayr, d-W (10)
Ch. Radar of Monty-Ayr, d-W (6)
Ch. Rombus Andante, b-W (3)
Ch. Ormandy's Westward Ho, d-W (2)
Ch. Masterpiece of Monty-Ayr, d-W (1)
Ch. Dulac Heathland's Commander, d-Col (8)
Ch. Bathwick's Bonnie, b-Col (1)
Ch. Rombus Astronaut of Lenster, d-Col (1)
Ch. Abraxas Ace of Aces, d-Col (1)
Ch. Agates Bronzino, d-Col (1)

Int. Ch. Dulac Heathland's Commander and Int. Ch. Kashdowd's White Rock of Coolyn Hill each went Best in Show in their first time shown in the United States. Ch. Cloudland White Mist and Ch. Haymarket Faultless were Canadian-bred, the five dogs of Monty-Ayr prefix were American-bred, and all the rest were imports from England.

Bull Terrier Club of America Specialty Show Winners (1971-1985)

1971 Held with Associated Terrier Clubs show February 14.
Judge: Marilyn Drewes
BOV Colored: Highland's Big Ben (Ch. Abraxas Ace of Aces ex Ch. Kearby's Maxwell's Gold Dust)
Breeders-Owners: Forrest and Agnes Rose

BOV White: Ch. Harper's Hemstitch (Souperlative Benbeau of Ormandy ex Harper's Highnote)
Breeders-Owners: Phil and Gloria Hyde

1972 Held with Associated Terrier Clubs show February 14.
Judge: Charles Meller
BOV Colored: Molyha Snip Snap Snorum (Ch. Abraxas Ace of Aces ex Can. Ch. Huntress of Molyha)
Breeder-Owner: Halina M.B. Molyneux

BOV White: White Rocket of Lenster (Phidgity Harper's High N Mighty ex Silverweed of Lenster)
Breeder: not given
Owners: Phil and Gloria Hyde

Best in Show winning father, Ch. Abraxas Ace of Aces, whelped 1965, by Eng. Ch. Ormandy's Ben of Highthorpe ex Abraxas Alvina. Isis Vabo Trophy, 1968. Bred by Miss V. Drummond-Dick and owned by Ralph Bowles.

Ch. Highland's Big Ben ROM, son of Ch. Abraxas Ace of Aces, owned by Forrest and Agnes Rose, one of the most successful Coloreds ever shown.

Best in Show winning son, Ch. Agates Bronzino, whelped 1967, by Ch. Abraxas Ace of Aces ex Agate's Lotus Elite. Bred by Mrs. M. O. Sweeten, and owned by Ralph Bowles and Charles Fleming. Specialty winner and Isis Vabo Trophy, 1969.

Ch. Highland's Bashful Dwarf ROM, a daughter of "Ben," owned by the Roses. A 1974 Specialty winner and best Colored bitch at the 1974 Silverwood.

1972   Held on Silverwood Weekend, Wheeling, Illinois, October 14.
Judge: Cecil Mann
BOV Colored: Ch. Molyha Snip Snap Snorum (Ch. Abraxas Ace of Aces ex
Can. Ch. Huntress of Molyha)
Breeder-Owner: Halina M.B. Molyneux

BOV White: Sunburst Solar System (Can./Am. Ch. Tantrum's Trad Lad ex
Can. Ch. Iella Desdamona)
Breeders: Mr. and Mrs. Gary J. Travers
Owners: Mr. and Mrs. Len P. Spicer

1973   Held with Associated Terrier Clubs show February 11.
Judge: Oliver W. Ford
BOV Colored: Rocky Barnabus of Taylorwood

BOV White: Ch. Banbury Borealis (Ch. Banbury Briar ex Souperlative
Meteor)
Breeder: Mabel Smith
Owners: Allan and Marie Gerst

Held with Montgomery County K.C., Ambler, Pennsylvania, October 7.
Judge: H. B. Bradbury
BOV Colored: Regina of Colostaurus (Can. Ch. Plaisance Seabryn Air
Marshall ex Can. Ch. Athena)

BOV White: Can./Am. Ch. Paupen's Mr. Wiggins (Can./Am. Ch. Maerdy
Moonstone ex Romany Rock Rose)
Breeder: Joseph J. Cowan
Owners: Paul and Penny Maier

1974   Held on Silverwood Weekend, New Castle, Pennsylvania, September 14.
Judge: Charles Meller
BOV Colored: Ch. Highland's Bashful Dwarf (Ch. Highland's Big Ben ex
Highland's Lady Jessica)
Breeder: Mary Rose
Owner: W. Weitz, Jr.

BOV White: Ch. Banbury Butter Rum (Ch. Trooper Duffy of Manchester
ex Ch. Banbury Charity Buttercup)
Breeder: W. E. Mackay-Smith
Owners: Harvey and Paula Shames

1975   Statistics Unavailable

1976   Held with Associated Terrier Clubs show, February.
Judge: Lucy Cress
BOV Colored: Senator of Lenster
Breeder: S. V. Morris
Owner: Ray Jones

BOV White: Banbury Bergerac (Eng./Am. Ch. Targyt Silver Bob of
Langville ex Ch. Harper's Hemstitch ROM)
Breeder: Ken Neumann
Owners: Phil and Gloria Hyde

Ch. Molyha Snip Snap Snorum ROM, another daughter of Ch. Abraxas Ace of Aces, owned by Halina Molyneux, 1972 Specialty winner.

Ch. Midnight Melody, daughter of Ch. Abraxas Ace of Aces, owned by Charles A. Fleming.

61

Can./Am. Ch. Regina of Colostaurus
ROM, owned by Gail Gordon, 1973
Specialty winner.

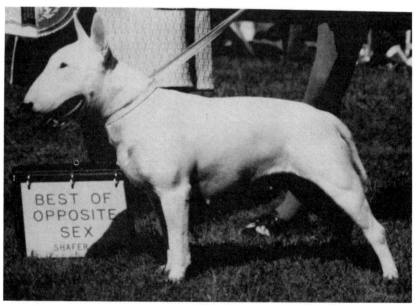

Can./Am. Ch. Sunburst Solar System ROM, owned by Mr. and Mrs. Len Spicer,
1972 Specialty winner.

Held in conjunction with the Montgomery County Kennel Club show, October 3.
Judge: Betty Strickland
BOV Colored: Broadside Music Maker (Ch. Papilio Pop Music ex Ch. Herschel Bull O'th Woods)
Breeder-Owner: Hon. David C. Merriam

BOV White: Tenacious Chadwells Kelly Gay (Ch. Tantrum's Trad Lad ex Chadwell's Naughtical Girl)
Breeder: V. Spencer
Owners: Len and Kathy Spicer

1977 Held with Associated Terrier Clubs show, February 13.
Judge: Cecil Mann
BOV Colored: Tantrum's Trickster (Ch. Chadwell Chamaco ex Georgian Diamond Lil)

BOV White: Ch. Tenacious Chadwell Kelly Gay

Held on Silverwood Weekend, Northbrook, Illinois, October 16.
Judge: Jon Cole
BOV Colored: Ch. Monkery's Sea Boots (Ch. Monkery Sea Link ex Monkery Snow Boots)
Breeder: Phyllis Holmes
Owners: Carl and Barb Pew

BOV White: Ch. Souperlative Verdict of Broadside (Eng. Ch. Jobrulu Jacqueminot ex Souperlative Trotwood)
Breeder: Eva Weatherill
Owner: Hon. David Merriam

1978 Held with Associated Terrier Clubs show, February.
Judge: Vera Sheridan Jackson
BOV Colored: Ch. Abraxas Ardeur (Eng. Ch. Romany Rio Colorado ex Eng. Ch. Abraxas Athenia)
Breeder: Violet Drummond-Dick
Owners: Don and Emily Russ

BOV White: Silver Screen's The Sheik (Ch. Banbury Briar ex Banbury Sonata of Crestmere)
Breeder-Owner: Paul Badger

Held in conjunction with the Ox Ridge Kennel Club show, September.
Judge: Eva Weatherill
BOV Colored: The Duke of Goodwood (Can. Ch. Plaisance Seabryn Air Marshall ex Molyha's Royal Casino)
Breeders: Mr. and Mrs. T. Tierney
Owners: Mr. and Mrs. Brooke Wason

BOV White: Kearby's Salvationist (Eng. Ch. Hollyfir's Devils Disciple ex Eng. Ch. Kearby's Major Barbara)
Breeder: Quita Youatt
Owners: Steve Schmidt and Toby Fish

Ch. Banbury Bouquet ROM, a daughter of Ch. Kashdowd Bounce, owned and bred by Winkie Mackay-Smith, a 1975 Specialty winner.

Ch. Banbury Boothia ROM, daughter of Sea Boots and mother of Benson. She is one of the top producing brood bitches in the history of the breed and completed her championship at the 1977 BTCA Specialty.

Ch. Banbury Benson of Bedrock ROM. Benson and various sisters and daughters dominated show rings for the first half of the 1980s and his offspring continue producing top Bull Terriers. As with all Banbury and Bedrock animals, they are owner-handled. The highest accolade Benson achieved was winning the Terrier Group at Westminster in 1983, a first for a Colored Bull Terrier. *Ashbey*

Ch. Ann Dee's Red Adair ROM. Considered by many to be the best red and white dog ever bred in this country, he was largely undefeated in the show ring, a top producing sire and a 1979 and 1981 Specialty winner.

Ch. Cannoro Claret ROM. A foundation bitch for Bedrock Kennels, "Liza" won a 1979 Specialty under Maureen Bell.   *Gilbert*

1979   Held with Associated Terrier Clubs show, February 11.
Judge: James Boland
BOV Colored: Ch. Aricon's Archimedes of Foyri (Eng. Ch. Hollyfir Dog in a Doublet ex Loreli of Nanabar)
Breeder: Eric Stanley
Owners: Ed and Terry Sussman

BOV White: Abraxas Apex (Eng. Ch. Badlesmere Bonaparte of Souperlative ex Maerdy Monalita of Abraxas)
Breeder: Violet Drummond-Dick
Owners: Ralph and Mary Bowles

Held in conjunction with the Montgomery County Kennel Club show, October 7.
Judge: Maureen Bell
BOV Colored: Ch. Ann Dee's Red Adair (Can./Am. Ch. Paupen's Mr. Wiggins ex Hollyfir's Coppernob)
Breeder: George Schreiber
Owners: Elaine Bernard and R. Angus

BOV White: Ch. Cannoro Claret (Eng./Am. Ch. Foyri Electrify ex Banbury Bobbin)
Breeder: Bernard E. McCann
Owners: Jay and Mary Remer

1980   Held with Associated Terrier Clubs show, February 10.
Judge: Cecil Mann
BOV Colored: Ragged Hills Backstroker (Eng./Am. Ch. Monkery's Meltdown Sea Shanty ex Ch. Ragged Hills Aurora)
Breeders: Peggy and Michael Arnaud
Owners: David B. Phillips and Peggy Arnaud

BOV White: Ch. Jobrulu Hosta (Eng. Ch. Souperlative Sunstar of Ormandy ex Jobrulu Jewel Orchid)
Breeder: Joan Kenway
Owners: Ralph Bowles and Louis Wellons

Held on Silverwood Weekend, Atlanta, Georgia, September 28.
Judge: Phylis Holmes
BOV Colored: Ch. Ragged Hills Backstroker

BOV White: Binkstone's Buckskin Maggie (Can./Am. Ch. Monkery's Buckskin ex Gilavon Glisse)
Breeders: G. and J. Binks
Owners: Dr. Robert Myall and Anne Hamilton

1981   Independent Specialty, Newark, New Jersey, February 8.
Judge: Robert Thomas
BOV Colored: Ch. Ann Dee's Red Adair

BOV White: Jacquenetta of Brummagem (Eng. Ch. Souperlative Jackadandy of Ormandy ex Mischief of Brummagem)
Breeder: Janet Furneaux
Owners: David and Anna Harris and Jack Degidio

Ch. Jobrulu Hosta. Imported by Ralph Bowles, this bitch was a jewel in the ring and a most striking bitch. She was the winner at a 1980 Specialty.

Can./Am. Ch. Binkstone's Buckskin Maggie ROM, a beautiful showy bitch and a well-deserved winner of the BTCA 1980 Specialty.

Ch. Abraxas Apex ROM, imported by Ralph Bowles. "Justin" was a showstopper at the 1979 Specialty. *Fall*

Held in conjunction with the Montgomery County Kennel Club show, October 4.
Judge: Edie Micklethwaite
BOV Colored: Ch. Banbury Benson of Bedrock (Ch. Souperlative Special of Ormandy ex Ch. Banbury Boothia)
Breeders-Owners: W. E. Mackay-Smith and Jay and Mary Remer

BOV White: Magor Midas Touch (Can./Am. Ch. Van Don's Silver Chancellor ex Bancoup Evan's Girl)
Breeders-Owners: Gordon and Norma Smith

1982 Independent Specialty, Newark, New Jersey, February 7.
Judge: W. E. Mackay-Smith
BOV Colored: Brigadore Barron of Bedrock (Ch. Ann Dee's Red Adair ex Ch. Cannoro Claret)
Breeders: Jay and Mary Remer
Owners: Jay and Mary Remer and Linda Bergstresser

BOV White: Westbrook Wild One (Ch. Ragged Hills Lady Killer ex Ch. Westbrook Wit's End)
Breeder: Drue King
Owners: Drue King and Merry Hobbins

Independent Specialty held on Silverwood Weekend, Long Island, New York, September 19.
Judge: George Jarrett
BOV Colored: Ch. Banbury Benson of Bedrock

BOV White: Eng./Am. Ch. Aricon's Chief Eye Shy (Eng. Ch. Brobar Backchat ex Aricon Spanish Eyes)
Breeder: Eric Stanley
Owner: Robert K. Thomas

1983 Held with Associated Terrier Clubs show, February 13.
Judge: Cecil Mann
BOV Colored: Ch. Banbury Benson of Bedrock

BOV White: Banbury Bendetta of Bedrock (Ch. Banbury Benson of Bedrock ex Ch. Woodrow Carrissa)
Breeders-Owners: W. E. Mackay-Smith and Jay and Mary Remer

Held in conjunction with the Montgomery County Kennel Club show, October 9.
Judge: Kenneth McDermott
BOV Colored: Ch. Banbury Benson of Bedrock

BOV White: Ch. Banbury Bendetta of Bedrock

1984 Held with Associated Terrier Clubs show, February 12.
Judge: Hon. David C. Merriam
BOV Colored: Ch. Cinema the Omen of Westbrook (Can./Am. Ch. Van Don's Silver Chancellor ex Westbrook Witchcraft)
Breeders: Drue King and Marie Ciaffa
Owner: Drue King

70

Can./Am. Ch. Magor Midas Touch ROM. Owned and bred by Gordon and Norma Smith, Midas Touch continues one of the most successful lines of dogs developed in North America. He was a 1981 Specialty winner and has produced outstanding puppies.

Ch. Cinema The Omen of Westbrook ROM, combining the finest Colored bloodlines of the Westbrook Kennels with the White lines of the Magor Kennels. The Omen was a very typy dog who won many times, including a 1984 Specialty.

BOV White: Ch. Banbury Bendetta of Bedrock

Held on Silverwood Weekend, Plymouth, Michigan, September 16.
Judge: David Harris
BOV Colored: Ch. Terriwood's Merrimac (Can./Am. Ch. Monkery's Buckskin ex Terriwood's Night Shadow)
Breeders-Owners: A. J. and J. G. Walker

BOV White: Iffinest Amadeus (Polytelis Silver Convention ex Iffinest Abbondanza)
Breeder: Margaret Burns
Owners: Steve Schmidt and Margaret Burns

1985 Held in conjunction with the Fort Worth Kennel Club show, Fort Worth, Texas, March 23.
Judge: Anita Bartell
BOV Colored: Ch. Nautilus Monsoon Moonray (Ch. Monkery's Moatvale Bracken ex St. Kay's Nautilus Afloat)
Breeder: Donna Aiello
Owners: Michael and Janel Wellons and Donna Aiello

BOV White: Iffinest Amadeus

Held in conjunction with the Montgomery County Kennel Club show, October 6.
Judge: Don Russ
BOV Colored: Ch. Banbury Sargent Major (Ch. Banbury Benson of Bedrock ex Banbury Anna Goldien)
Breeders: Mr. and Mrs. Goldien and W. E. Mackay-Smith
Owner: Rick Battaglia

BOV White: Ch. Banbury Barnstormer (Can./Am. Ch. Van Don's Silver Chancellor ex Ch. Souperlative Sequoiah Sequin)
Breeders: W. E. Mackay-Smith and Margaret Burns
Owners: Matthew and W. E. Mackay-Smith

7

The Trophy Winners

$\mathbf{T}$ROPHIES offered by the Bull Terrier Club in England have been many and have done much to sustain interest in the breed, as they have been well publicized.

The first important such trophy was the Regent Trophy, offered by Dr. G. M. Vevers. Each year, the Committee of the Bull Terrier Club selects the dogs to compete, selection being made from among the dogs or bitches first shown the year preceding the actual selection at the Open Show of the Bull Terrier Club, usually in February. The judging is done by a panel of three, selected from the Committee of the Bull Terrier Club. It is as a mememto of this win that the replica of the original bronze model, in Royal Nymphenburg porcelain, is awarded.

A trophy for the Best of Opposite Sex to the Regent Trophy winner was offered by the Golden State Bull Terrier Club, beginning in 1953.

The Ormandy Jugs are offered for competition within each sex. That is, there is one Jug for competition of dogs only and one for bitches only. Competitors are selected by a committee of three from among the best dogs and bitches of the past year exhibited at championship shows. Since 1957, selection has automatically included all those who have completed their championship during the preceding year. The actual selection from among these competitors is made by a different committee of three. An inscribed plaque is given as a memento of the win. A contestant defeated one year may be invited to compete the next year.

The Regent Trophy, awarded for the best dog or bitch first shown at a Championship show in the year preceding the award. Winner receives a plaque, and all competitors receive a medal.

The Ormandy Jugs, presented by Raymond H. Oppenheimer to the Bull Terrier Club (England) in December 1946 as trustees for the breed. Presented to celebrate the record of Ch. Ormandy's Dancing Time. The original jug was presented by the Lord Mayor of London to Joseph Watte in 1666 for recovering important documents belonging to the city during the Great Fire of London.

Eng. Ch. Abraxas Audacity, the winner of Best in Show at Crufts, and the Regent Trophy in 1970.   *Fall*

Regent Trophy Winners (1970-1984)

1970 Ch. Abraxas Audacity (dwr)
     (Ch. Romany River Pirate ex Ch. Abraxas Athenia)
     Breeder-Owner: Violet Drummond-Dick

1971 Ch. Abraxas Aristo (dwr)
     (Woodrow Frosty Flake of Ormandy ex Ch. Abraxas Athenia)
     Breeder-Owner: Violet Drummond-Dick

1972 Abraxas Achilles (dwb)
     (Ch. Ormandy's Archangel ex Ch. Abraxas Athenia)
     Breeder-Owner: Violet Drummond-Dick

1973 Monkery's Delantero Moonride (dwb)
     (Ch. Monkery's Caspian ex Delantero Lunar Princess)
     Breeder: Mrs. M. B. Howard-Williams
     Owner: Phyllis Holmes

1974 Ch. Badlesmere Bonaparte of Souperlative (dwr)
     (Ch. Maerdy Maestro of Ormandy ex Souperlative Booksale Angel's Tears)
     Breeder: Mrs. J. Shaw
     Owners: Eva Weatherill and Raymond Oppenheimer

1975 Ch. Curraneye Schoolgirl (bwb)
     (Ch. Souperlative Sunstar of Ormandy ex Curraneye Lively Lady)
     Breeder-Owner: Edie Micklethwaite

1976 Ch. Jobrulu Jacobinia (dwb)
     (Ch. Badlesmere Bonaparte of Souperlative ex Jobrulu Xotica)
     Breeder-Owner: Joan Kenway

1977 Charlsdon Commander (dwb)
     (Ch. Badlesmere Bonaparte of Souperlative ex Charlesdon Little Peach)
     Breeder: Mrs. C. Boam
     Owners: Mr. and Mrs. J. Swigs

1978 Jill of Brobar (bwb)
     (Ch. Souperlative Jackadandy of Ormandy ex Brobar Elan)
     Breeders: Mr. and Mrs. Arthur Miller
     Owners: Mr. and Mrs. J. M. Whitham

1979 Harper's Holiday (bw)
     (Ch. Souperlative Jackadandy of Ormandy ex Hoya of Harpers)
     Breeders: Miss Graham-Weall and D. Vick
     Owner: Mrs. Carruthers-Smith

1980 Ch. Quilla of Quillon (dwr)
     (Ch. Jobrulu Jacobinia ex Jobrulu Camellia)
     Breeder: Joan Kenway
     Owners: Mr. and Mrs. B. Sait

1981 Contango's Classy Dame (bwb)
     (Ch. Sequoiah County Game ex Court Gem of Contango)
     Breeder-Owner: Joy Schuster

1982 Ch. Maximillian Bully Boy of Jobrulu (dwb)
     (Ch. Souperlative Jackadandy of Ormandy ex Pontybully Sonata)
     Breeder: Mr. Bath
     Owners: Joan Kenway and Mr. and Mrs. Carroll

Ch. Ormandy Souperlative Chunky, whelped 1958, Best in Show in England. Regent Trophy, 1960. Owners, R. H. Oppenheimer and Miss E. M. Weatherill.

Eng. Ch. Abraxas Aristo, Regent Trophy 1971.

Fall

Eng. Ch. Badlesmere Bonaparte of Souperlative, winner of the Ormandy Jug and the Regent Trophy in 1974. This dog was, in many ways, the finest dog I have ever seen. He has been an important sire with very desirable bloodlines.

Charlesdon Commander, winner of the Regent Trophy in 1977, one of Bonaparte's exceptional sons, loaded with type and personality. *Fall*

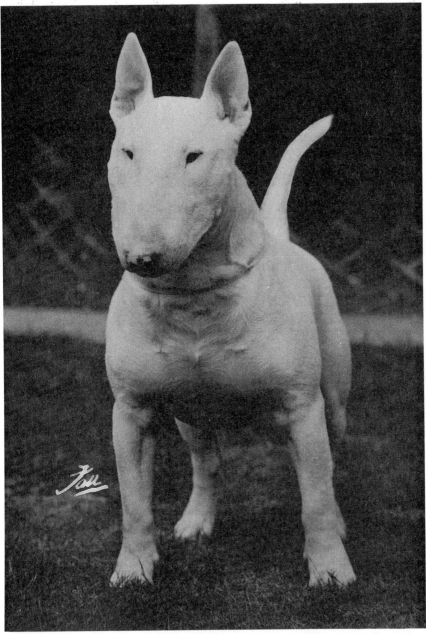

Eng. Ch. Jobrulu Jacobinia, one of the Jobrulu brothers. He won the Regent Trophy in 1976.
Fall

Ch. Monkery's Delantero Moonride, Regent Trophy winner for 1973.

Eng. Ch. Agate's Sweet Sauce, winner of the Ormandy Jug for Bitches in 1972.   *Fall*

1983 Ch. Bella Bianca Jackenna (bw)
(Ch. Souperlative Jackadandy of Ormandy ex Moatvale Morning Glory)
Breeder: G. Scott-Barrs
Owners: Mr. and Mrs. K. W. Higgins
1984 Ch. Ghabar Crusader (dwb)
(Eng./Am. Ch. Catrana Eye Opener of Aricon ex Brobar Silver Satin of Ghabar)
Breeders-Owners: Mr. and Mrs. R. Edmond

Best of Opposite Sex to the Regent Trophy

1970 Ch. Uglee Snow Blossom of Lenster (bwb)
(Ch. Monkery's Mr. Frosty of Ormandy ex Ch. Uglee Apple Blossem)
Breeder: Mrs. Chamberlain
Owners: Mrs. Mankin and Miss Graham-Weall
1971 Ch. Souperlative Laura (bbw)
(Ch. Romany River Pirate ex Ch. Souperlative Rominten Rheingold)
Breeder: Eva M. Weatherill
Owner: Bill Harding
1972 Ch. Pontybully Pearl (bwb)
(Harper's Headmaster of Lenster ex Pontybully Promise)
Breeder: C. J. Waterman
Owner: N. Alden-Smith
1973 Ch. Woodrow Minx (bwr)
(Ch. Monkery's Caspian ex Souperlative Wren of Woodrow)
Breeder-Owner: Helen Powe
1974 Ch. Brobar Elite (bwb)
(Ch. Maerdy Maestro of Ormandy ex Brobar Horatia)
Breeders: Mr. and Mrs. Arthur Miller
Owners: Mr. and Mrs. I. D. Porter
1975 Ch. Kearby's William (dwb)
(Ch. Hollyfir's Dog in a Doublet ex Ch. Kearby's Rosemary)
Breeder-Owner: Quita Youatt
1976 Ch. Kearby's Temptress (bbw)
(Ch. Hollyfir's Devil's Disciple ex Ch. Kearby's Major Barbara)
Breeder-Owner: Quita Youatt
1977 Ch. Brobar Clever Clogs (bw)
(Ch. Hardra's Prince Charming ex Brobar Elan)
Breeders-Owners: Mr. and Mrs Arthur Miller

NOTE: AS OF 1978, THE GOLDEN STATE TROPHY IS AWARDED TO THE BEST WHITE BITCH IN THE REGENT TROPHY COMPETITION.

1978 Ch. Jill of Brobar (bwb)
(Ch. Souperlative Jackadandy of Ormandy ex Brobar Elan)
Breeders: Mr. and Mrs. Arthur Miller
Owners: Mr. and Mrs. J. M. Whitham

1979 Harper's Holiday (bw)
(Ch. Souperlative Jackadandy of Ormandy ex Hoya of Harpers)
Breeder: D. Vick
Owner: M. Caruthers-Smith
1980 Kearby's Merry Dancer (bwb)
(Ch. Kearby's Black Buck ex Miriam of Kearby)
Breeders: Quita Youatt and G. Ellis
Owner: Mrs. S. Johnson
1981 Ch. Abraxas Count-On-Me (dbw)
(Ch. Hardra's Prince Hal ex Abraxas Achillea)
Breeder-Owner: Violet Drummond-Dick
1982 Ch. Silver Rose of Charlesdon (bwb)
(Ch. Souperlative Jackadandy of Ormandy ex Charlesdon China Rose)
Breeders: Mr. and Mrs. Anderson
Owners: Mr. and Mrs. Duggan
1983 Ch. Segreda St. Christopher of Dajan (dwb)
(Ch. Souperlative Explorer of Ormandy ex Segreda St. Clair)
Breeders: Mr. and Mrs. Huguenin
Owner: Janet Furneaux
1984 Bodyline of Brobar (bwb)
(Marton's Marauder ex Brobar Honeysuckle)
Breeders: Mr. and Mrs. G. Steels
Owners: Mr. and Mrs. Arthur Miller

Coverwood Casket

(for Runner-Up in the Regent Trophy—first awarded in 1965)

1965 Ch. Corinthian Silver Queen of Ormandy (bwr)
(Ormandy Souperlative Bar Sinister ex Ch. Ormandy's Duncannon Double Two)
Breeder: Raymond Oppenheimer
Owner: H. B. Bradbury
1966 Ch. Contango Clever Me (bwb)
(Ch. Ormandy Souperlative Bar Sinister ex Ch. Contango Quelle Chance)
Breeder-Owner: Joy Schuster
1967 Ormandy's Corinthian Clipper (bwb)
(Ch. Ormandy's Ben of Highthorpe ex Ch. Corinthian Silver Queen of Ormandy)
Breeder: H. B. Bradbury
Owner: T. J. Cochrane
1968 Ch. Abraxas Athenia (bwr)
(Ch. Monkery's Mr. Frosty of Ormandy ex Abraxas Souperlative Viola)
Breeder-Owner: Violet Drummond-Dick
1969 Ch. Ormandy's Caviar (dwb)
(Ch. Ormandy's Archangel ex Ch. Ormandy's Corinthian Clipper)
Breeder: T. Cochrane
Owners: Mr. and Mrs. O. Jensen

Eng. Ch. Curraneye Schoolgirl, winner of the 1975 Regent Trophy. This bitch is an example of the fine type produced by the Micklethwaites.

Eng. Ch. Curraneye Wonderba of Debirus, runner-up in 1984 to the Ormandy Jug for Bitches and a star of the 1985 show ring.

Ch. Jill of Brobar, winner of the Regent
Trophy in 1978.   *Fall*

Eng. Ch. Silver Rose of Charlesdon, winner of the 1982 Ormandy Jug for Bitches.

1970 Romany River Music (dwb)
      (Ch. Romany River Pirate ex Contango Cantata)
      Breeder: Joy Schuster
      Owners: Miss Montague-Johnstone and M. Williams
1971 Ch. Souperlative Laura (bbw)
      (Ch. Romany River Pirate ex Ch. Souperlative Rominten Rheingold)
      Breeder: E. M. Weatherill
      Owner: W. R. E. Harding
1972 Ch. Snow Mountain of Lenster (dwr)
      (Ch. Harper's Howda of Lenster ex Ch. Uglee Snow Blossem of Lenster)
      Breeders-Owners: Mrs. Mankin and Miss Graham-Weall
1973 Ch. Woodrow Minx (bwr)
      (Ch. Monkery's Caspian ex Souperlative Wren of Woodrow)
      Breeder-Owner: Helen Powe
1974 Ch. Brobar Elite (bwb)
      (Ch. Maerdy Maestro of Ormandy ex Brobar Horatia)
      Breeders: Mr. and Mrs. Arthur Miller
      Owners: Mr. and Mrs. I. D. Porter
1975 Ch. Keyhole of Brobar (bwb)
      (Recnad Silver Oak ex Pollyanna of Brobar)
      Breeder: Miss Fielding
      Owners: Mr. and Mrs. Arthur Miller
1976 Ch. Kearby's Temptress (bbw)
      (Ch. Hollyfir Devil's Disciple ex Ch. Kearby's Major Barbara)
      Breeder-Owner: Quita Youatt

NOTE: AS OF 1977 THE COVERWOOD CASKET IS AWARDED TO THE
BEST DOG IN THE REGENT TROPHY COMPETITION.

1977 Charlesdon Commander (dwb)
      (Ch. Badlesmere Bonaparte of Souperlative ex Charlesdon Little Peach)
      Breeder: Mrs. C. Boam
      Owners: Mr. and Mrs. J. Swiggs
1978 Ch. Contango Come On Jack (dwb)
      (Ch. Souperlative Jackadandy of Ormandy ex Contango Chat Me Up)
      Breeder-Owner: Joy Schuster
1979 Ch. Barrowboy of Badlesmere (dwb)
      (Ch. Segreda White Warlord ex Badlesmere Bryony)
      Breeders: Mr. and Mrs. Frost
      Owner: Mrs. J. Shaw
1980 Ch. Quilla of Quillon (dwr)
      (Ch. Jobrulu Jacobinia ex Jobrulu Camellia)
      Breeder: Joan Kenway
      Owners: Mr. and Mrs. B. Sait
1981 Ch. Abraxas Count-On-Me (dbw)
      (Ch. Hardra's Prince Hal ex Abraxas Achillea)
      Breeder-Owner: Violet Drummond-Dick

Eng. Ch. Segreda St. Christopher of Dajan won the Ormandy Dog Jug and the Coverwood Casket in 1983. This dog had as fine a rear as could be.

Eng. Ch. Moatvale Knight Valiant, winner of the Ormandy Jug for Dogs in 1979. A very typey brindle with less than good hindquarters.

Eng. Ch. Quilla of Quillon, winner of the
Regent Trophy in 1980.   *Fall*

Eng. Ch. Bella Bianca Jackenna, winner of the 1983 Regent Trophy.

1982 Ch. Maximillian Bully Boy of Jobrulu (dwb)
      (Ch. Souperlative Jackadandy of Ormandy ex Pontybully Sonata)
      Breeder: Mr. Bath
      Owners: Joan Kenway and Mr. and Mrs. Carroll
1983 Ch. Segreda St. Christopher of Dajan (dwb)
      (Ch. Souperlative Explorer of Ormandy ex Segreda St. Clair)
      Breeders: Mr. and Mrs. Huguenin
      Owner: Janet Furneaux
1984 Ch. Ghabar Crusader (dwb)
      (Eng./Am. Ch. Catrana Eye Opener of Aricon ex Brobar Silver Satin
      of Ghabar)
      Breeders-Owners: Mr. and Mrs. R. Edmond

Ormandy Jug Winners—Dogs (1970-1984)

1970 Ch. Abraxas Audacity (dwr)
      (Ch. Romany River Pirate ex Ch. Abraxas Athenia)
      Breeder-Owner: Violet Drummond-Dick
1971 Maerdy Mycropolis (dwb)
      (Souperlative Benbeau of Ormandy ex Maerdy Mona)
      Breeder-Owner: Bill Morgan
1972 Abraxas Achilles (dwb)
      (Ch. Ormandy's Archangel ex Ch. Abraxas Athenia)
      Breeder-Owner: Violet Drummond-Dick
1973 Monkery's Delantero Moonride (dwb)
      (Ch. Monkery's Caspian ex Delantero Lunar Princess)
      Breeder: Mrs. M. B. Howard-Williams
      Owner: Phyllis E. Holmes
1974 Ch. Badlesmere Bonaparte of Souperlative (dwr)
      (Ch. Maerdy Maestro of Ormandy ex Souperlative Booksale Angel's Tears)
      Breeder: Mrs. J. Shaw
      Owners: E. M. Weatherill and Raymond Oppenheimer
1975 Ch. Hollyfir's Devil's Disciple (dwr)
      (Ch. Maerdy Maestro of Ormandy ex Ch. Sweet Thursday of Hollyfir)
      Breeders: Mr. and Mrs. Jack Mildenhall
      Owner: R. Hill
1976 Ch. Jobrulu Jacqueminot (dwr)
      (Ch. Badlesmere Bonaparte of Souperlative ex Jobrulu Xotica)
      Breeder-Owner: Joan Kenway
1977 Charlesdon Commander (dwb)
      (Ch. Badlesmere Bonaparte of Souperlative ex Charlesdon Little Peach)
      Breeder: C. Boam
      Owners: Mr. and Mrs. J. Swiggs
1978 Ch. Contango Come On Jack (dwb)
      (Ch. Souperlative Jackadandy of Ormandy ex Contango Chat Me Up)
      Breeder-Owner: Joy Schuster

Eng. Ch. Contango Come On Jack, winner of the Ormandy Jug for Dogs and the Coverwood Casket in 1978, an exceptional dog in a year of phenomenal bitches.

Eng. Ch. Souperlative Silhouette, winner of the Ormandy Jug for Bitches in 1979. "Dolly" is Eva Weatherill's house pet, constant companion and a joy to behold.   *Fall*

Harper's Holiday, winner of the Regent Trophy in 1979, a daughter of Jackadandy who like so many of his champion offspring produced no puppies and died prematurely. *Fall*

Eng. Ch. Happy Hippolyta, winner of the 1980 Ormandy Jug for Bitches, another Jackadandy daughter who died prematurely.

1979 Moatvale Knight Valiant (dbw)
       (Ch. Souperlative Jackadandy of Ormandy ex Moatvale Minuet)
       Breeder: Miss McCombie
       Owner: T. Walton
1980 Meregis Jack Knife (dwr)
       (Ch. Souperlative Jackadandy of Ormandy ex Hollyfir's Merry Kate)
       Breeders-Owners: Mr. and Mrs. R. Bates
1981 Ch. Aricon's Chief Eye Shy (dwr)
       (Ch. Brobar Backchat ex Aricon Spanish Eyes)
       Breeder: Eric Stanley
       Owner: Robert K. Thomas
1982 Ch. Maximillian Bully Boy of Jobrulu (dwb)
       (Souperlative Jackadandy of Ormandy ex Pontybully Sonata)
       Breeder: Mr. Bath
       Owners: Joan Kenway and Mr. and Mrs. Carroll
1983 Ch. Segreda St. Christopher of Dajan (dwb)
       (Ch. Souperlative Explorer of Ormandy ex Segreda St. Clair)
       Breeders: Mr. and Mrs. Huguenin
       Owner: Janet Furneaux
1984 Ch. Faithfield Royal Sovereign (dwb)
       (Ch. Catrana Eye Opener of Aricon ex Laselle Rebecca of Faithfield)
       Breeders-Owners: Mr. and Mrs. A. Coupe

Ormandy Jug Winners—Bitches (1970-1984)

1970 Ch. Iella Cinderella (bwr)
       (Ch. Monkery's Mr. Frosty of Ormandy ex Valkyrie Zenith)
       Breeder-Owner: E. S. T. Hughes
1971 Ch. Souperlative Laura (bbw)
       (Ch. Romany River Pirate ex Ch. Souperlative Rominten Rheingold)
       Breeder: Miss E. M. Weatherill
       Owner: W. R. E. Harding
1972 Ch. Agate's Sweet Sauce (bwr)
       (Ch. Ormandy's Caviar ex Ch. Agate's Amethyst)
       Breeder-Owner: Margaret Sweeten
1973 Ch. Woodrow Minx (bwr)
       (Ch. Monkery's Caspian ex Souperlative Wren of Woodrow)
       Breeder-Owner: Helen Powe
1974 Ch. Brobar Elite (bwb)
       (Ch. Maerdy Maestro of Ormandy ex Brobar Horatia)
       Breeders: Mr. and Mrs. Arthur Miller
       Owners: Mr. and Mrs. I. D. Porter
1975 Ch. Keyhole Kate of Brobar (bwb)
       (Recnad Silver Oak ex Pollyanna of Brobar)
       Breeder: Mrs. Fielding
       Owners: Mr. and Mrs. Arthur Miller

1976 Souperlative Evanly of Sax (bwb)
(Ch. Maerdy Maestro of Ormandy ex Ch. Souperlative Scrumptious of Ormandy)
Breeder: E. M. Weatherill
Owner: T. Degg
1977 Ch. Brobar Clever Clogs (bwb)
(Ch. Hardra's Prince Charming ex Brobar Elan)
Breeders-Owners: Mr. and Mrs. Arthur Miller
1978 Jill of Brobar (bwb)
(Ch. Souperlative Jackadandy of Ormandy ex Brobar Elan)
Breeders: Mr. and Mrs. Arthur Miller
Owners: Mr. and Mrs. J. M. Whitham
1979 Ch. Souperlative Silhouette (bwb)
(Ch. Souperlative Jackadandy of Ormandy ex Souperlative Scrumptious of Ormandy)
Breeder-Owner: E. M. Weatherill
1980 Ch. Happy Hippolyta (bwb)
(Ch. Souperlative Jackadandy of Ormandy ex Eldo's Camilla)
Breeder: J. Wilson
Owner: R. Mitchell
1981 Contango's Classy Dame (bwb)
(Ch. Sequoiah County Game ex Court Gem of Contango)
Breeder-Owner: Joy Schuster
1982 Silver Rose of Charlesdon (bwb)
(Ch. Souperlative Jackadandy of Ormandy ex Charlesdon China Rose)
Breeders: Mr. and Mrs. Anderson
Owners: Mr. and Mrs. Duggan
1983 Ch. Bella Bianca Jackenna (bw)
(Ch. Souperlative Jackadandy of Ormandy ex Moatvale Morning Glory)
Breeder: G. Scott-Barrs
Owners: Mr. and Mrs. K. W. Higgins
1984 Bodyline of Brobar (bwb)
(Marton's Marauder ex Brobar Honeysuckle)
Breeders: Mr. and Mrs. G. Steels
Owners: Mr. and Mrs. Arthur Miller

8

The AKC Standard
—an Introduction

THE first record we can find of a purely American standard for judging the Bull Terrier appeared in the June 30, 1915 edition of the *American Kennel Gazette,* official publication of the American Kennel Club.

However, in the October 31, 1915 issue of the *Gazette* there was published a different version of this American Standard, preceded by the explanation that "Inadvertently there was sent us by the secretary of the Bull Terrier Club of America an incorrect standard, and same appeared in the June 30, 1915 issue. We now append the correct standard as approved by the Bull Terrier Club of America."

A comparison of the two versions of this American Standard leads to the conclusion that there were differences in the thinking back of the two versions that reflected serious conflict in opinions on type. These differences were as follows:

First Version: Muzzle should be neither square nor snipey, but should present a rounded appearance as viewed from above.

This seems to be obviously a different and not as clear way to define the egg-shaped head. It recalls the description of the head in the Standard of the Bull Terrier of Scotland, 1904.

Second Version: Muzzle wide and tapering, but without such taper as to make the nose appear pinched or snipey.

This type of head was contemporaneously often referred to as the "coffin-shaped" or "brick-shaped" head. It holds to the type head with a straight profile as called for by early Standards. Some prominent fanciers of the time considered that the term "down-ness" given in the Standard referred to expression, and not to any curvature of the profile. In fact, in the 1930s one breeder and judge so highly regarded the straight profile that he insisted that a Roman finish to the nose was a disqualification and judged his dogs accordingly.

This newer Standard on the head took the development of the breed away from the direction in which it had been going, the direction being followed by English breeders. In the States, egg-shaped heads were inevitably produced, but were immediately discarded. They were not wanted as they were not considered to fit either the Standard or the fashion. The ideal head became that of Ch. Haymarket Faultless (Best in Show at Westminster 1918). A headstudy of Faultless was carried at the beginning of the Bull Terrier column in the *Gazette* until 1938, when it was replaced by a picture closer to the head type being imported by American breeders.

Another interesting difference in the two versions was the matter of weight. The first version stated "Weight is not a matter of importance, so long as a specimen is typical." The second version specified "From 12 to 60 pounds inclusive."

It is rather an astonishing thing to learn that at the time English breeders were developing the great heads and stocky bodies that were so to influence American breeders in future years, and Lord Gladiator and his descendants were setting new standards of greatness, American breeders were turning their backs on this natural evolution and breeding a type that degenerated until the English imports came on to dominate the shows in their own persons and get. It is especially astonishing when one recalls the admission of English breeders at the start of the century that more and better Bull Terriers were to be found in America then than in all of England.

American breeders misguidedly went to great efforts to lengthen heads, which gradually weakened the muzzle and led to the oft-quoted expression "couldn't bite through a biscuit." Together with length of head was inevitably produced a leggy, narrow dog with the very characteristics that Mr. Pegg decried in the English dogs of 1907.

Around 1930, a tendency to ignore the American standard began to manifest itself. More and more dogs with uncropped ears were being shown, despite the fact that the Standard called for a cropped ear. In fact, the Bull Terrier selected for the American Kennel Club's official book of the standards, *The Complete Dog Book,* Ch. Comfey, had an uncropped ear, even though the Standard given in that very same volume (1936) called for a cropped ear.

In 1954, at the annual meeting of the Bull Terrier Club in England, it was suggested that a new Standard be drawn up. A Committee was formed, with Raymond Oppenheimer as Chairman.

In 1956, the English Standard was about complete. It was a model of simplicity and clarity. I saw the opportunity for a new American Standard and wrote Mr. Oppenheimer asking if I could copy the "new" English Standard, and he responded affirmatively. I contacted the officers of the Bull Terrier Club of America and some breeders, and all agreed it was a great idea. They felt that the English breeders who formulated the Standard had done such an excellent job that there was no need for another committee to duplicate their work, especially since a Committee of the BTCA appointed in 1952 to revise the Standard could not even agree on the head.

The new Standard was proposed and presented in its exact English form at the meeting held in July, 1956. Three changes were voted and the new Standard was approved unanimously.

The American Kennel Club unofficially stated that several changes would be necessary before the Standard could be approved. One of these changes provided for a separate Standard for each variety, rather than a combined Standard. I wrote Mr. John Neff, then Executive Vice-President of the American Kennel Club, stating that "any attempt to modernize our Standard has been met with suspicion. This is the proposed new English Standard, word for word."

At the regular Fall meeting of the Bull Terrier Club of America, the new Standard was voted in unanimously and adopted August 30, 1956. The American Kennel Club approved it on December 11 of the same year.

As was to be expected, there was some criticism of the new Standard. Peculiarly enough, a good part of that criticism was directed at phrases that are practically identical with those of the old Standard.

One of the outstanding features of the new Standard is that attention is concentrated upon what a dog *should be,* rather than on what it *should not be.* Judges guided by the Standard will do a better job because they know what to look for. Judges who look for what a dog should *not* be, will never increase their knowledge and will be constantly exposing ignorance because they have not learned to recognize a good dog.

In eliminating a listing of faults, the Standard credits the judge with the common sense and ability, as well as the responsibility, to learn what to look for. Most of our bad judging (and bad breeding) comes from concentrating on faults rather than virtues. If the advice of those who put accent on faults were followed, the greatest Bull Terriers ever born would never have been bred.

In his column on Terriers in the October 1964 issue of *Popular Dogs,* Dr. E. S. Montgomery, famous judge and breeder (Monty-Ayr prefix) wrote:

> Some years ago the Bull Terrier Club of America revised the Standard of Perfection. It then set, and still sets, a precedent and a target for *all* breed clubs. The Standard tells only what a good Bull Terrier should look like, . . . not what it should not look like.

The publication of the English Standard was delayed for three years, until 1959. It is, in general, much the same as the American.

Further revision to the American Standard was made and approved as of September 10, 1968. Two changes were made.

In the 1956 Standard, the provision for Color in the White Bull Terrier had read:

> *The Color should be pure white, though markings on the head are permissible. Any markings elsewhere on the coat shall disqualify.*

This was revised to read:

> *The Color is white though markings on the head are permissible. Any markings elsewhere are to be severely faulted. Skin pigmentation is not to be penalized.*

The 1968 Standard also made *blue eyes* a disqualification in both the White and Colored varieties.

A further revision was approved in 1974. In the paragraph on *Color* for the Colored variety, the sentence which read: *Preferred color, brindle,* was amended to read: *Other things being equal, the preferred color is brindle.*

To help the reader in his understanding of the Standard, we have included diagrammed pictures illustrating some of its main points. A few words regarding the dogs used as models in these pictures may be in order.

The dog used as model in the picturizations taken straight·head-on and straight from the rear was selected because of his lack of exaggeration —his points are easy to understand because his type lies between the extremes of terrier and Bulldog. These are poses rather difficult to secure and are not ordinarily as flattering as those taken from a slight angle. Other pictures may show dogs with a greater curvature of profile, a more exaggerated ear placement, a greater spring of rib, but none that in their entirety gives such a pleasing impression of type and balance. A judge keeping this dog in mind as a modest ideal will also not go too far astray.

The skeleton has been superimposed upon the same front and rear pictures in order to better show the relationship between the actual flesh one sees and the underlying bone structure. In order to avoid the confusion of too many lines, most of which would help but little in an understanding of fundamental structure, only the principal bones have been shown.

Ch. Marko of Monty-Ayr, bred and owned by Dr. E. S. Montgomery, handler, William Snebold.

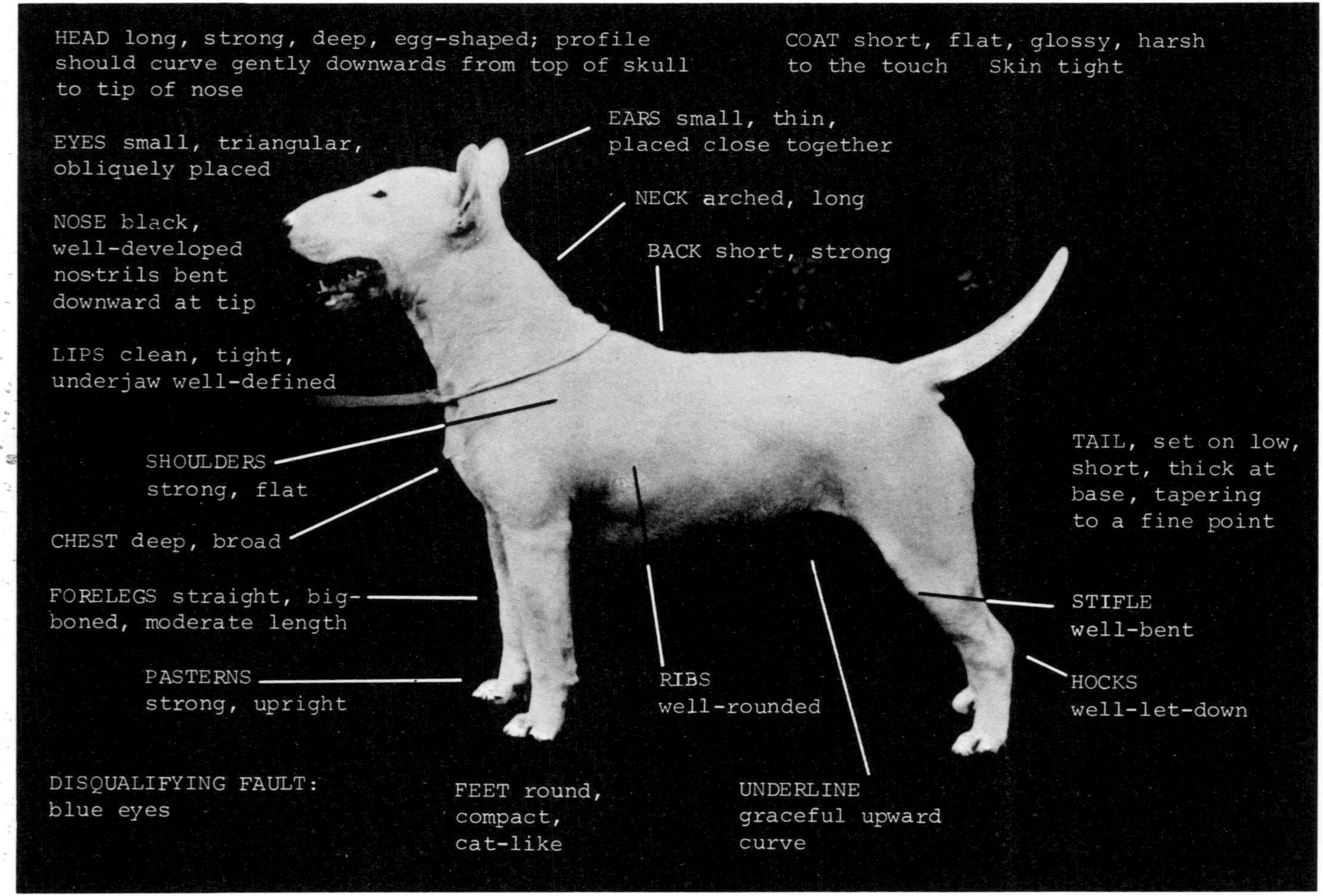

HEAD long, strong, deep, egg-shaped; profile
should curve gently downwards from top of skull
to tip of nose

COAT short, flat, glossy, harsh
to the touch Skin tight

EYES small, triangular,
obliquely placed

EARS small, thin,
placed close together

NECK arched, long

BACK short, strong

TAIL, set on low,
short, thick at
base, tapering
to a fine point

STIFLE
well-bent

HOCKS
well-let-down

NOSE black,
well-developed
nostrils bent
downward at tip

LIPS clean, tight,
underjaw well-defined

RIBS
well-rounded

UNDERLINE
graceful upward
curve

SHOULDERS
strong, flat

CHEST deep, broad

FORELEGS straight, big-
boned, moderate length

PASTERNS
strong, upright

FEET round,
compact,
cat-like

DISQUALIFYING FAULT:
blue eyes

9

Official Breed Standard
of the Bull Terrier

As adopted by the Bull Terrier Club of America, and
approved by the American Kennel Club, July 9, 1974.

THE Bull Terrier must be strongly built, muscular, symmetrical and active, with a keen determined and intelligent expression, full of fire but of sweet disposition and amenable to discipline.

WHITE

The Head should be long, strong and deep right to the end of the muzzle, but not coarse. Full face it should be oval in outline and be filled completely up, giving the impression of fullness with a surface devoid of hollows or indentations, i.e. egg-shaped. In profile it should curve gently downwards from the top of the skull to the tip of the nose. The forehead should be flat across from ear to ear. The distance from the tip of the nose to the eyes should be perceptibly greater than that from the eyes to the top of the skull. The underjaw should be deep and well defined.

The Lips should be clean and tight.

The Teeth should meet in either a level or in a scissors bite. In the scissors bite the upper teeth should fit in front of and closely against the lower teeth, and they should be sound, strong and perfectly regular.

99

The Ears should be small, thin and placed close together. They should be capable of being held stiffly erect, when they should point upwards.

The Eyes should be well sunken and as dark as possible, with a piercing glint and they should be small, triangular and obliquely placed; set near together and high up on the dog's head. Blue eyes are a disqualification.

The Nose should be black, with well developed nostrils bent downwards at the tip.

The Neck should be very muscular, long, arched and clean, tapering from the shoulders to the head and it should be free from loose skin.

The Chest should be broad when viewed from in front, and there should be great depth from withers to brisket, so that the latter is nearer the ground than the belly.

The Body should be well rounded with marked spring of rib, the back should be short and strong. The back ribs deep. Slightly arched over the loin. The shoulders should be strong and muscular but without heaviness. The shoulder blades should be wide and flat and there should be a very pronounced backward slope from the bottom edge of the blade to the top edge. Behind the shoulders there should be no slackness or dip at the withers. The underline from the brisket to the belly should form a graceful upward curve.

The Legs should be big-boned, but not to the point of coarseness; the forelegs should be of moderate length, perfectly straight, and the dog must stand firmly upon them. The elbows must turn neither in nor out, and the pasterns should be strong and upright. The hind legs should be parallel viewed from behind. The thighs very muscular with hocks well let down. Hind pasterns short and upright. The stifle joint should be well bent with a well developed second thigh.

The Feet round and compact with well-arched toes like a cat.

The Tail should be short, set on low, fine, and ideally should be carried horizontally. It should be thick where it joins the body, and should taper to a fine point.

The Coat should be short, flat, harsh to the touch and with a fine gloss. The dog's skin should fit tightly.

The Color is white though markings on the head are permissible. Any markings elsewhere on the coat are to be severely faulted. Skin pigmentation is not to be penalized.

Movement. The dog shall move smoothly, covering the ground with free, easy strides, fore and hind legs should move parallel each to each when viewed from in front or behind. The forelegs reaching out well and the hind legs moving smoothly at the hip and flexing well at the stifle and hock. The dog should move compactly and in one piece but with a typical jaunty air that suggests agility and power.

100

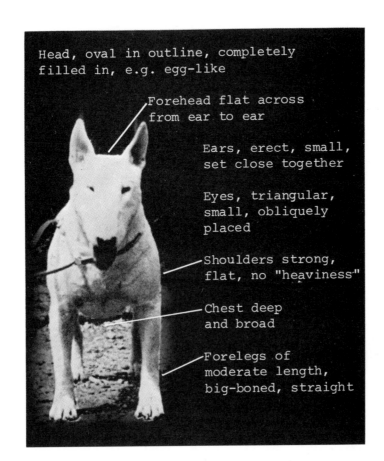

Head, oval in outline, completely filled in, e.g. egg-like

Forehead flat across from ear to ear

Ears, erect, small, set close together

Eyes, triangular, small, obliquely placed

Shoulders strong, flat, no "heaviness"

Chest deep and broad

Forelegs of moderate length, big-boned, straight

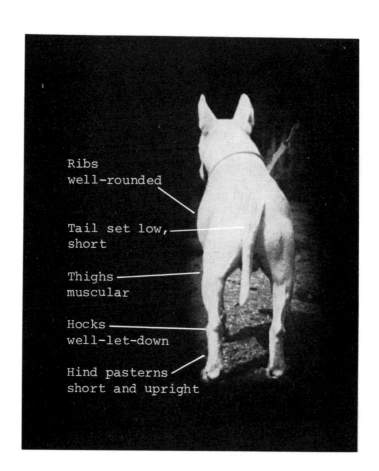

Ribs
well-rounded

Tail set low,
short

Thighs
muscular

Hocks
well-let-down

Hind pasterns
short and upright

102

Faults. Any departure from the foregoing points shall be considered a fault, and the seriousness of the fault shall be in exact proportion to its degree, *i.e.* a very crooked front is a very bad fault; a rather crooked front is a rather bad fault; and a slightly crooked front is a slight fault.

DISQUALIFICATION:
Blue eyes.

COLORED

The Standard for the Colored Variety is the same as for the White except for the sub-head "Color" which reads:

Color. Any color other than white, or any color with white markings. Other things being equal, the preferred color is brindle. A dog which is predominantly white shall be disqualified.

DISQUALIFICATIONS:
Blue eyes.
Any dog which is predominantly white.

Raymond H. Oppenheimer with Ch. Ormandy
Souperlative Chunky and Ch. Burson's Belinda.

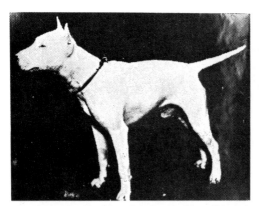

Ch. Haymarket Faultless (left) Best in Show, Westminster, 1918. Ch. Argent Arrogance, (right) a
California Best in Show winner a half century later. These dogs all show the evolution of type
through the years.

10

The Four Variations in Bull Terrier Type

by Raymond H. Oppenheimer

T HERE are today four distinct types of Bull Terriers to be seen in the show ring, and a careful study of photographs back to the early days convinces me that these four types have always existed since the breed first took recognizable shape. What is more, three of these types quite clearly reveal the separate and distinct ancestry from which the Bull Terrier originated.

Many people both inside and outside the breed deplore this diversity, but I believe keen students of Bull Terriers find it one of the breed's greatest charms, because it admits a considerable number of possible permutations and combinations which breeders can employ in seeking to achieve their ideal, an ideal which varies from breeder to breeder which provides that spice without which any activity sinks into a dull monotony.

Let us now examine these four types and classify them, with an example of each:

First, there is the Bull Terrier with the accent on "Bull," an obvious and magnificent specimen of this being Ch. Beech House Ballyhooligan.

Next, we show the Bull Terrier with the accent on "Terrier," and here we need not look further than the outstanding Ch. Kowhai Uncle Bimbo.

Third, is the above Bull Terrier with the accent equally divided between the two words. A splendid example of this is Ch. The Sphinx.

Last, we have the "Dalmatian" type. I must make it clear that I mean no reference here to ticks. Anyone who is in doubt as to what I am trying to explain should study the photo above of the great Dalmatian Ch. Snow Leopard. If they will mentally give him a Bull Terrier's head and a pure white coat, they will see at once the similarity in build to certain famous Bull Terriers, though naturally the Bull Terriers are heavier. A good example of this type is Ch. Ormandy Souperlative Snowflash.

Three types show clearly the three breeds which were used in building up the Bull Terrier, i.e., Bulldog, English Terrier, and Dalmatian, while the fourth type is a blend of the other three.

Each of these types has its devotees, but the fascinating thing is that history teaches us—and personal experience confirms—that all four types are necessary to keep the breed progressing. A breeder who will not use the "Bulls" soon finds his line beginning to lose substance; if he will not use the "Terriers" he finds his line beginning to lack corkiness and fire; if he will not use the blended types he finds his line beginning to lack balance; while if he will not use the "Dalmatians" he is soon in trouble with a lack of reach and style.

In many books on breeding one will find the advice that it is a mistake to mate extremes together in the hope of getting something halfway between, because the puppies will normally take after one parent or the other. This advice is excellent where one is dealing with what, for want of a better expression, I will call specific physical features; e.g., it would certainly be ridiculous to mate together a dog whose feet turned out and a bitch whose feet turned in with the fantastic hope of having puppies whose feet turned neither in nor out. But where the question is one of proportions or "type," in this context, the uniting of extremes is often exceedingly successful, since the characteristics involved are ones which blend. For example, if one mates together a well-bred "Bull" and a well-bred "Dalmatian," it is distinctly exceptional to get a litter as "Bullish" or as "Dalmatianish" as either parent—and, although many geneticists will frown in displeasure at this statement, it is a demonstrable fact, and one the appreciation of which will help breeders immensely in their efforts to obtain the builds they require.

Once this fact has been understood, there is really no more one need say, provided that the breeder's eye is accurate in assessing the proportions of those animals with a view toward choosing their mates.

The hallmark of a good judge and the greatest gift which a breeder can possess, is the ability to appreciate a good dog or bitch of any one of these types. When judging I have always tried to guard against any tendency to lean towards any particular type. By this I mean that I try to concern myself only with the dog's physical perfections or imperfections. In this connection I always find the criticism, often heard at shows, that such-and-such a judge has not stuck to one type not only senseless, but also proof that the critics themselves cannot know what they are talking about, since no judge should leave out a top class Bull Terrier even if it is the type for which the judge has a personal predilection.

However, I want to utter one serious word of warning. Bull Terriers can be so extreme in type, towards the Bulldog, or towards the Dalmatian, or towards the Terrier, as to cease to conform at all to the general type outlined by the Bull Terrier Standard. I should not like anyone to read into what I have written a suggestion that departures of so violent a nature are good or are even to be excused by judges. The four types of which I speak are really subdivisions, within the general type, and a smooth-coated, pure white Borzoi or its opposite, a Bulldog with a Bull Terrier head, should not be tolerated by any judge or breeder who knows the job.

A good judge should be prepared to assess, without prejudice, any Bull Terrier whose variation in type remains within limits legitimately covered by the wording of the breed Standard, but should equally be prepared to deal, without mercy, with any animal, however well made, which departs too far from the accepted Standard to be reasonable.

Type is and must be the prime essential of every breed, since, in the final analysis, it is only type which differentiates one breed from another or the purebred from the mongrel.

Now to pass from the general to the particular. Correct Bull Terrier type as we see it in England is a blend between the Terrier and the Bulldog, onto which is added the various specific points as set out in our Standard. A departure from that correct type towards an undue emphasis of the Terrier or Bulldog characteristics is very bad, as is any Houndy tendency, because we feel that the dog immediately ceases to conform to the basic demands of the Standard which was grounded upon the conceptions of those who produced the original White Bull Terrier.

I have spoken of a blend and in that connection I should make it clear that in our view, the blending not only applies to individual tendencies but also, most important of all, to the proportions. These agree proportions are not simply the outcome of the whim of some bewhiskered ancestor of the modern fancier. They are, on the contrary, based upon sound mechanical knowledge as to what best constitutes theoretically the ideal fighting machine. With that in mind, the framers of our Standard demanded width of chest for stability, shortness of back to give maneuverability and quick turning power, and enough length of foreleg for reach and agility. Onto these proportions they added the other necessary points, e.g., correct shoulders, strong hindquarters, and so on, to complete the perfect fighter.

In addition, there were some points added for purely aesthetic reasons (such as a white coat, no wall eyes and other points which we all know), until there emerged the picture of a splendid animal, complete in every detail and of a type quite unmistakable.

Look at the full face. The head should appear long and strong and it should be oval or egg-shaped; that is to say, it should be filled up everywhere so that the surface has no hollows or bumps. There should be a minimum of loose skin, especially around the throat and mouth, while the forehead should be flat from ear to ear and not domed or peaked like a gnome. The cheeks should be flat and clean—not coarse and lumpy. The ears should be on top of the dog's head, fairly close together and should be capable of being held by the dog stiffly erect, when they should point upwards and neither sideways nor forwards. When all these features are present, the head gives a general impression of smoothness—almost as if it had been "blown up" with an air pump.

In profile the head should form nearly an unbroken line curving slowly downwards from the top almost to the end of the nose, where it should— for the last half inch or so—curve down a little more steeply, producing that feature generally referred to as the "Roman finish." Continuing in profile, the head should give an appearance of depth and should look neither shallow nor bird-like, nor should the profile to be so exaggeratedly curved or angulated as to cause the dog to look like some kind of sheep. The head should be in proportion to the rest of the dog.

One other feature of paramount importance is the dog's eye and more particularly, expression. The eye itself should be as nearly black as possible and it should be well sunk into the head. The opening into which the eye is sunk should be high upon the dog's head so that the distance from the nose to the eye is perceptibly greater than that from the eye to the top of the head. Further, the opening should be small, triangular, and, above all, slanting so that it points upwards and outwards. With these features the dog will have the true Bull Terrier expression which, for me, contains something of the gay, proud, mischievous, and grave, and much of the impassive, repelling, and inscrutable.

The Bull Terrier should have a wide chest with straight front legs and clean shoulders (i.e., shoulders that are not rounded or bulgy when looked at head-on). They should be firmly attached to the dog's body and the shoulder blades should be well laid back. A line drawn from the front and bottom of the shoulder blade to the top and back of it should point up over the middle of the dog's back and not directly upwards only just behind his head. When the shoulder blades are thus laid back, the dog's neck comes into its body in a clean sweep and not at that very unattractive near right angle which spoils so many quite nicely arched necks. A neck that is reachy, arched and muscular, and sweeps smoothly into the line of the back is one of the most distinguishing marks of a good Bull Terrier.

Looking down on the dog's back, the spring or bowing of its ribs should be plain to see and it should be much wider across the back than across the loins. Looked at sideways, the dog's brisket should be much nearer the ground than its belly. It is this formation which gives an appearance of lowness to ground as opposed to the ill-balanced, Bulldoggy, stunted appearance of so many with too short legs.

110

Continuing to look at the dog sideways, its back should be short, strong, and level to the loin, where there should be a slight rise (or roach), after which the line should curve smoothly downwards and be set off nicely by the tail, which should be attached low down. It should taper from base to tip and be carried parallel to the ground. Beneath this should come well-muscled, broad hindquarters leading to a well-bent stifle and a well-angulated hock, giving almost an impression as if the dog were slightly crouched to spring. Another important attribute of a well-made dog is that the various parts of the body should be in proportion to each other. That is to say, the length of the leg should be in proportion to the width of the dog, to its length of back, and so on, and it is of paramount importance that the dog should **neither be nor look disconnected.**

Finally, when the dog moves, the front and hind legs should travel parallel, straight toward the observer and straight away. The dog should cover the ground easily with a swinging, springy stride, the front legs reaching out well forward and the hind legs flexing easily at the stifle and hock. The dog should move smoothly, truly, and strongly from the hip, carrying itself proudly and in one piece.

So far I have only dealt in detail with head, make and shape, and proportions. If we add big and round but not coarse bone, strong "cat" feet, a temperament obedient but full of go, and muscles rippling beneath a shining coat, we shall have gone a long way to describing a dog in which every feature is in proportion to all the others. Then the predominating impression will be not of some outstanding point, but of general all-round excellence approaching the Standard's description of "a strongly built, muscular, active, symmetrical animal, with a keen determined expression, full of fire but of sweet disposition, amenable to discipline."

No one has ever bred the perfect Bull Terrier, no one ever will, but in the struggle to approach the unattainable lies the source of so much happiness to so many. In the foregoing words I have tried to paint a picture of the unattainable which we in England are trying to approach.

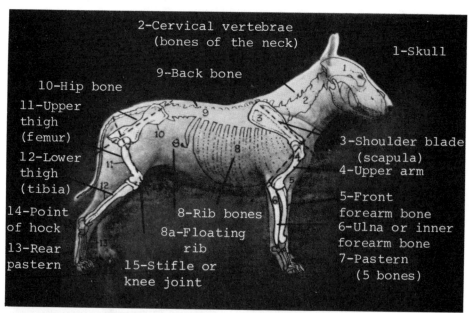

2-Cervical vertebrae
(bones of the neck)

1-Skull

9-Back bone

10-Hip bone

11-Upper
thigh
(femur)

12-Lower
thigh
(tibia)

14-Point
of hock

13-Rear
pastern

3-Shoulder blade
(scapula)
4-Upper arm

5-Front
forearm bone
6-Ulna or inner
forearm bone
7-Pastern
(5 bones)

8-Rib bones
8a-Floating
rib
15-Stifle or
knee joint

1-Scapula

2-Upper arm

3-Inner bone
of forearm
4-Front bone
of forearm

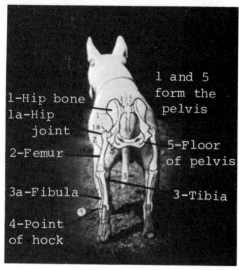

1-Hip bone
la-Hip
joint

2-Femur

3a-Fibula

4-Point
of hock

1 and 5
form the
pelvis

5-Floor
of pelvis

3-Tibia

112

11

Skeleton of the Bull Terrier Analyzed

by T. J. Horner

An understanding of the main parts of the skeleton is necessary to a proper understanding of how a dog is put together under the flesh and muscle. In order to explain more fully the points depicted on the preceding two pages, it would seem a good idea to include the comments of T. J. Horner, which appeared in an early Bull Terrier Club Annual, *since this is the best explanation I have seen. A foremost journalist and judge in England, Mr. Horner was then one of the leading Bull Terrier breeders, and his "Tartary" prefix is well known in the breed.*

Y EARS ago, Bull Terrier breeders and judges were almost wholly concerned with the finishing touches to the breed—downfaces and fill-up, dark eyes, fine, tick-free coats, small neat ears, etc.; in other words, they were more concerned with the icing than the cake. It is only fair to say that in those days there were a few hardy individualists who preached make and shape, soundness and character. But theirs were voices crying in the wilderness and few heeded them, certainly not the winning owners who were content to strive for bigger and better downfaces, leaving make and shape to those cranks who were interested in it. And who can blame them? For were not the biggest winners the possessors of the best downfaces? A little before World War II there was a sudden awakening of interest in substance, and it was soon decided that a Bull Terrier could be an outstanding specimen without an outstanding head, provided it had enormous substance. Before long, clever breeders combined good heads and great substance, but then found that even the best Bull Terriers were still lacking in that subtle something which makes a dog look right from any angle. It was at this stage that a real interest in make and shape began to take hold of the fancy, which has led to the marked improvement so apparent in the breed today.

There is nothing secret or occult about make and shape: indeed it is a fascinating subject that can be an enormous help to breeders in their efforts to produce that perfect Bull Terrier. The skeleton is the key to make and shape, which in all normally shaped breeds is approximately the same, varying only in proportions as type varies in different breeds.

So many people boggle at the words "make and shape" and turn glassy-eyed at mention of the skeleton, that I think it is time to drag it out of the cupboard. Let's take a closer look to see just how it is put together and some of the ways in which it can get out of shape. To be really successful as breeders and judges, it is essential that we should know something about the foundations on which we are trying to build our ideal. No one would try to build a house from the roof downwards, and it seems to me unreasonable to expect to breed a Bull Terrier by considering only heads, leaving the rest to chance and good feeding—as so many have done in the past.

The skull should have an egg-like appearance with great strength under and between the eyes. There should be a distinct downward inclination from the brow forward, but no stop; nor should there be any angle or abrupt falling away at this point. The Standard calls for an egg-shaped head—and eggs do not have angles. The underjaw should be deep, strong and in proportion to the rest of the skull. The teeth should be level, even and the jaws fitting to give that vice-like grip so characteristic of the breed. Crooked teeth, as well as under- and overshot jaws weaken this grip and therefore are faults.

The neck, which is an extension of the backbone, should be long and strong enough to give the dog a proud carriage of the head and provide great strength and mobility in action. Too long a neck unbalances and weakens the dog, too short a neck detracts from mobility and gives a stuffy appearance foreign to the breed.

The forequarters consist of the shoulder blade, upper arm and forearm, the pasterns and the foot, and the joints which couple them together. The feet should be small, thickly padded, closely knit, and should point straight forward, standing or moving. The pasterns, which are the dog's shock-absorbers as well as providing a flexible joint between the feet and the forearm, should be short, strong, upright, and yet have a certain elasticity. The forearm with the pastern and foot forms the foreleg, which should be straight viewed from any angle, and placed well under the dog, but should not turn out nor be so closely knit to the body as to restrict movement.

The upper arm is the bone which slopes obliquely forward from the elbow to the point or base of the shoulder blade. The ideal is a long upper arm forming a right angle with a long shoulder blade when the dog is standing normally. A short upper arm leads to a steep shoulder placement, very common in our breed and often accompanied by excess muscle on shoulders, loose elbows, and a short neck giving the animal a thick Bulldog-like appearance and very restricted action.

Shoulder blades should be long and set well back and also inclined inwards toward the withers. This formation allows a long, arched neck, broad at the base and tapering gracefully into the skull, without loss of strength. Extremely steep shoulders are sometimes accompanied by a long neck which completely lacks arch, in extreme cases curving in toward the front of the dog. This is a ewe neck and a very ugly fault. Upright shoulders often are accompanied by a dip behind the withers, well laid back shoulders seldom are.

The chest should be broad with the brisket coming well below the elbow.

The body of the dog is in three parts. First, the back and barrel, consisting of the section from the point of the withers to the last rib, includes the ribs themselves which should be deep, well-rounded and carried well-back. The back should be short and level and the underline of the ribs should show a graceful curve from the point of the chest up into the loins. The loins form the second part of the body and reach from the last rib to the croup—the point at which the pelvis is attached to the spine. The loins should be short, broad, and slightly arched. There should be a distinct "cut up" or rise in the underline of the belly, and the flanks should be clearly defined. Lack of these points produces a "sausage body" in which chest and belly are the same depth and chest and flanks the same thickness—a bad fault and all too common in the breed. Third, the croup, from the end of the loin to the root of the tail, should continue the arch of the loins and curve slightly downward to the tail, which should be set on low, be short, thick at the root and taper to a fine point. It should be flexible and free of breaks or kinks.

The hind legs are attached to the body by the pelvis, a large bone plate which is attached to the spine at the end of the loin. At its lower extremities are two ball and socket joints which fit into the upper ends of the hind legs. The hind leg consists of the femur and the tibia, the upper and lower long bones which are connected by the stifle joint. The tibia is connected to the back pastern by the hock joint and by the pastern to the foot.

115

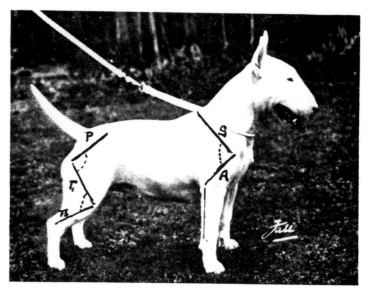

S.4   The bones angled correctly

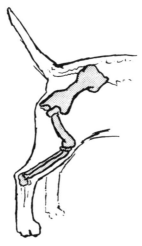

S.5   Well bent stifle

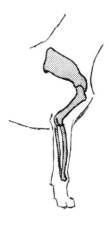

S.6   Shoulder well laid back

A study of the accompanying pictures and diagrams will show the correct angle of the bones to each other in both the fore and hind limbs. In all cases, widening the angle has a detrimental effect.

Compare the shoulder in picture S.4 with that of S.7. In S.4 the angle of the shoulder to the upper foreleg is approximately 90° which is correct. In S.7 it is wider giving the characteristic upright shoulder.

The hindquarters in S.4 and S.8 show how opening the angle gives a straight stifle joint, because the pelvis is insufficiently angled to the upper thigh.

S. —Shoulder (Scapula)

A. —Upper Foreleg

P. —Pelvis

T1. —Upper Thigh

T2. —Lower Thigh

S.F.—Stifle Joint

S.7   Upright shoulder   **S.8**   Straight stifle

117

The top of the femur fits into the socket of the pelvis at the hip, and the all-important angulation of the hind leg depends on the angle at which the pelvis is attached to the spine. The ideal—again we assume the dog to be standing normally—is halfway between vertical and horizontal, about 45° to the spine. This position permits the dog to reach well forward and allows ample drive from behind. A pelvis set at a steep angle—more nearly vertical—tends to shorten the leg bones, reduce the length of stride forward and back. The angles at the stifle and hock will then give a short, choppy, stilted hind action, very common in extra short-bodied dogs. This is usually accompanied by very steep shoulder placement and gives a Bulldoggy appearance. The opposite condition, when the pelvis is set at too flat an angle, produces overangulation. Here the dog's leg bones are unduly lengthened and the bend of stifle unduly exaggerated. The dog's hocks are pushed too far behind, as seen in some German Shepherd Dogs. This gives a weak, uncontrolled action, but is seldom seen in Bull Terriers. Even with the pelvis in the right position, unless the angles at stifle and hock are approximately correct, the dog will still be unbalanced and will be unable to move with freedom and drive. The correct angles at stifle and hock are those which in any given dog—whether tall or short on leg, long or short in body—bring the stifle joints well forward under the dog, and the hocks a little further to the rear than the root of the tail. To some extent these angles are governed by the length of femur and tibia. The whole conformation of the hind legs is dependent on all component parts being in harmonious proportion to each other so the dog both looks and is firmly balanced on its feet and is able to move freely and strongly from the hocks. In some cases these angles are almost non-existent, giving the formation known as "straight in stifle." When the line from the hip to the foot is nearly vertical, it has the effect of pushing the dog's latter end up and gives a dip in the back and a complete inability to move with freedom and drive.

Hocks should be well defined and remain parallel both standing and moving. The distance between them should be in proportion to the general width of the dog—they should look neither close nor wide apart. The back pasterns should be short, strong, and upright, with the hind feet rather smaller than the forefeet.

The entire skeleton should be closely knit together and the dog should move all in one piece.

No one will ever breed a perfect Bull Terrier, but if breeders will bear the skeleton in mind when planning matings, they will have a far better chance of achieving the impossible than if they leave it to rot in its traditional cupboard.

12

Analysis of Bull Terrier Structure

by Herbert H. Stewart

Mr. Stewart, an artist and an engineer, owned Bull Terriers for some forty-five years. He is the breeder of Ch. Buccaneer, three times Best Bull Terrier at Westminster, and is internationally known as an authoritative judge who knows type thoroughly. He was among the very first to understand and appreciate the trend toward the modern type of Bull Terrier. His sketches and remarks, originally published in Bull Terriers of Today, *are so fundamental to a proper understanding of what to look for that they are reprinted here.*

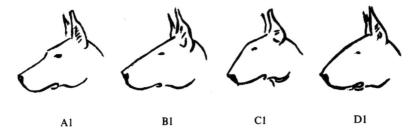

| A1 | B1 | C1 | D1 |

SHAPE OF HEAD: The above heads are all of the same length, the only difference being in downface. A1 is a poor type head, still encountered in the show ring. B1 is a much better type head, brick shaped; the top is practically straight. C1 shows a false type of downface induced by 'angulation.' This type head is not as powerful as D1 and is always accompanied by a high eyebrow which is a fault. It is, however, a step in the stage of evolution towards D1. D1 shows downface; this head looks shorter than A1 and B1 because fill and arc lend an optical illusion. This type head usually has a deeper, stronger underjaw which gives a further illusion of shortness. Now to assure yourself that the drawings all show heads of the same length and proportions, measure them.

A2   B2   C2

In A2 notice how the lack of fill and the wide skull give an appearance of coarseness, whereas in C2, with the same width, the "egg-shape" gives a clean feeling despite the tremendous space for leverage where the jaw joins the skull. In B2, although the skull is clean and the expression is good, note how much weaker the head appears even though it looks to be longer.

E1   F1   G1

EYES: The eye gives the Bull Terrier its characteristic expression. E1 shows a small triangular eye that is placed as in an Airedale; there is no Bull Terrier expression here. F1 shows a deep-set round eye; again there is no Bull Terrier expression and would be none, no matter how small the eye was. G1 shows an eye slanted down towards the nose—this is a true Bull Terrier eye, properly placed, and gives the true Bull Terrier expression. No matter how small, well shaped, and deep set an eye may be, it is a poor Bull Terrier eye if it is not slanted as in G1.

120

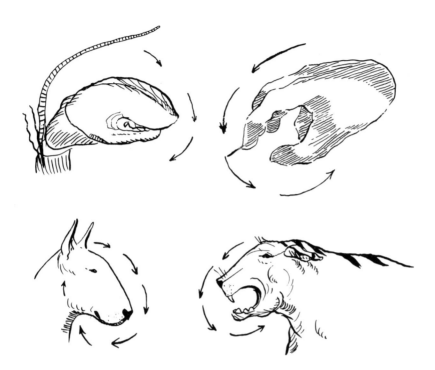

DOWNFACE is probably the most important development of the Bull Terrier of today. It is more than expression—it is an actual curvature of the top of the head or, as the English Standard puts it, "The profile should be almost an arc from the occiput to the tip of the nose . . . almost egg-shaped."

This "downface" is not a fad. It is the key to a stronger muzzle than the Bull Terrier ever had before. Most all powerful, flesh tearing animals have a downface, as this gives leverage. The arrows in the sketches indicate the flow lines of the power.

Note that the lobster has two claws, one long and thin for grasping like a pair of tongs, the other larger and thicker, used for crushing. Take a look at a Stillson wrench, the only kind that has enough leverage to unscrew a rusted pipe. Also at your own hands when they grasp something. Sort of lobster claw-like, are they not?

Note how much fill and downface there is in the head of a tiger. Then transfer this physical aspect of jaw power to the head of the Bull Terrier; see how man's selective breeding has taken this mechanical principle developed by nature and used it to give the Bull Terrier a stronger yet at the same time a more beautiful head than it ever before possessed. One might almost see that "fill" and "downface" are a natural in the breed because sometimes it pops up most unexpectedly and in a big way.

121

BODIES are of two general types. One is short, chunky, rather low set and compact, as shown at the left. The other is long and rangy, high on leg, as shown at the right. It is obvious which gives the greater impression of power and fast action at close quarters. The rangy type may be a pretty dog, but is apt to be weedy, flat sided, with head and body too narrow. Either a straight or an angular head is likely to go with the rangy dog, whereas true downface seems to be linked more with the chunky type.

FRONT should show straight legs, a powerful chest and clean shoulders. Compare the sense of power shown by the dog at the left with the narrow-chested, rangy type shown at the right. Remember that the Bull Terrier packs the most power in the least space—and should always look like a powerful, active dog, full of courage and spirit and giving the impression of having the will and the ability to meet any emergency.

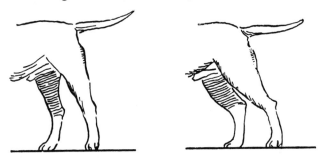

REAR should be powerful. Once again, see how the broad dog gives the impression of a powerful rear, whereas the rangy dog looks as if it has less power. POWER WITHOUT COARSENESS IS THE KEYNOTE TO BULL TERRIER CONFORMATION.

STIFLES should be well rounded and hocks well let down. Note how the high hock and straight stifle at left give an impression of weakness,

122

whereas the rounded stifle and well-let-down hock at right give an impression of strength. Also note how the high-set tail at left looks weaker than the low-set tail at right and contributes to a poor tail carriage.

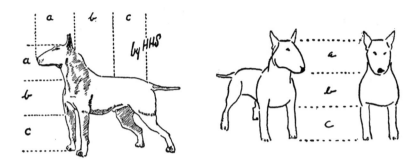

PROPORTIONS of the Bull Terrier divide themselves into three masses. Mr. Stewart illustrates this clearly in sketches we reprint from an early Annual of the Bull Terrier Club of England. The text accompanying the sketches says in part, "The Bull Terrier can be divided into three approximately equal parts. This makes the Bull Terrier head greater in proportion to its body than the heads of most other breeds, a fact which we appreciate as very important. Most artists unfamiliar with the breed, or lacking appreciation of it, seem to miss this point and always get the head too small, and most times, the legs too long.

Now let us look at the whole dog. This dog's proportions give balance. This dog looks game. Note that the chest is not only wide but deep—This is a powerful dog able to move fast at close quarters and to turn on a dime, rather than one which would excel on the race track.

Ormandy's Bar Sinister, winner of the Stud Dog Prize for 1965 and 1966. Not shown because he was a partial unilateral cryptorchid (one testicle normal and fully descended into the scrotum, and the other partially descended). Bar Sinister was otherwise a dog of unparalleled excellence. Bred for his virtues, he produced two Regent Trophy winners, two Ormandy Jug winners, and other toppers.

Ch. Ormandy's Thunderflash, son of Bar Sinister.

13

Superficial Faults and Their Significance

by Raymond H. Oppenheimer

Because it so graphically underlines the point we have made of breeding for what one does like, rather than against what one does not like, we include this article from Mr. Oppenheimer's book "After Bar Sinister." This book, and the earlier "McGuffin and Co.," are classic works on the breed that every Bull Terrier enthusiast will want to own. They are published by The Dog World Ltd., Ashford, Kent, England.

THE appearance in the ring of a dog with a mark on his tail, the award to him of a Challenge Certificate and of a reserve-best-of-sex card and his selection as a competitor for the major Trophies, at one time did, as might have been expected, set off a controversy.

As usual, those who are most alarmed and excited over the problem are the same sort of people who thirty years ago would have frothed at the mouth over ticks, over a few misplaced teeth, over slightly soft ears or any other of the superficial faults.

The truth of the matter is that pink noses, incorrect mouths, soft ears, light and wall eyes, unilateral cryptorchidism and marks behind the collar are only seven different facets of the same problem, that of the polygenic recessive and how to deal with it.

Events over the years have proved beyond a doubt that a policy which puts a taboo on any single fault is disastrous so far as breed progress is concerned. In fact it is only fair to say that had some of the breeders not been more far-seeing than some of the legislators our breed certainly and many others probably, would be thirty years behind the advanced position they have now reached.

An appreciation of this fact is absolutely fundamental to progress, and what is most required of judges is that they shall calmly and dispassionately assess the virtues and the faults of each animal which comes before them, balancing the one against the other. I have said that a variety of shortcomings in our breed is only different facets of the same problem. Let us now examine the lessons of history in this respect and see if they bear out what I have written.

The great Brigadier, when he first appeared in the ring, had an extremely pink nose. The superficialists, in other words those who could not see the wood for the trees, made the same fuss over his pink nose as had since been made over other similar defects. If they had their way, he would never have won a prize and would therefore scarcely have been used at stud. Yet this pink nose caused no concern whatever in subsequent generations.

Twenty or thirty years earlier, in fact, a dog with such a nose never would have been seen in public.

Let us pass on from there to incorrect mouths. Mrs. Schuster never bothered to show Contango Cobblestone because he was undershot and the then climate of opinion said he would never win a prize nor be used at stud except by the percipient breeder. Miss Montague-Johnstone was one of the far-seeing and by using him produced Romany Rivet, dam of Reliance. Miss Weatherill and I never troubled to show Souperlative Soap Bubble because of her mouth. Many people would never have bred from her either for the same reason, magnificent bitch though she was. Had she been discarded there never would have been a Snowflash.

Next let us move on to light and/or wall eyes. The Knave had a light one. The dams of the Sphinx and Starshine had wall eyes. What a tragedy it would have been if these three first-class animals had never been used or if the two latter had never been bred!

Before the last war, ears such as Princeling's would have condemned him to life as a pet. If he had not been used there would never have been a Barbelle, a Rheingold, a Silver Bob or a dozen others.

Exactly the same principle applies in the case of Bar Sinister, one of whose normal brothers had more unilateral cryptorchids descended from him than have come down from Bar Sinister himself.

Over the years I am happy to say a more rational attitude has been adopted toward the first five of these defects with great success and profit to the breed and we must hope that increased knowledge will help the Kennel Club to a more sensible and constructive handling of the testicle problem in due course.

Let us now return in conclusion to the point which started us off, namely to the question of marks behind the collar.

Souperlative Amelia Bebe was a good bitch but she had a black spot on the root of her tail. She was mated and produced the great Spurrell. I cannot, offhand, remember anything by Spurrell nor indeed anything descended from him in the first two or three generations which was marked behind the collar. Yet, in total contrast, I could name at least a dozen animals descended from Ben, of which Tracval's Barney Boy is indeed one, which are marked behind the head. There is no mark behind Ben, known to me anyway, for endless generations, in fact not till we get back into the dim ages with Hampstead Heathen.

What this demonstrates, as do all other similar cases, is that there is no sense whatsoever in refraining from breeding from *really top-class* animals carrying one of these polygenic recessives unless one is able also to avoid using any of their relations since these, even if on the surface unaffected, are very likely to transmit the defect. As this is the case, no good but actual harm is done if first-class animals are barred from the ring or the prize list while their less good contemporaries can win the highest honors, especially since such a ban encourages faking which soon becomes widespread.

There is, moreover, the basic fact that for very straightforward genetic reasons a dog with outstanding virtues and outstanding faults is arithmetically more likely to transmit virtues than faults, because virtues (in our breed anyway) are, in the genetic sense of the term, dominant, while faults are recessive. At the worst, if one mates two animals, one of which has one of the defects on which I have written, it could only be even money on it reappearing in the puppies. It is three to one on such an animal transmitting a virtue. Therefore, those who will not take chances in breeding are always stacking the odds against themselves as compared with breeders who will take chances.

To sum up, fanciers should maintain an entirely dispassionate attitude to all faults and all virtues. Breeders, judges and critics alike should bear in mind that the entire problem revolves 'round a sensible balancing of faults against virtues.

The breed Standard makes the position extremely clear when it states very plainly and simply that any departure from the list of desired points is a fault and that the seriousness of the fault should be in exact proportion to its degree.

In other words, how badly undershot or overshot a mouth is, how soft the ears are, how pink the nose is, how big is the mark behind the collar, how blue or how light is an eye or how abnormal are the testicles, has to be balanced by breeder or critic against the virtues of any animal which carries such faults.

The basic point at issue is how bad are the points, superficial or indeed anatomical, carried by any animal and how do they compare with his or her virtues. The good judges and the clever breeders will work out the answers to best advantage and history will support the decisions which they reach.

Many people seem to forget that in breeding for the show ring the object must be the production of outstanding animals. So long as this is achieved, it does not matter how many faults the less-good puppies have from a show point of view, provided that they are typical, healthy and good tempered.

In order to breed outstanding animals one must use dogs and bitches with outstanding virtues. If these virtues can best be found in animals that have superficial aesthetic faults as well, then they must be used, and by skillful selection the faults are discarded in future generations and the virtues retained.

14

Judging a Bull Terrier

T HE Bull Terrier is certainly one of the most difficult breeds of dogs to judge, as virtually every judge of them will tell you. Why is this the case?

The Bull Terrier evolved from different types of dogs and today varies widely in acceptable type. The result is a dog which cannot be judged like any other. How does one go about evaluating its qualities with consistency?

The objective in judging is to identify the dog which most exemplifies the essence of a Bull Terrier as defined by the official Standard. Ability to identify this essence is not learned from reading books or from talking to breeders, but rather by seeing and handling many dogs of both good and poor quality. We refer to this essence as type and it comprises all physical and mental attributes of the dog. In Bull Terriers, the head is certainly the single most important physical feature. It distinguishes a Bull Terrier from any other breed and is a keystone of type. Sound quarters, proper body shape and the other physical properties are all of vital importance. Temperament is of paramount importance and must be stressed.

A significant improvement in Bull Terriers began to develop in the United States during the late 1960's. This was accomplished by a small number of astute and conscientious breeders whose influence was so great that today's dogs descend almost entirely from their lines, departing completely from earlier American stock.

These new breeders imported great dogs from England and elevated the breed to new heights. There are now many good animals with similar

129

degrees of faults, virtues and type, making judging all the more difficult because rarely is there only one worthy winner.

Most Bull Terriers have at least one or two clear physical faults. But the two greatest faults a dog can have are a bad temperament and lack of type. The two leading White stud dogs of the last few years had bad mouths. They also had the great virtue of distinct breed type and both had superb temperament!

In comparing Bull Terriers in the ring, what is to be rewarded? Those with type should stand out. Let us suppose you have a dog with a massive head and a bite slightly off, great substance but with weak movement and no other glaring faults or outstanding virtues. Standing next to him is a bitch with a less good head but with a good bite, good body lines and good movement. How do you choose which is the better? A breeder judge would tend to reward the stronger head, forgiving the off-mouth and the weak movement. An all-breed judge would tend to put up the bitch because of her better movement and lack of bad bite. You have in fact a toss-up and either choice could be supported.

Consider now, two animals with moderate quality heads, straight shoulders, bad hind ends and long backs. This is what one is more likely to find. In a head of moderate quality, the bite should be good. Only in an exceptional head can an off-bite be permitted. An animal with straight shoulders must then have good bone and tight feet with a straight front. But a straight shoulder accompanied by a crooked front or lack of bone must be more heavily penalized. Straight shoulders usually appear with long backs, which is tolerated more with bitches than with dogs. Rear assemblies are of vital importance and strengths and weaknesses occur in the hips, thighs, stifles, hocks and feet. The Bull Terrier must first have a well-muscled hind end and good stifle joints, without exception. If the pelvis is rotated too far forward or too far back, it will result in close and/or cow-hocked movement behind. Close rear movement is a less serious fault than lack of muscle or weak stifles. Thus, in evaluating the two animals, you must weigh the various virtues against the faults in order of importance. This order must be based on sound principles of breeding.

It is also important to mention the difference in judging Coloreds versus Whites. Only in the United States are the varieties judged separately and it is likely that before long, the Bull Terrier Club of America will realize the importance of combining the varieties. Judging will then become far more difficult.

Because of white markings which occur on most Colored dogs, an optical illusion occurs. These illusions work both for and against the appearance of the dog. For this reason it is important that the judges feel the animals thoroughly with their hands. Your hands must confirm the truth your eyes tell you.

130

Ch. Coolyn North Wind, winner of the BCoA Specialty
1939 and 1940, Isis Vabo Trophy 1939, 1940 and 1941.

Eng. Ch. Raydium Enterprise of Ormandy, believed to be the largest English
champion, weight 70 lbs.

131

A profile appears dippy with an unfavorable crooked blaze. The muzzle appears weak with a large eye mark or moustache. On the other hand, a broad blaze and muzzle can enhance the head with extra power. A white collar well into the shoulder gives a long, more desired neck line. Too much white on the front legs causes the elbows to look out and too little causes the feet to look too big.

When moving a Colored, have a good look at the markings on the hind legs in the event of apparently faulty movement. Uncomplementary markings on the stifles and hind legs can cause the illusion of bad movement.

Coloreds tend to look smaller and coarser than Whites. Look carefully though, as the markings can cause a misinterpretation of the overall dog.

The most important virtues of this breed have been those which have taken the longest to develop, including strength of head, correct front and rear quarters, and soundness of temperament. These will be the most easily lost if not recognized and rewarded accordingly.

15

Breeding Bull Terriers

WHY is it that so often top stock will be imported into the United States—and peter out within two or three generations? Why is it that even in England, where the very best studs are available to everybody within a reasonable distance and at a low cost, some breeders in over twenty years of active breeding have never bred a champion? Why is it that some breeders will have at least one worthy champion in almost every litter? Is it luck—or is it something else?

Basic Reasons for Success or Failure

The whole foundation of breeding is so fluid that it is possible to cite numerous important exceptions to every rule that can be advanced, and so cast doubt upon its validity. However, when we analyze the reasons for the success or the lack of success of the individual breeder, we find that there is one reason which will stand up in a sufficient number of cases to warrant the most careful consideration—and which will come as close to proving itself as is possible with any breeding idea. That reason falls into two parts:

1. The average (and unsuccessful) breeders will breed *against* what they do *not* like and not *for* what they do like. That is, they will breed *against* the bad rear and poor backline that they do *not* want instead of for the great head and expression that they *do* want.

2. Too many breeders do not know a good dog when they see one: they can recognize common faults apparent in any breed, but they have not

trained themselves to recognize the virtues of type that we have previously discussed. It is absolutely vital to be able to recognize such virtues if one is to be a successful breeder or a capable judge.

Listen to comments around any judging ring. The "expert" comment is usually a savage criticism of the top dogs—straight stifles, bad movement, crooked fronts, etc. Seldom indeed is there any recognition of a strong, square underjaw; of a beautifully shaped cat-foot; of a properly shaped and placed ear; of the balance and spirited movement that is the birthright of a good Bull Terrier. The average breeders unconsciously train to see the bad in a dog rather than the good, and so faults assume a far greater importance in their eyes than they should.

Take, for example, Int. Ch. Kashdowd's White Rock of Coolyn Hill, a truly great dog in England who won both the Regent Trophy and the Ormandy Jug; who in the United States went Best in Show, all breeds, when he was first shown July 17, 1954; and who, after being shown sixty-eight times, had chalked up ten Best in Show awards, all breeds, and twenty-four Terrier Group firsts—a remarkable record for any breed. Such comments were heard about him as "too short in head," "body too long," "moves badly in rear," "front is crooked," "bad ears," etc. Time after time the dog defeated every other Bull Terrier sent against him, placed nearly every time in the Terrier Group, and was piling up a Best in Show record that had never even been approached in Bull Terriers. It became obvious that the "experts" did not know what they were talking about.

That pattern of inability to recognize virtues is so common that further examples are not necessary—they are apparent on every hand and in every breed. Now, when this inability to recognize virtues is carried over into breeding, we begin to see why the breeder who cannot recognize the virtues to breed to, but who breeds against common faults, is doomed to failure. One may need to improve heads—but will refuse to breed to a great headed dog who may have a poor rear. Or if one does by chance breed a great headed bitch, she will be discarded because of her faults. So we gradually lose virtues which are so precious and so rare, and breed poorer stock with each generation.

If the ideas of the relatively unsuccessful breeders had been followed by the successful breeders, the greatest Bull Terriers ever bred would never have been whelped.

Take, for example, the English Ch. The Sphinx—the first Bull Terrier to twice top the breed at Crufts. His dam had a blue eye, as did the dam of one of England's greatest studs and Ormandy Jug Winner, Ch. Ormandy Sylveston Starshine. Or take the English Ch. Ormandy Souperlative Snow Flash, a Regent Trophy winner—his dam was undershot; this dog sired the sensational litter sisters Ch. Phidgity Snow Dream and Ch. Phidgity Flashlight of Wentwood.

Mrs. Drury L. Sheraton, one of our truly great authorities, told me many years ago never to consider any Bull Terrier without this mating in its pedigree—Ambassador and Ivy Gladiator. But Ambassador had two blue eyes! Ambassador was the sire of the great Ch. Cylva Belle and she was the aunt of Ch. Rhoma, whom some consider the best bitch ever bred. Indeed, if this dog with two walleyes had never been mated to Ivy Gladiator, it would have been a sad loss to the breed.

When a certain virtue is so hard to get as it is in Bull Terriers, that virtue must be grasped whenever it occurs, even though it may mean the temporary toleration of great faults. If the virtue is not grasped, it will disappear.

I am inclined to think that sometimes a fault may not be due to heredity but to feeding or environment. For example, loose feet or a crooked front may be due to rickets resulting from lack of proper food or sunshine. Cowhocks may come from much standing on the hind legs during puppyhood. "Out-at-shoulder" may come because a puppy is constantly leaning down to look under something to get a better look at the outside world.

We all know that the parts of puppies grow at different rates of speed. That is, ears grow faster than the rest of the body; the underjaw grows more slowly than the upper jaw, as indicated by the fact that badly overshot puppies often wind up with a perfect bite. (Yet an undershot puppy at three months may have a level bite at eight months.) If sickness strikes a puppy so that growth is affected at the time a certain part would normally be developing, that part may never have the opportunity to grow into normal proportion.

Support for the preceding paragraphs was found in an article in *Ladies Home Journal* called "The Uninsulted Child." It discusses a theory first stated by Dr. Theodore H. Ingalls, Associate Professor at the Harvard School of Public Health, and the article is well worth reading. In a nutshell, this theory states that shock or illness to the mother during human pregnancy can affect the unborn child so that it may come into the world with a physical deformity even so serious as Mongoloidism. Dr. Ingalls also voices the theory that any effect on the supply of oxygen during pregnancy can result in mental defects, miscarriage, or death within a few weeks after birth. He advises against an airplane trip of any duration during pregnancy. (This indicates that a bitch in whelp should not be flown to its new home.)

The "Genetic Shadow"

The mating of two dogs with perfect fronts will sometimes produce a litter with mostly bad fronts. Why? Why will the mating of good headed

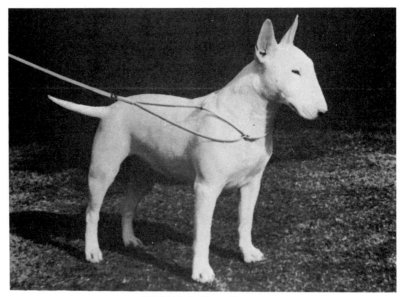

Ch. Phidgity Snow Dream

Ch. Souperlative Summer Queen

136

stock often produce progeny with poor heads or the mating of poor headed dogs sometimes produce a dog with a great head? There is a scientific basis for all unexpected results which make the best laid plans "gang oft aglee."

Every dog is actually two dogs. One is the dog visible to the eye. The other is the invisible but powerful "genetic shadow" of that dog—the make-up of the genes which determine characteristics of the progeny. In this make-up of the genes, the family is of greater importance than the individual dog in the majority of cases. It is rare that a sire will stamp himself visibly on his offspring. Probably one of the best examples of throwing his likeness was the Boxer, Ch. Bang Away of Sirrah Crest.

Let us consider some of the many practical examples of genetic problems we have all experienced.

Marks on the head are recessive. For several generations all parents and offspring may be pure white. Suddenly, head marks may appear. In fact, it is entirely possible that every one in the litter may be marked even though there are several generations of pure White stock.

Sometimes a body mark will appear from stock that for generations has had no body marks. Where such markings come from, and why, nobody really knows. As they are a recessive trait, the conditions may have momentarily become favorable for their reappearance.

A non-genetic reason, and one that experienced breeders are familiar with, is that there is a constant tendency to pull towards the past—it is the "drag" of the breed, and it is particularly strong in Bull Terriers where there is such a wide variation in size and type.

It is this "drag" that explains why so often American breeders will import top stock only to find that within two or three generations they will be back where they started from. The reason for the loss of quality has already been explained—offspring may be selected for qualities of a day gone by. Therefore, selection is made of the worst breeding stock in the litter—at least so far as type is concerned—and the breeding program will go down hill rapidly.

Down-hill speed may be further accelerated by the breeder who gets a great head or other rare and desirable quality accompanied by a blue eye, a cowhock, or other fault. If they refuse to breed such a specimen, the great head will be quickly lost from the line, and litters of nonentities will result.

There are four points on which every successful breeding program is based:
1. Selection.
2. Perseverance.
3. Knowledge of type. (The ability to recognize a good one.)
4. An understanding of how a line is built.
Let us take an example. An intelligent breeding is made, and the

resulting litter is not what was expected—there is nothing on the surface worth retaining. So the entire litter is sold and the breeder tries another mating, quite likely with the same result.

That litter which, from its physical appearance, holds no promise is quite likely to be full of promise because of the unseen genetic forces that have been brought into it. The "genetic shadow" probably has been strengthened and improved. Perseverance in the breeding program is almost certain, sooner or later, to result in success. As each successive breeding is made, the "genetic shadow" of what is wanted becomes stronger and stronger until the desired characteristics almost have to pop out. (Provided, of course, that the breedings have been made intelligently and with a full knowledge of the family lines involved.)

An examination of the pedigrees of great dogs of the past will testify to that basic principle we have been discussing. A pedigree may be full of gods of no great show importance—but suddenly the "genetic shadow" becomes so strong and so improved that the line will start to produce truly great ones.

This brings us back from a different angle to that important fact we discussed in a previous chapter—to breed for virtues and not for an absence of faults. It cannot be too strongly emphasized that if a virtue is not bred for, it will be lost. If only breeders would realize the importance of that principle and hold fast to it, everybody who tries to breed better dogs would benefit and much faster progress would be possible.

Here is another fact whose importance is not generally realized: the fault in the dog with great virtue may not appear in the subsequent litter and, in fact, may occur less often in future litters than it will if a dog without that fault is used.

A good example of the workings of that principle was Ch. Coolyn Bailfire, a great American sire of the thirties who gave champions to breeders who never before had bred one—and that in a day when Bull Terrier champions were far harder to make than they are today. Yet, many breeders refused to use him because he had soft ears, and at that time poor ears were a very bad fault. Despite his physical lack, in his "genetic shadow" this dog was strong for good ears and generation after generation traced their good ears back to him. I doubt if he ever threw more than three offspring who did not have unusually good ears, and I further doubt if there was any sire of his generation who threw such a high percentage of good ears. Those who did not use Bailfire missed a great breeding opportunity.

What makes the whole subject of genetics difficult to grasp is that there are very few if any characteristics governed by a single gene. We learn *how* things happen and *why* they happen, but know far too little about *how to make them happen.*

We have no accurate list of dominant or recessive characteristics, and things may not always be as they appear. A fault may be caused by environment or feeding, as previously mentioned, or by both, and so may be disregarded in any breeding program. However, even if the theory of bad feeling and environment is finally proven beyond question—and I have seen much evidence to support it—the fact remains that the line may have a tendency towards the fault and require only a favorable atmosphere to develop it.

We do know that bad mouths, ticks, and walleyes are recessive. Other characteristics may be both dominant and recessive. Since a characteristic may be governed by a number of genes, the combinations of what may come out are almost endless, both for good and for evil. If one tries to be more theoretical than practical, one can easily get lost in a bewildering maze. It is all far more complicated than when dealing with the simplicities of Mendel's peas. The best thing to do is breed for the virtues and avoid the faults, but to put up with a fault when this is the only way a virtue can be held or acquired.

An interesting summary of dominant and recessive traits has been worked out by the Eugenics Record Office staff as follows:

Dominant Traits

1. The trait does not skip a generation.
2. On the average, a relatively large number of the progeny are affected.
3. Only affected individuals carry the trait.
4. With traits of this sort, there is less danger of continuing undesirable characteristics in a strain than is the case with recessive traits.
5. The breeding formula for each individual is quite certain.

Recessive Traits

1. The trait may skip one or more generations.
2. On the average, a relatively small percentage of the individuals in the strain carry the trait.
3. Only those which carry a *pair* of determiners of the trait will exhibit it.
4. Those carrying only one determiner can be ascertained only by mating, hence there is much more danger of insidiously contaminating the strain than is the case with dominant traits.
5. The trait must come from both sides of the family.

In the scheme of breeding to establish a line, inbreeding, outcrossing, and line breeding each has its proper place.

Ch. Coolyn Bailfire, famous sire of the 1930s. Bred by Mrs. Jessie Bennett.

Ch. Souperlative Masta Plasta of Ormandy

Ch. Ormandy's Ben of Highthorpe

Bull Terriers whose genetic shadow produced champions for many kennels.

140

Let me emphasize—select for what you want on the basis of knowing what is usually thrown by the stock used. A dog who generally throws good heads is quite likely to throw good heads with your bitch. If he often throws bad ears, he will probably throw bad ears with your bitch, unless her "genetic shadow" for ears is strong enough to overcome his deficiency.

Take plenty of time to study what is needed and what dogs are most likely to give it. Work to a planned program, not to a series of haphazard matings, and the gods are likely to send their sweetest smiles in your direction.

Learn About Breeding

If you purchased your Bull Terrier with an eye towards breeding and showing, there are many excellent books available to help you. You may also be fortunate enough to live near a kennel club that offers conformation classes for dog owners wishing to learn how to handle their own dogs at shows. Your dog's breeder or other Bull Terrier people can also be very helpful in getting you started in this fascinating hobby. If your show dog is also of breeding quality (and some may not be), you must do a considerable amount of background work before the actual mating. The best book, by far, to assist the novice breeder is DOGS AND HOW TO BREED THEM, by Hilary Harmar. Don't just borrow a copy, buy one. You'll refer to it over and over again in the years to come.

Breeding is not an undertaking that one should view lightly. If, however, you have done preliminary study and have a quality bitch, then you are on the right track. Talk to your dog's breeder and others knowledgeable in the breed before deciding on a stud. Study several of the books and try to develop a level of knowledge regarding different bloodlines. See the stud in person whenever possible. Do not rely on photos alone. They can be very deceiving.

Do not take your responsibilities to the breed lightly. You must provide your bitch and her puppies with the best possible care. You must adhere to acceptable breeding and sales practices. **It is irresponsible to undertake a breeding just to have puppies to sell.** You should breed carefully planned, well thought out litters only, and don't breed at all if there is a shortage of good homes available. Your puppies exist only because you planned the breeding between their parents. Your responsibility to them does not end when they are sold! A reputable breeder maintains an interest in the welfare of his puppies throughout their entire lives. You must be prepared to take dogs back, if need be. If a puppy develops a temperament or physical problem of a hereditary nature, you must be willing to give a replacement pup or a refund. Sometimes you will find that, in spite of your best efforts in screening the buyer, you have placed a pup in a situation that is far less than desirable. You must summon all the nerve you can muster and somehow get the dog back. Sometimes you will have to help find a new home for an adult dog that has never been housetrained or disciplined and is virtually unadoptable due to the neglect of its former owners. All of this comes with the job. If you don't think you could handle all of these extra hassles, DON'T BREED!

A lazy or unethical breeder cannot hope to earn the respect or cooperation of other breeders who have the best interests of the breed at heart. There is no tolerance within established breeding circles for opportunists.

On the other hand, if you evince a willingness to learn and listen, if you show proper concern and attention to your animals, and come into dog breeding with a good attitude, you'll find other breeders willing to help you in any way possible. Before you know it you'll have a fascinating hobby and new friends who share your interests and love of the breed!

Some Breeding Do's and Don'ts

DO make sure your bitch is in excellent health. Let your vet check her prior to breeding, just to make sure.

DO screen puppy buyers carefully. Trust your intuition when in doubt.

DO worm and vaccinate puppies according to your vet's instructions and on time.

DON'T breed a bitch earlier than her second heat, or before she is physically mature.

DON'T breed a bitch more than once a year.

DON'T leave a whelping bitch unattended. Have your vet on call in case of emergency.

DON'T give out your address to anyone who asks peculiar questions.

DON'T advertise puppies for sale in the newspaper.

DON'T breed unless you have the facilities, time and finances to do it properly.

In Closing

One day you'll look at your dog and it will dawn on you that the gangly, awkward puppy of a few months ago has somehow blossomed into a beautiful adult. Hopefully, your dog will be all you've ever hoped, intelligent, loving and handsome too! If you've done the best you can to raise your puppy properly, train the dog consistently and love him or her dearly, there's no reason why you shouldn't have pleasure for many years to come.

From puppyhood until old age, Bull Terriers will ask only one thing of you . . . to be your chum. Include them in your activities and be sure to spend some time every day with them alone . . . brushing, playing fetch or maybe just a quiet walk in the woods. This is doubly important with old dogs whose eyes and ears may be failing. Let them know you're still there, still caring even though those games of fetch are no longer possible.

Eng. Ch. Romany Reliance. Sire, Ormandy Sunny Day. Dam, Romany Rivet. Reliance won the Ormandy Jug in 1947, the first year it was established.

Ch. Phidgity Phlasher
of Lenster

Ch. Romany Romantic
Vision, Phlasher's half
brother.

Ch. Ormandy Souperlative
Princeling, a Phlasher
son.

A family of Bull Terriers who influenced many bloodlines on both sides of the Atlantic.

16

Twenty Basic Breeding Principles

by Raymond H. Oppenheimer

THERE are numbers of different breeding methods, some good, some bad. I never presume to tell fanciers what is the right method because there is no such thing. Outstanding success can be achieved and has been achieved in a variety of different ways, so all I am going to do is to make some suggestions which I think helpful and to warn against certain pitfalls which trap too many of the unwary:

1. Don't use indiscriminate outcrosses. A judicious outcross can be of great value, an injudicious one can produce an aggregation of every imaginable fault in the breed.

2. Don't line breed just for the sake of line breeding. Line breeding with complementary types can bring great rewards; with unsuitable ones it will lead to immediate disaster.

3. Don't take advice from people who have always been unsuccessful breeders. If their opinions were worth having they would have proved it by their successes.

4. Don't believe the popular cliché about the brother or sister of the great champion being just as good to breed from. For every one that is, hundreds are not. It depends on the animal concerned.

5. Don't credit your own dogs with virtues they don't possess. Self-deceit is a stepping stone to failure.

6. Don't breed from mediocrities; the absence of a fault does not signify the presence of its corresponding virtue.

7. Don't try to line breed to two dogs at the same time; you will end by line breeding to neither.

8. Don't assess the worth of a stud dog by his inferior progeny. All stud dogs sire rubbish at times; what matters is how good their best efforts are.

9. Don't allow personal feelings to influence your choice of a stud dog. The right dog for your bitch is the right dog, whoever owns it.

10. Don't allow admiration of a stud dog to blind you to his faults. If you do you will soon be the victim of auto-intoxication.

11. Don't mate together animals which share the same fault. You are asking for trouble if you do.

12. Don't forget it is the whole dog that counts. If you forget one virtue while searching for another you will pay for it.

13. Don't search for the perfect dog as a mate for your bitch. The perfect dog (or bitch) doesn't exist, never has and never will!

14. Don't be frightened of breeding from animals that have obvious faults so long as they have compensating virtues. A lack of virtues is the greatest fault of all.

15. Don't mate non-complementary types. An ability to recognize type at a glance is a breeder's greatest gift; ask the successful breeders to explain this subject—there is no other way of learning. (I would define non-complementary types as ones which have the same faults and lack the same virtues.)

16. Don't forget the necessity to preserve head quality. It will vanish like a dream if you do.

17. Don't forget that substance plus quality should be one of your aims. Any fool can breed one without the other!

18. Don't forget that a great head plus soundness should be another of your aims. Many people can never breed either!

146

19. Don't ever try to decry a great Bull Terrier. A thing of beauty is not only a joy forever but a great Bull Terrier should be a source of aesthetic pride and pleasure to all true lovers of the breed.

20. Don't be satisfied with anything but the best. The second best is never good enough.

Best in Show winner Ch. Ferdinand of Ormandy, whelped 1939, by Ch. Ormandy's Mr. McGuffin ex Ch. Bedran Snow White. Pictured with his owner, Mrs. Mabie.

A whelping box should be both practical and comfortable for the bitch and her puppies. The box pictured provides security for the pups and a place for mom to "get away from it all."

148

17

Whelping

by Winkie Mackay-Smith

WHELPING is perhaps one of the most natural functions of the bitch and yet it seems to be one of the most perplexing to the owner. This article covers the natural sequence of whelping, gives a few pointers on how to assist and mentions a few of the more common problems to which Bull Terriers are prone.

First of all, it is possible to shut the bitch in the barn, garage, or basement with a whelping box and let her do it all on her own. By doing this, we assume the natural risks, i.e.: several or all of the puppies might be lost in the process or the bitch might have trouble with delivery. We must also remember that most brood bitches are house or kennel dogs and have been raised in an entirely unnatural manner. Taking all of this into consideration, I am assuming that we wish to reduce the risks and increase the chances of survival for both bitch and puppies.

Approximately sixty-three days following conception, the bitch is due to whelp. The time span of pregnancy varies in individual bitches sometimes as much as a week, and the date of conception is never positive as a bitch can conceive from any given mating up to thirty-six hours afterward. Rather than counting on a particular date, you should calculate sixty-three days from the first mating and sixty-three days from her last mating, adding three to five days variation each end, and you will end up with a period of about ten days during which your bitch will naturally whelp.

Several signs indicate the impending event. First of all, about five to seven days before whelping the bitch suddenly looks less full and tight, especially in the loin area high behind the last rib. At the same time she seems to bulge more in the lower abdomen. This is caused by the relaxation of the muscle tissue prior to whelping. The vulva will also become enlarged and flaccid during this period. The next sign appears twelve to twenty-four hours before the actual whelping starts. There is a significant drop in the bitch's temperature. The normal rectal temperature is 100-100.5° and will drop to 98-99.5° . At this point the bitch will usually, but not always, refuse her food. A slight shivering or trembling sometimes occurs with the drop in temperature and can become quite violent and pronounced as the whelping time draws closer. As the uterus starts to contract, the bitch will become uncomfortable, walking about, scratching in her bed, panting, and making frequent trips to evacuate her bladder and bowels. When she actually starts into hard labor, you will hear breaks in the panting as she pushes, her sides will contract, and she will lift her tail as she bears down. She should take twenty minutes to one hour to produce the puppy after she starts pushing.

When the puppy is presented, the area just above the vulva will get hard and bulge. At this point I kneel next to the box with a towel in hand, and as the puppy slips out (usually head first in a membrane sac followed immediately by the umbilical cord and placenta) pick up the puppy, membrances, placenta and all in the towel. Quickly strip the membrane back away from its head, and with the puppy wrapped in the towel, left hand under its stomach and right forefinger firmly behind its head, swing it from shoulder height in an arc downward between your knees. The centrifugal force expels the fluid from the respiratory tract and is an especially useful procedure for puppies that are a bit blue and not breathing properly when they first come out of the membrane. I then unfold the towel (with the puppy in it) by the bitch's head and let her eat the placenta, biting the cord off and licking the puppy for a minute or so. If the puppy seems vigorous, I then put it to the bitch to nurse. If the puppy is limp and has no interest in nursing after fifteen-twenty minutes from delivery, I give it a few drops of glucose (Karo syrup) and water with a medicine dropper. This generally gives it enough energy to nurse in a few minutes.

Generally the bitch will produce her puppies at twenty minute to hourly intervals, and as she starts to bear down on the next one, I put the previously born pup(s) in a box with a heating pad so she doesn't send them sprawling during delivery. I also put clean newspaper on top of the wet spot from each delivery which keeps the bed clean and dry without disturbing the bitch too much. In between deliveries several or all of the puppies are returned to the bitch to nurse. The nursing facilitates the whelping as it stimulates uterine contraction, and the presence of the puppies comforts the bitch.

When all of the puppies have been delivered, the bitch will simply relax and have no more contractions. If she has any contractions, seems disturbed and no puppy appears, it is best to check with your vet to determine whether or not there are any more puppies in her uterus. After whelping, the bitch will usually accept some milk and glucose with a slice or two of bread in it.

The bitch's temperature goes up after whelping to 101-103°. Take her temperature at least twice daily, and consult the vet if it gets higher than 103°. Normally, there will be a blackish uterine discharge. If it becomes pinkish, puss-filled or foul smelling, it indicates an infection of the uterus, or perhaps an undelivered, decomposing fetus.

The first day or so after whelping, the bitch's stools will be loose and blackish green due to the digestion of the placenta. The fact that the bitch refuses food twelve hours before whelping, empties her bowels close to whelping, and eats the placenta of her whelps which have a nutritious and laxative effect on the empty bowel, completes a natural and sensible sequence.

A syndrome which seems to be peculiar to Bull Terriers is a faulty calcium metabolism in early lactation which, rather than producing classic signs of eclampsia, produces an hysteria in which the bitch pants excessively, becomes increasingly anxious and active, carries the puppies in her mouth and generally loses track of her surroundings and function. This can be rectified by subcutaneous injections of calcium gluconate @ 5 ml, repeating whenever the symptoms recur. Warning: most vets will discourage this treatment as the bitch is not exhibiting classic eclampsia, but the reaction seems to be unique to Bull Terriers and the injections usually cause regression of symptoms.

We have had very few instances of this problem in the last five or six years, possibly due to the fact that we have stopped supplementing the pregnant bitches with calcium. It was explained to me by a veterinarian that excessive calcium in the diet of a pregnant bitch is excreted by her system, and that when she whelps, this excretory system is slow to reverse. When the bitch whelps and begins lactation, her system suddenly requires absorption of calcium while she is still in the process of excreting it. This, of course, results in systemic calcium deficiency for the first two days of lactation, until the system reverses and catches up with the increased demand for calcium.

Management of the Bitch and Puppies

During pregnancy the bitch should be fed her regular meals. We also feed non-fat powdered milk, reconstituted with water and poured over the meal. During the latter part of pregnancy, it is best to divide the daily meal

151

into two feedings, morning and afternoon, as the bitch will be unable to ingest large quantities. During this period the bitch will also have to urinate more frequently due to the pressure on her bladder. Very often the bitch will be unable to last the whole night, so some arrangements should be made to cope with this if she is living in the house.

About two weeks before whelping time, the bitch should be introduced to the quarters in which she is expected to whelp. We whelp ours in a spare bedroom which is quiet for the bitch, and also comfortable for the attendant who will be spending a good bit of time there. Her bed can be put into the whelping box so she gets used to sleeping there.

Whelping boxes differ enormously in construction and elegance. We find a practical size to be about thirty-six inches square with twelve inch high sides and a plywood bottom. We cut a u-shaped piece out of one side so the bitch can come and go without hurting herself. Ours has four posts, about three feet high, at the corners so we can hang a bedsheet or canopy over the box. A card table placed over the whelping box with a sheet or bedspread over it will serve the same purpose. This seems to quiet the bitch after she has whelped and keeps the area warm and draft-free.

For the actual whelping, thick layers of newspaper are put in the floor of the box, and fresh newspaper added on top as the bitch whelps. About four hours after the bitch has finished whelping she will generally have to be taken out to urinate. While she is out I take out the newspaper and put in a piece of foam rubber cut to exactly the size of the floor of the box. On top of this I put a piece of carpet, which is the same size. (I have read reports of indoor-outdoor carpet reacting adversely to urine, and scalding the skin of the pups.) Between the foam rubber and the carpet I use a large size heating pad set on low. This I put in the middle of the box as it encourages the puppies to huddle in the center and helps to avoid the bitch mashing them against the side of the box when she changes position.

I do not personally advocate the use of a heat lamp for two reasons. First, newborn puppies are extremely heat sensitive, that is, they are drawn to warmth. In the normal state they will be drawn to the mother, who is significantly warmer than the rest of her surroundings. Using a heat lamp creates a dispersed warmth which causes the puppies to have no stimulus drawing them to the mother. Puppies under a heat lamp will end up sleeping scattered around the edges of the whelping box, which is very frustrating for the bitch who wants to have them huddled near her. Secondly, the heat from the heat lamp is hard to regulate and usually overheats the bitch while maintaining warmth for the puppies. The heating pad creates a locus of warmth where the puppies can congregate, but is not overwhelming for the bitch, as she can lie next to it rather than on it, and still have a natural proximity to her litter. If the bitch consistently seems to push puppies to the side and lie on them, a whelping rail can be used. I have found that often the bitch will be frustrated by the whelping rail and dig and paw at any puppy under it. In either case, we remain with the bitch and puppies for several days during which we can rescue any puppies on which she inadvertently sits.

The puppies' nails should be clipped at ten days and once a week thereafter until they are six weeks old.

The bitch will lick the puppies during the first several weeks and keep the box clean. The puppies can urinate and defecate only when the bitch licks them, so she can usually keep up with the cleaning. Between two and three weeks the puppies will start standing alone, and at this point they can urinate without the stimulation from the bitch. This makes for a wet floor, and we put newspaper under the carpet, and change the carpet as well every day. I like the carpet for the puppies as it gives them some traction when they are learning to walk, and I know that the bitch must appreciate the carpet and foam rubber pad, as she is in the box most of the time.

At three weeks and then ten days later I worm the puppies. They start getting a tablespoon of scraped beef per day at this time, and the worm medicine can be fed right along with the beef. Between three and four weeks we start feeding high protein baby cereal with Esbilac and honey, graduating to puppy biscuit, powdered milk and ground beef around five to six weeks. This is fed from two to five times a day, depending on the appetite of the puppies and amount of nourishment they are getting from the bitch. Some bitches produce so much milk that the puppies simply are not interested in cereal and milk until they are four to five weeks old. Other puppies will dive into a meal of cereal, meat and milk at three weeks old. Sometimes one or two of the puppies in a litter will be hungry and the others won't.

During lactation the bitch should be fed twice a day. The content should be high in fat, protein and carbohydrate to supply the necessary nutriments for milk production. We feed biscuit, bread, milk, processed cheese and raw ground beef with calcium supplement. Often the bitch will accept the food only when hand fed, especially the first week. Please do not leave the bitch unattended with a bowl of food or a bone if the puppies have access to the food as well. Many bitches who are otherwise model mothers will snap at puppies approaching their food dish. The amount of food should increase as the bitch's appetite increases until weaning. We then cut back a bit on the fat and carbohydrate as her milk production decreases.

Most bitches will lose their coat between three and five weeks after delivery. The hair becomes dry and will often shed out leaving the bitch quite bald until the new coat grows in.

Weaning can begin at five to six weeks. It is important for the puppies to be eating well from a dish before they are weaned. During weaning, they should be separated from the bitch for several hours (increasing the time separated each day by one half to one hour), then fed a meal before the bitch returns to them for nursing. She can remain with them for an hour or so and then be separated from them again and the same procedure applied. By six to seven weeks the puppies should be having five meals a day unless they have puppy biscuit available, free-choice at all times. They should have their meat, milk, and supplements twice a day.

18

The New Arrival

THE joyous day has arrived and you're off to pick up your Bull Terrier puppy from the breeder.

Many breeders let their pups go off to their new homes at around eight weeks.

An important thing to keep in mind is that puppies go through a "fear imprinting stage" usually in their eighth and ninth weeks of life. During this stage they are particularly sensitive to loud noises. Because of this stage and also because the pup will not have had all of his vaccinations, it is a good idea to keep the pup in his immediate home environment. No outings where the pup could be exposed to loud noises or to other puppies and dogs which haven't been fully immunized. The pup will have enough adjusting to do in his "new home" with his "new family" to keep all parties busy for a couple of weeks.

The first day or two in a new home is likely to be confusing and stressful to a young puppy. Try to make it as easy as possible. Although all of your friends will be anxious to see your new pet, discourage visits until the pup has had a few days to settle in. Feed the same diet at the same times. Do not allow a lot of rough play or excessive handling until the pup has become adjusted to the new environment. Keep him away from other dogs except those in your own household. He should not be exposed to strange dogs or areas where they defecate until the entire series of puppy shots has been completed. Make sure the pup is getting enough time to nap frequently. Remember, this is only a baby!

155

Your water may temporarily affect stools if it is markedly different than at the kennel where the pup was raised. This will straighten out in a few days, after he has become acclimated to it.

In most cases, the breeder will provide a feeding schedule along with a recommended diet. Free choice feeding is not recommended as it tends to promote a picky eater as well as adding complications to the housebreaking routine. Bull Terriers can be prone to allergies so it is best not to feed a diet with a lot of chemicals or preservatives. A fat Bull Terrier puppy is not a healthy one. Because of their great bone and substance they will be more prone to sprains, strains and breaks if kept too heavy during the developmental first year.

A growing puppy is boisterous and playful and will want you to roughhouse with him. You must remember that while he is growing he may not be as tough as he looks. You must be careful not to let him do a lot of leaping and jumping until he is mature, especially if he is a heavyweight puppy. His bones and muscles are still developing and cannot stand a lot of stress and strain. Many Bull Terriers injure themselves severely between the ages of four to ten months, simply because their owners have allowed them to jump after frisbees or play rough and tumble games with a larger dog. The best games to play at this time are those that do not involve any sort of leaping. Also, if you intend to show your dog, don't play tug-o-war with it while it is still immature. Your dog's bite could be affected enough to make a difference in the show ring.

Any new puppy owner must become fully aware of the responsibilities regarding proper raising and nutrition.

The period of growth from eight weeks until maturity is an awkward stage in dogs as it is in humans. Like teenagers, puppies grow in spurts, sometimes rather unattractively! Have no fear, eventually your dog will develop into the fine specimen you've envisioned! Of course, dogs cannot blossom unless you provide the proper nutrition. This is probably the most expensive part of puppy raising, but one which will repay you in the end. Cutting corners and feeding cheap substitutes will only hamper development and puppies will never reach full potential. Your dog is programmed, genetically, to mature in a certain way. If fed properly and given quality care, it will mature to be as good as its breeding will permit. However, the best bloodlines the world cannot compensate for the effects of poor diet and care in a growing puppy. You've undoubtedly paid a fair sum of money for your dog. Why not provide the essentials of proper growth? Your dog does not have to be a show dog to be a good representative of the breed . . . and a healthy, well-raised dog exudes the glow of good breeding and care, even if he or she isn't a champion. If you do your part, you'll be justly rewarded with a beautiful, radiant animal that you can be proud to own.

Planning for the New Puppy—A Shopping List of Essentials

Most of the items listed can be purchased in your local pet supply store. You can also order many of them at discount prices through pet supply catalogs.

Crate (See section on housebreaking to see why we list this as No. 1 on our list!) Recommended types: Vari-Kennel 300 (med.), 400 (lrg.) or 500 (giant). Also good are Central Metals cages in sizes comparable to the Vari-Kennels. Whatever type of crate you buy, make sure it is STURDY and that the latches and hinges are strong. A cheap dog crate will not hold up and could even be dangerous to the dog.

Stainless Steel Dishes, you'll need two. The 2½ quart size is just about right for most adult Bull Terriers. Never use plastic dishes as they can be chewed up and the pieces, if swallowed, could kill your dog. Same goes for aluminum.

Nylon Web Collar, buckle type. NEVER LEAVE A CHOKE COLLAR ON A DOG EXCEPT WHILE TRAINING! Nylon web is durable and strong and won't stain the coat as leather will. You can buy a lightweight, less expensive one for a puppy, but an adult should have a good, sturdy, heavyweight collar.

Nylon Web Lead, six foot is best. A puppy will need a lighter lead. For this, a nylon show lead is good. Don't buy a chain lead for a Bull Terrier . . . it's very rough on your hands.

Old Blankets or rugs for bedding in the crate. Sometimes a good supply of dog bedding can be found at yard sales and flea markets. Also useful are the carpet samples that measure about 1½' × 2'. Most Bull Terriers, however, will appreciate something they can dig around in, and so old blankets are ideal.

Toys, We only recommend two types of toys for Bull Terriers. Every Bull Terrier should have a large size CRESSITE (English Rubber) ball and a giant size NYLABONE. No other brands or types of dog toys will hold up under the wear and tear that they'll get from a Bull Terrier's jaws. Even tennis balls can be torn up and the pieces swallowed. CRESSITE and NYLABONE are well-known brand names, easily found at any pet store. Don't buy cheap imitations.

We feel that rawhide chewbones are not suitable toys for Bull Terriers. We came to this conclusion after nearly losing a bitch who had a piece of rawhide toy lodged in her throat. Had we not been at home, she would have died. In fact, she was already turning blue when we found her. If you think your dog needs something to chew on, give him a Nylabone or a few large dog biscuits. Leave the rawhide toys to dogs with less powerful jaws.

Likewise, we list any sort of bone as a no-no. You must remember that

This curious Bull Terrier puppy sees something she wants.

Bull Terriers can chew up and swallow pieces of things that the average dog can't even put a dent in! Bones can splinter and cause injury to the esophagus. Too many bones can also cause blockage of the intestines. Of course, the dog can also choke on them! It is far safer to stick to "Bull Terrier-proof" toys than to risk an accident. Any sort of toy, however, must be large enough that the dog cannot swallow it.

At Home

We listed the most essential piece of equipment for raising a Bull Terrier puppy as a crate. The crate should be in the house when the puppy arrives home. A proper size crate will give the pup a lifelong home of his own. A proper size would be a Vari-Kennel #300 which is a medium size or a Vari-Kennel #400 which is a good size for most adults. If you have a particularly large Bull Terrier you may want to get a Vari-Kennel #500. Metal crates are also available in corresponding sizes. Puppies particularly seem to prefer the metal crates to be covered with a blanket over the top, down the back and partially covering the sides. This makes a more den-like atmosphere.

New dog owners often feel that putting a dog in a "cage" is cruel. Actually, a crate is "cruel" only if misused or too small. Let's go into this further.

When used properly, a crate is a most useful tool; we feel it is essential for fast, effective housetraining. A proper sized crate gives your dog a "room of his own" when non-doggy friends come to visit. It is the safest way to transport a dog to the vet or to training classes. At home, the crate door can be removed or tied open and the crate becomes a "den" for your dog to retreat to for a snooze. It is a place where he can hide his toys or escape the poking and prodding of small children. No Bull Terrier owner should be without a crate. Many breeders refuse to sell a dog without one—for good reasons!

Getting a small puppy used to being crated may be frustrating for a day or so. Don't give in! Like anything else, you must be patient and understanding, but FIRM! The pup will most likely "carry on" for a while the first few times he is crated. You must remember, however, that it is not the CRATE he is protesting, but the separation from you. NEVER, NEVER, NEVER break down and remove him from the crate while he is fussing! If you give in, he has won round one and you will only be prolonging the ordeal. Sooner or later, he will settle down. If you give in to his temper tantrums, you will only teach him that by crying and carrying on he will eventually get his way. This is a basic principle of dog training. NEVER LET THE DOG MANIPULATE YOU! NEVER!

To help him adjust to the crate, you can feed him a few times in the crate before actually closing the door. Once you have gotten him used to

159

being in the crate with the door open, you can give him a toy or a few biscuits and close the door. Hopefully, he will be occupied with his toy and will take the confinement in stride. If he fusses, however, just carry on as usual without making any special fuss over him. If he is crated where he can see you, he will not feel quite so put out. At least he'll know he hasn't been abandoned. Ignore the wails and whines as best you can. He'll get over it. When he finally settles down, then you can remove him.

Never use the crate as punishment. You must always make the association as pleasant as possible so the pup will accept the crate as his own private quarters. Comfy bedding and enough room to move around will make the crate more pleasant for him.

Housebreaking

To use the crate to housebreak your puppy, follow the guidelines listed below:

1. Crate the puppy when you are not actively playing with or observing him. Allowing the pup complete freedom of the house before he is fairly trustworthy is counterproductive and unfair to the immature pup. Not only will it be impossible to be consistent in his training, but if you don't keep an eye on him he may get into real trouble. . . like chewing on a lamp cord.

2. For very young puppies (8-12 weeks) the crate should not be too large. A puppy will avoid soiling his bed if at all possible, but in a huge crate he will be able to retreat to a far corner and not have to live with his errors!

3. Do not expect perfection from a tiny pup. Like any infant, he will have his limits. You can, however, make things much easier for him if you give him ample time to relieve himself. It IS cruel to confine a tiny puppy to a crate for such extended periods of time that he is forced to soil his bed. Remember, the natural instinct to keep the "den" clean is the key to housetraining. If you pervert this basic instinct, you will make the job of housetraining much more difficult, if not impossible. If you know you must leave the puppy unattended for a long time, fix him a pen or exercise area in which he can stay. A young pup will have to go out frequently and should be taken outside or to the exercise area almost hourly, and even once or twice during the night. (Nobody said dog training is easy!) Once he is over 12 weeks old, you can take him out every two or three hours.

4. Always take the puppy out the very first thing in the morning. If you wait until you've dressed you probably will have a mess to clean up. Waste no time. A puppy will have to go out as soon as he wakes up.

5. The puppy will also have to go right after eating. If you have been playing with him for more than five or ten minutes, give him a chance to go out, especially if he loses interest in the game and starts to sniff around.

160

6. Withhold water and food after 8:00 PM and take the puppy out the very last thing at night. Don't rush things . . . give him plenty of time. While outside, remember that he is there to perform and not to play . . . if you distract him from the matter at hand, you may have a mess to clean up later! A fenced yard, portable run or outdoor exercise pen will give him a little more freedom to take care of business. Every dog, however, should also learn to relieve himself while on leash.

7. Keep the crate near your bed at night if your puppy is very young. It is unrealistic to expect a tiny puppy to "hold it" all night. By having him near you, you will be able to hear if your pup whines to go out. As they get a few weeks older, they'll be able to last longer.

NOTE: Never put any dog or puppy in a crate when it is wearing a choke collar. The "live" ring of the collar can easily catch on the wire bars or door latch and if the dog struggles or panics, it will surely strangle. Choke collars are meant to be used for training and ONLY while training. If you must leave a collar on your dog, use the nylon web type that buckles. Choke collars aren't called CHOKE collars for nothing!

If your puppy has not passed a stool recently and you just KNOW he has to go but suspect he is not concentrating hard enough on the matter at hand, you can help move things along by the OCCASIONAL use of an infant suppository. After using the same spot in the yard a few times, he'll get the idea. Always praise profusely when things progress properly.

It's very easy to teach the puppy the word "out." When you're getting ready to take the pup out to relieve himself, say his name and "out." As you open the door, repeat "out" so he makes the connection between the word and the door. When he relieves himself, say "good out." Very soon you'll be able to ask the pup if he has to go out. He will cock his head and it will be no time before he'll go for the door when he hears the word. Your puppy will have a different whine for "I have to go out," and "I'm tired of being in here." As you become more familiar with your pup, you'll be able to understand its verbal and non-verbal communication with you.

Choosing a Veterinarian

A vital element in preparing for your new puppy is finding the right vet. If you have not had previous association with a veterinarian that you know and have faith in, you can ask local dog breeders or the area all-breed kennel club for a referral. Most often, the vet used by area dog breeders is the best, most up-to-date available. Breeders of valuable show dogs will not patronize a vet who doesn't keep abreast of current developments in his field.

If the vet you choose doesn't seem to like Bull Terriers, or does not answer your questions to your satisfaction, look elsewhere. Your dog may live to be twelve or fifteen years old and you will need a veterinarian with whom you can establish a rapport. He may not be familiar with the Bull Terrier breed, but he should at least not be afraid of the dog or assume it is a fighting dog! He or she may think your dog is a Pit Bull . . . the two breeds are commonly confused. This is an excellent opportunity to explain the difference and make a new friend for the breed as well!

The first time you take your Bull Terrier to visit the vet, take along the vaccination and worming records your breeder gave you. This will enable the vet to continue vaccinations and fecal tests on schedule.

If you live in an area where heartworm is a problem, you will need to give your dog heartworm preventative, usually in tablet form. Your vet will probably require a yearly blood test to check for the microfilaria that indicate heartworm infestation. Ask your vet about putting your new puppy on the preventative when you take him in for his first check-up. Without precautions, your dog could become seriously ill or die if he becomes infested with heartworms.

In recent years, a new health problem has developed . . . PARVO-VIRUS, commonly referred to as "Parvo." A highly contagious virus, Parvo is usually spread through contact with infected dogs or their feces, but can also be carried on your clothing or shoes. It can kill immature, debilitated or elderly dogs within hours of the first visible symptoms. Puppies that get Parvo rarely survive. Older dogs may live through it if in basically good health otherwise. The first symptoms of Parvo include depression and lack of appetite. Severe and persistent vomiting will occur, followed by extreme diarrhea and a temperature of 104-106 degrees. Diarrhea may be bloody and very foul-smelling. Because of the loss of fluids from vomiting and diarrhea, a dog with Parvo will quickly become dehydrated. At the very first indication that your dog is not feeling well, waste no time in getting him to your vet. Delay of even a few hours may make the difference between life and death. Many dogs die of Parvo because their owners wait too long to seek help. It is better to have the dog examined right away and have it turn out to be nothing more than a bellyache, than to wait until the dog is devastated and dying.

With Parvo, as with Distemper and other contagious dog diseases, prevention is the best solution. However, at this writing, an infallible vaccine for Parvo has yet to be developed. The vaccines currently available will provide a degree of protection in an otherwise healthy, worm-free dog, but the duration of protection is uncertain and varies with the different types and brands of vaccine. To make things worse, it is now believed that the dam's maternal immunity is transmitted to her puppies with the first milk. This immunity may last just a few weeks or up to two or three months. It may vary even among puppies of the same litter! The problem lies in the

162

Ch. The Ink Spot of Nelloyd as a four-month-old puppy.

These two best friends begin an adventure together in their yard.

fact that any vaccinations given to young puppies may protect them from Parvo IF the maternal immunity has dissipated. However, if the puppy still has some immunity from its mother, this maternal immunity will block any protection the pup might derive from the vaccination! So, the breeder or owner will assume that, because the pup has had its Parvo shots, it is protected, when in fact the maternal immunity may have blocked the vaccinations. Therefore, once the maternal immunity wears off, the puppy is left virtually unprotected. To counter this problem, many breeders are now advocating a vaccination program for young puppies which entails vaccinating with killed vaccine every three weeks from age six weeks to four months. At four months, the puppy can receive a vaccination with modified live virus which will last at least six months. Until a more stable vaccine is developed, it is best to revaccinate with the modified live vaccine every six months, particularly if your dog will be shown, boarded, attending training classes, or will be exposed to stray or loose dogs in your neighborhood. Regardless of vaccination, however, it is unwise to take your puppy to parks and public areas frequented by dogs until the pup has had the modified live vaccine. Try to keep strays and neighborhood dogs from coming into your yard. Wash your pup's living area often with a solution of one part Clorox to thirty parts water. So far, bleach water is the only disinfectant known to be effective in killing the virus. If you have been walking where dogs congregate, clean your shoes with bleach water before coming into the house. If you follow a regular schedule of fecal testing (every month for pups under six months old, then every three months), and worm your dog as needed, you can help your dog fight off Parvo should it become infected. Because Parvo attacks the intestinal lining, a dog with worms is at a great disadvantage.

In addition to Parvo vaccination, your puppy will need vaccinations against Distemper, Hepatitis, Leptospirosis and Parainfluenza. These are usually all combined into one shot. A young puppy may get a Measles shot at six weeks, then two DHL-P shots, at nine weeks and twelve weeks. Your vet may elect to give the Parvo shot with the DHL-P or space them a week apart. The puppy will also need a Rabies shot at six months of age and every three years thereafter. Most vets will send you a reminder through the mail when your dog is due for shots, but do not rely on this. Far better that you keep track of this detail yourself and make sure you present your dog on schedule!

Last But Not Least

It is a sad commentary on our times when we cannot safely leave a dog unattended in a car or yard without having it stolen. Bull Terriers are prime targets because they are commonly mistaken for Pit Bulls, which are, sadly, a "hot item" among unscrupulous sorts. Pit Bulls and Bull Terriers, when stolen, are usually needed for the "game testing" of fighting dogs. What that means is that your dog will be used as a sort of "sparring partner" for a pit dog to test the other dog's desire to fight. Needless to say, your Bull Terrier, a hundred years removed from the dog pits, will not fare well. A measure of caution and common sense can help you to protect your dog from this horrible fate. If you leave your dog unattended in a car or public place you are asking for trouble. Even your fenced yard or dog pen is not safe if it is visible from the road or your dog is left out while you are not home. Bull Terriers have been stolen from dog shows, from kennels, and even from a breeder's basement puppy pen while she was at work! Avoid discussing your dog with anyone who asks too many questions. Certainly don't give out your address. Staffordshire Terrier and reputable Pit Bull breeders have been dealing with this problem for a long time.

Many now tattoo their dogs and even puppies before they're sold. Bull Terrier clubs are now sponsoring tattoo clinics for Bull Terrier owners. Tattoo identification will not keep your dog from being stolen, but if you let the fact be known that your dogs are tattooed, chances are that the dognappers will look for an easier mark. A tattoo provides positive identification if the dog is recovered. It will also help humane societies and veterinarians trace lost or injured dogs, as most vets and shelters have access to the tattoo registry hotline numbers. We strongly suggest that you have your new puppy tattooed as soon as you get it. Contact your vet or nearest Bull Terrier regional club for more information.

You can have your dog tattooed with your social security number or a special code number issued by a tattoo registry. Before tattooing, contact one of the nationwide registries (I.D. PET or NATIONAL DOG REGISTRY) for information. Once your dog's number is registered, you will be provided with a door decal (WARNING: TATTOOED PETS) and a metal collar tag that will draw attention to the tattoo inside the dog's flank. The tag lists a toll-free number that anyone finding a tattooed dog can call. The dog's tattoo number will then be run through a computer which will provide the owner's name, address and phone number! Needless to say, this can really be a deciding factor in helping you find your dog, should it ever get lost. Tattooing and common sense are the best ways possible to protect your pet.

It should go without saying that a Bull Terrier or any dog should never be allowed to run loose or be off-lead in an unfenced area. Some dog owners get very complacent about this after a while and usually eventually learn the hard way. Perhaps this point is best illustrated by a story about a tragic event that happened to us just before Christmas, 1981 . . .

We had placed a young male Bull Terrier named Elmo with Mike, the boyfriend of our kennel assistant, Karen. Elmo and Mike seemed made for each other. Elmo badly needed someone to roughhouse with and Mike admired the dog's spunky personality. One of the conditions of the placement was that Mike must provide Elmo with a fenced yard or dog run in which to exercise. We knew that Mike's family had a Labrador previously that had been killed by a car and we would not consider placing Elmo with them unless they would keep him confined to their yard. Karen assured us that Mike's family had been heartbroken at the loss of their pet and had vowed never to let it happen again. So Mike and his father built a sturdy pen for Elmo and promised that he would be taken there regularly during the day for exercise. Mike took Elmo home in August and all went well for several months. Then one snowy night in December, Karen called us, in tears. Elmo had been hit by a car and she needed the number of the emergency veterinary clinic near my house. We provided the number and waited anxiously. About a half an hour later, a car pulled up outside. Elmo was stretched out on a blanket on the back seat . . . the family was distraught . . . "Could we see if he might still be alive?" . . . They thought he had stopped breathing, but didn't want to believe it was so. Allan lifted the dog's head in his hands then laid it gently down and walked away. Elmo was dead, just two weeks short of his first birthday.

When something like this happens, you want answers. You want to know why such a stupid and unnecessary thing should ever have happened! We later found out that the family had been very good about taking Elmo out to his pen while the weather was nice, but when snow accumulated and the temperature dropped it became a "hassle" to walk him out to his pen. It was just a lot easier to simply open the door and let him out. They thought he was being good about not leaving the yard. What they never considered was the impulsive nature of the average Bull Terrier puppy. A lovely young dog died because of the laziness of his owners. Some people just never learn.

If you have any intention of being lax in the supervision of your animal, please do the breed a favor . . . don't get a Bull Terrier! The days when dogs could run loose are long past. If you don't want to accept the responsibility of proper care or the "inconvenience" of having to walk the dog or the expense involved in purchasing a dog run or fencing . . . you don't deserve one of these fine animals and you most certainly will not get one from me!

166

19

The First Year

MANY people refer to Bull Terrier pups as terrors and shark-like with respect to their teeth. This breed is very much orally fixated especially during teething. They need bones to constantly massage the gums. A fresh marrow (shin) bone every day is in order. Be sure not to give the knuckle part of the marrow bone, as it will splinter or break off and can cause serious damage internally. Remember that Bull Terriers have extremely strong jaws. Never give chicken, steak, chop or rib bones!

When your puppy begins to teethe, at around four months of age, you should check his mouth frequently to make certain no puppy teeth are impeding the development of the adult teeth. Sometimes a puppy tooth will not fall out and will share its space with the adult tooth, causing the permanent tooth to come in crooked or out of line. It is especially important to keep a close eye on the teeth if you intend to show the dog. Also, puppy teeth may begin to decay or cause an abcess if they remain in place longer than intended. Your vet can remove any offending tooth that may be causing problems. Give your puppy a Nylabone to chew on and most of the puppy teeth will eventually come out on their own.

You may notice during teething that your puppy's previously erect ears become periodically floppy. The puppy's calcium is now going to the teething process and sometimes the ears will soften in this stage. Normally, as the adult teeth finish coming through, the ears will return to their erect stature. If they do not, consult your breeder about having the ears taped.

Some puppies will need help with their ears at three to four months of age. If your puppy carries ears high or at half mast, they will probably go up on their own, or with a light one- or two-day taping. Most breeders begin taping a puppy's ears at three months if they are especially heavy or large and lie flat like a Labrador Retriever's ears. Since the puppy begins to lose puppy teeth at around four months of age, ears that are already standing may droop for a while but will usually stand again without assistance, once the teething period is over and the body is less stressed. If your pup's ears don't seem to be going up at all by age three months, consult your breeder. He or she will know, from past experience with the bloodlines, whether you should begin to tape or let it go for a while. There are as many ways to tape ears as there are breeders, and every Bull Terrier person you talk to will have a different opinion on the matter. We've tried several methods, but find the procedure outlined below to be simple and easy on the dog's ears:

Buy a package of Dr. Scholl's Moleskin (as used on human feet, available at the drugstore). Make sure to get the lightweight type that is flannel-like on one side and sticky on the other. Also buy a roll of 3-M Nylon first-aid tape, available at the drugstore. Nylon tape doesn't pull the hair off the ears when you remove it. Don't use regular adhesive tape. If you can't find the nylon tape, masking tape is a better alternative. You will also need some rubbing alcohol, a few cotton balls and several wooden matches with the heads cut off, or Q-tips.

1. Clean the inside of the ear flap (NOT ear canal) with alcohol dampened cotton balls. The object is to remove any dirt or oils that will keep the moleskin from sticking.

2. Cut four pieces of moleskin exactly the same size and shape. It might help to have a pattern. You want a shape that if approximately the same size and shape of the inner ear flap, but round off the edges. Generally, a four-month-old pup would require a triangle that is roughly 1¼ inches or so at the base and perhaps 2 inches on the other two sides.

3. Cut your matches or Q-tips to a length of 1½ inches or so. Allow three for each ear brace. Place them on the sticky part of one piece of moleskin so that they meet at the top and fan out at the bottom. Place another piece of moleskin fuzzy side down over the matches so as to sandwich them between the two pieces of moleskin. You should have one side with the fuzzy material exposed, the other side should be sticky.

4. Fit the moleskin "brace" into the ear. If it extends too far into the inner ear, cut some off the bottom. You don't need to support anything except the ear flap.

5. Gently fold the two sides of the ear inward together so as to form a sort of cone. Using nylon tape, wrap ear SNUGLY, but NOT TIGHTLY from the bottom to the tip, leaving an opening at the bottom and at the top for air circulation. Repeat on the other ear, even if it is standing.

168

"So *that's* what the rest of the world looks like!"

6. You should now have two cone-shaped "appendages" protruding from your dog's head. More likely than not, these will stick out to the sides, so you must stabilize them on top of the head to aid in proper ear set. Using more nylon tape (or you can use adhesive tape here, it might even work better) wrap around the base of one ear, cross the top of the dog's head, encircle the base of the other ear, then back again to the starting point. Repeat. You need to form a "bridge" at the base of the two ears to hold them in the proper position on top of the head. With a small piece of tape, wrap around the bridge between the two ears to keep it from unraveling.

7. Leave this on from three to five days. Keep the ears free from water. Your dog may dig at the tapes at first but will usually leave them alone if you distract him with a special toy or goodie. Repeat the taping if necessary, but allow a rest of a few days between tapings if the ears appear sore.

Making certain that your dog is in good health and nutritionally fit will aid in ear development. A dog with a diet deficiency will have problems developing properly.

Sometimes you, as a Bull Terrier owner, will have to go against your vet's advice. This happens most often when diet and ear taping are discussed. Vets are used to dealing with average dogs that do not require the quality of bone and substance that a well developed Bull Terrier should have. The average vet will suggest that you feed your puppy a "well-balanced" commercial brand of puppy food. While this may be fine for Poodles or Collies, it generally is not the ideal food for a growing Bull Terrier puppy. Follow the diet instructions provided by your breeder. They know through experience what makes good healthy bone and optimal substance on a Bull Terrier.

Ear taping is another common point of contention. Most vets feel that unless the ears are cropped, they don't need help or support and will eventually stand on their own. Being unfamiliar with the history of the breed, they do not know that the natural prick ear is a fairly recent development in this breed and so it is not unusual for a puppy to require some taping to get the ear standing erect. Most breeders do not allow an ear to droop past three, or at most four months without taping it. Some Bull Terrier puppies will never need to be taped, but many of the heavyweights or pups with large ears will need a little help. Some vets confuse the breed with Pit Bulls and American Staffordshire Terriers and will swear that a Bull Terrier's ears should be cropped! Whatever you do, make sure that is NOT what your vet has in mind if you do let him or her work on your puppy's ears!

As with any breed of dog, there is always the possibility that sooner or later your dog will become involved in a fight. Any breed will scrap, however, with Bull Terriers, like their cousins the Pit Bulls and Staffordshires, the danger lies in the fact that they are capable of doing serious damage to an opponent in a short amount of time. Every effort must be made to avoid a conflict with another dog, for certainly it will always be the Bull Terrier's "fault" in the eyes of the public, even if the other dog attacked him.

If your dog should become involved in a fight with another dog, you must know how to break it up quickly and safely. Don't rely on the usual techniques of yelling, throwing things, beating with brooms or dousing with water. Bull Terriers will rarely take much notice. Under no circumstances ever attempt to pry the combatants' jaws open with your hands, as you will most certainly be accidentally bitten in the process. The best way to break up a dog fight is to be prepared . . . ALWAYS keep a sturdy nylon web or leather collar on your dog. The collar will serve as a handle to grab in case of a scrap. The main objective in breaking up a fight is to disentangle your dog as soon as possible from the fracas and pitch him into an open car, separate room or whatever . . . to keep him from jumping back into the fight. Unless your dog has gotten into it with another Bull Terrier, most likely the opponent will "head for the hills" as soon as he is freed. To get your dog to let go of the other dog, follow this procedure:

1. Grasp your dog firmly by the collar, taking care to keep out of the way of the other dog's jaws. If someone is helping you, slip a leash or rope noose-fashion over the other dog's head. Have your helper stand by ready to pull the other dog away from the scene. Twist with all your might on your dog's collar. The object is to cut off his air supply temporarily. While twisting the collar, try to shove his nose INTO the other dog. Sooner or later he will need to take a breath and will have to open his mouth to do so. Be prepared! The moment he gasps for air, yank him away and remove him from the scene.

2. If you are in the unfortunate position of having to break up a fight on your own, use the choking technique as outlined above and pray that the underdog wants to escape and not continue the brawl. If, however, your dog has gotten into a scrap with an aggressive dog, you have a big problem! Try to noose the dog that doesn't seem to have a hold on the other dog. Secure the lead or rope to something strong. Then grasp your dog and choke him off. As soon as he lets go, remove him from the area. I have heard that smelling salts or ammonia on a rag will help break up a serious fight, but unfortunately these items are never available when you need them!

If your dog has gotten into a fight with another dog, check him closely for puncture wounds and lacerations that may become infected. It may be wise to have your vet take a look, as antibiotics will probably be necessary to ward off infection. If you know who owns the other dog, you should let them know that their dog may be injured so that they can get veterinary attention for him.

Needless to say, it is much simpler and safer to avoid conflicts at any cost. Do not take your dog where you know there will be many dogs running loose. Even with your Bull Terrier on leash, you never know when a loose dog will try to provoke a fight. A dog who has never had the opportunity to get into a scrap will be much less interested in accepting a "challenge" than one who has gotten a taste of it. Try to insure that your Bull Terrier is never in a position where he can become involved in a fight . . . even if he is only trying to defend himself.

In the home, as well, one must be sensible in preventing situations which can trigger a fight. At the risk of making this breed seem dangerous or difficult to live with, I must stress that certain situations may arise where even the most compatible housepets will fight.

If you have more than one dog, remember that all pets crave attention and may compete for affection or food. This can lead to some nasty fights. Be cautious, too, in situations where one or both dogs may become overly excited . . . such as in greeting visitors, competitive games, or barking at intruders. In the height of excitement, one dog may attack the other. I know that sounds terrible, but it is a fact to consider if you intend to keep a Bull Terrier with another dog. If you allow your dogs to play together, keep an eye open for any sign of irritability or fatigue that may turn a game into a nasty brawl. Stop the game as soon as things appear to be progressing past the fun stage.

Needless to say, NEVER leave your Bull Terrier alone with another animal unsupervised. When you are not home, they must be put into separate rooms or crates. There have been too many sad tales of dogs who have grown up together, and have been good friends, yet have gotten involved in serious arguments. I recall one tragic instance where the owner went to work and left her Bull Terriers, a male and two bitches, alone together in the house. When she returned, she found the male had been attacked and killed by his companions. Don't be so foolish as to assume that because your dogs never fight that they never will. Even the best of friends sometimes have disagreements.

If confining your pets every time you leave the house doesn't agree with you, then you should not consider adding a Bull Terrier to your household. Bull Terriers can be wonderful with other dogs, even cats and other animals, but never forget that they are terriers and are very capable of killing another animal should a conflict arise. Ownership of Bull Terriers, like any breed, does have some drawbacks. Some breeds need continual grooming, others may have physical problems . . . Bull Terriers need supervision and control. This must be a very serious consideration before obtaining one, especially if you have other animals.

Kenneling Your Bull Terrier

If you find you will have to board your Bull Terrier, try to choose a kennel that has had previous experience with the breed. Some kennels are not properly equipped to handle a Bull Terrier and some have a definite bias against the so-called "fighting breeds." It is much safer and kinder to your dog to leave it with someone who can care for him properly. If your dog's breeders live nearby, they may be able to board the dog for you. If not, perhaps you can work out a mutual dog-sitting arrangement with another Bull Terrier owner whom you know and can trust to take proper care of your dog. Do not board your dog with your veterinarian unless the vet has boarding facilities separate from the clinic. Veterinary hospitals are for sick dogs, not boarders.

Six to Twelve Months

As your Bull Terrier approaches maturity, you will have to make some decisions regarding the future. If purchased strictly as a pet, now is the time to set a date with your veterinarian for neutering or spaying. Pet quality dogs should not be used for breeding. If you have any doubt in your mind, consult your dog's breeder and respect his or her decision. If you bought your dog from an established breeder, he will be able to give you an idea of the quality of puppies your dog might produce, based on past experience with the line. If he or she recommends not breeding the dog, don't. Remember, your pet quality Bull Terrier is not necessarily a poor specimen of the breed . . . it might, however, have faults that conscientious breeders are trying hard to eradicate. Please help to protect the breed by not breeding your dog if this is the case. If you bought a pet because you wanted a good companion and chum, let it be just that.

There are so many reasons why pet quality animals should NOT be bred, it's easier to make a list:

1. Males used at stud frequently forget their house manners. A stud dog is more inclined to wet down your couch than an untried dog. It's simply instinct. He's marking out his territory!

2. An un-neutered dog will usually become more aggressive towards other dogs, especially other males. He may have been mellow before, but he may now regard the other males as threats to his "domain."

3. An experienced male will actively seek a way to escape from his yard when there's a bitch in season in the neighborhood. If you think he doesn't know about her, you're kidding yourself!

This month-old youngster shows a beautiful clean head, well-placed eyes, and good bone and feet. The nose is just starting to blacken up. (Bull Terrier puppies are usually whelped with all-pink noses, and pink streaks may remain for months.)

This puppy has an unusually good chest, heavy round bone, excellent conformation throughout. But his eyes are not well placed, fill seems a bit lacking, and the chances are that he will not develop into good show type.

A young puppy, about two months old, bred by Miss D. Montague Johnstone. Note the fill, strength of jaw, the good bone and feet, the well-bent stifle, and good back line. A puppy like this would be a very good gamble indeed.

174

4. Stud dogs will fret when a female in season is nearby. Your dog may refuse to eat, resulting in unwanted weight loss. He may also howl all night, resulting in angry neighbors!

5. Pet owners sometimes think that any dog offered at stud will have an active career. That just isn't so. Only a very few top quality dogs are in demand. If your dog hasn't proven himself in the show ring, he may only be used once or twice, by other pet owners. That may be just enough experience to ruin him as your housepet. Is it worth it?

6. Neutering will eliminate or decrease the probability of developing various health problems. Neutered dogs have no risk of cancer of the testicles, and lowered risk of prostate cancer.

Have your pet male neutered before he is one year old. Neutered dogs don't metabolize calories as quickly as un-neutered dogs do, therefore, you must adjust his food intake after neutering. If you watch his diet, there is absolutely no reason for him to become overweight. Neutered dogs become obese because their owners continue to feed the same amount of food after neutering as prior to the operation.

7. The heat seasons of the average unspayed female dog can be a nuisance to the pet owner. Aside from the normal copious discharge and resulting mess, you may also find every male dog in the neighborhood camping on your doorstep. This may result in fights between the suitors, ruined shrubbery, howling, and possibly even a bite from a Romeo who resents your attempts to shoo him off! Your bitch may not be her normal, loving self either! You'll have to watch her like a hawk to insure that she doesn't escape and become bred accidentally.

8. The breeding of a bitch is not to be taken lightly. It is hard work! The idea of substantial monetary gain is laughable. If you keep an accurate record of expenditures (stud fee, shipping, feeding, vet care, loss of wages while off work to attend the litter) you will see that even with an easy, uneventful whelping of four or five LIVING puppies, you will be lucky to break even. If something goes wrong . . . the bitch needs a Caesarian (fairly common in this breed), the puppies don't thrive and you lose some or all of them, or if the mother has no milk and you must hand-feed every few hours, you will soon find your "profit" going down the drain. It is unrealistic to expect to make money raising Bull Terriers.

Aside from catastrophies, raising a litter is not very pleasant work! You will lose a lot of sleep the first few days after whelping because even the best Bull Terrier mothers may be a little anxious after whelping and may step on or lie on their pups. Needless to say, someone will have to be with the new mother and her litter for AT LEAST a week, around the clock, to keep an eye on things. Frequently, the litter will require close observation for even the first two or three weeks. You simply cannot expect to go to

175

work as usual, or out to dinner or to a movie and expect to raise the whole litter to weaning age.

If you don't have the time, stamina, stomach and finances to raise a litter properly, DON'T DO IT!

9. An unspayed bitch runs a significantly higher risk of developing breast cancer as she gets older. To lower this risk, she should be spayed before she is two years old. Spaying after this time has less effect on the incidence of the disease.

Bad Habits

As your puppy matures, there may begin to develop some habits you find less than charming. Some of these may be outgrown, such as chewing when going through teething. Others, like jumping on people and barking incessantly, reflect a lack of discipline or boredom. Both can be corrected with a little understanding of the problem. We recommend basic dog training to help eliminate these habits before they become too difficult to break.

One bad habit that is quite common in Bull Terriers is tail chasing. It quickly becomes a serious problem, partially because new owners think it is so cute . . . at first! When it becomes obsessive behavior, it isn't so entertaining anymore! It is not clear what causes a dog to chase its tail. Many Bull Terriers seem to do it just for fun, but it can also be the byproduct of excessive confinement (boredom) or due to a physical problem (impacted anal sacs). Take the dog to the vet first to rule out a possible physical problem. If the dog checks out okay you must consider the problem to be behavioral in nature and take steps to correct it. Some Bull Terriers will become so obsessed with tail chasing that they seem to do nothing else! In extreme cases, the dogs may become neurotic. . . chasing continuously until their physical and mental health is impaired. Don't let it get to that point. When you first see the puppy beginning to develop a chasing habit, distract him with a toy or start another game. If he ignores you and persists, a stern reprimand is in order. You must be consistent. Don't scold or punish one time and then laugh the next. Dogs will take laughter and lack of reprimand as encouragement to continue. Once established, tail chasing is a very difficult habit to break.

You may find your dog is a great attention getter when you are out for a walk. You may be approached by people interested in your dog's "fighting ability." It is best to cut these people short and give them no information whatsoever regarding your dog, except to mention that he couldn't fight his way out of a paper bag! If you are walking, do not invite theft by immediately heading for home. You may be observed. I do not want to make the new dog owner apprehensive of every curious stranger on the street, but I must stress common sense in dealing with those who ask the wrong questions.

In Ohio, Florida, California, and several other states, legislation has been proposed which would make ownership of American Pit Bull Terriers and Staffordshire Terriers restricted or outlawed in certain counties. This is a dark omen for Bull Terrier owners as well because so many people confuse the breeds. In addition to anti-"Bull-breeds" legislation, there is a growing trend to severely restrict or penalize ownership of ANY breed! As a dog owner, and especially as a BULL TERRIER owner, you have a responsibility to make sure your dog does nothing which would reflect badly on the breed or on dogs in general. If you want to keep the peace in your neighborhood, do not allow your dog to be a nuisance to your neighbors. Do not allow him to run loose, terrorizing neighborhood pets. You could find yourself in court if he dispatches the neighbor's cat! Do not permit excessive barking in your absence. Introduce him to your neighbors, stressing that he is NOT a fighting dog and poses no danger to the community. Every new friend you make for your dog is also a new friend for the breed . . . and in this day and age the Bull-and-Terrier breeds need all the friends they can get!

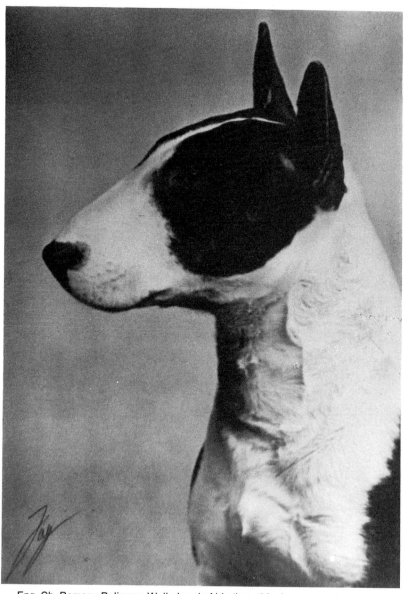

Eng. Ch. Romany Reliance. Well ahead of his time, this dog was a champion in 1946 and was used to great advantage by the greatest Colored breeders of the time. Today, many credit him as being the foundation for the modern Bull Terrier head. *Fall*

20

Development of the Modern Head

by Raymond H. Oppenheimer

IN 1919 there were many proud and mighty male Bull Terrier lines in both the United States and Britain in which generation succeeded generation in aristocratic triumph: Ch. Norcross Patrician, Ch. Haymarket Faultless, and on to Ch. Norcross Thunderer, Ch. Mascotte Cheeky, Ch. Bloomsbury Cheeky and on to Ch. Coolridge Grit of Blighty, Ch. White Noel and Ch. Krishna. Hampstead Heathen, Robert the Devil, Ch. St. George, Ch. John Ridd and on to Ch. Lord Teddy. There were so many of them and they were so strong and widespread that the onlooker gazing at any one of them might well have exclaimed with Macbeth, "What! will the line stretch out to the crack of doom?"

Certainly it must have seemed that the answer was "Yes," and yet even at that moment those with keen eyes might have seen a cloud "no bigger than a man's hand" from which such a deluge of outstanding champions was to come that in twenty short years every rival male line had been totally submerged.

Lord Gladiator

In 1918 the Great War was reaching its climax when a Bull Terrier was

179

Lord Gladiator, whelped in 1918, was generally credited with being the source of the modern Bull Terrier head.

Another view of Lord Gladiator. The dog shows obvious faults, but his virtues changed the course of the breed.

whelped in London with a head far in advance of anything seen before. This dog, bred by the late W. J. Tuck and called Lord Gladiator, started upon his stud career and launched a tail-male line that was to crush its rivals with a speed and ruthlessness that any Juggernaut might have envied.

At first, not unnaturally, nothing very dramatic occurred. Gwent Graphite in the first generation was a good but not outstanding dog. However, his son, Ch. Crooke's Great Boy, was outstanding, though no more so than others had been, but in his turn he did shake up the pundits a little when he sired Ch. White Rose Girl, Egyptian Goddess, and Ch. Galalaw Benefactor, all of which were obviously exceptional. From then on the line gathered pace and power until by 1936 it was clearly dominant.

At this moment, when almost all opposition had already been crushed anyway, except for Ch. Maldwyn, Ch. Midhurst Mercury, and Defender of Monshireval, who were fighting to maintain the Hampstead Heathen line, Lord Gladiator brought up his heaviest guns; in 1937 came Ch. Raydium Brigadier and the Colored Ch. Romany Rhinestone; in 1938, Ch. Velhurst Vindicator; in 1939, Ch. Ormandy's Mr. McGuffin; and that was the end. These four trampled upon their few remaining rivals and Lord Gladiator reigned supreme.

Keen students of the breed naturally had all along been asking themselves whether the increasing dominance of Lord Gladiator's line was chance or whether it was the workings of certain definite laws of inheritance applicable to all Bull Terriers and which would therefore prove valid in other cases.

Lord Gladiator was by Ch. Oaksford Gladiator ex Ch. Lady Betty. Each was by Bloombury Czar and his claim to fame lay in his exceptional head. In fact, otherwise he was a comparatively ordinary dog. It followed then if his value was not chance, the success of his descendants must indicate that a great head, even though accompanied by some unsoundness, was a continuing and valuable asset to a line. At this point observers noted three interesting and complementary facts: First, that the breeders who ignored heads in the search for soundness were soon in trouble. Second, that those who used heads and risked some unsoundness were very successful and often got soundness too. And third, that lines that were weak in heads very quickly petered out.

It was only a very short step from that to the inference that good heads were most probably governed by hybrid dominant factors; i.e., they carried with them in recessive form the factors for plainer and plainer heads, and that the breed would always "recede" to the plainer type unless great care was taken to preserve the head which artists had for years portrayed as the ideal but which no one had ever thought fully attainable until Lord Gladiator appeared.

Eng./Am. Ch. Rambling Rose of Foyri ROM, as powerful a head as one would find on a bitch.

Ch. Ragged Hills Lady Killer, an exceptional head for any time. This is from the 1970s.

Ch. Banbury Blizzard of Bedrock, a weak profile on a dog who is otherwise virtuous. This dog would not win in the Specialty ring, but in the all-breed ring he was tops for two years.

Ch. Brummagem Barcarole ROM, a 1985 shot which shows a head which is as close to the standard as has been produced, not overcooked, but very clean and classical.

At this point I want to touch very lightly upon the Mendelian law which says that if a dominant factor is present it always manifests itself. That is true if the dominant factor is present in the body cells, but (although I have never seen it stated categorically in a book on genetics) my experience has led me to believe that dominant factors can be absent in the body cells and yet be present in the reproductive cells. That is the only practical explanation I can find of how certain animals pass on factors known to be dominant which they themselves do not possess and it is the only workable theory I can find to explain how some Bull Terriers can transmit great heads although they themselves have very ordinary ones.

I am aware that there is a school of thought which believes that great heads are produced by a process akin to that which produces *agoutism* in rabbits, but I have not found this a workable explanation.

Anyway, for practical purposes I think breeders will do well to accept this theory until a better one is propounded and to draw from it the conclusion which is demonstrable from the records—that there is no hope at all of great headed puppies unless at least one of the grandparents had a great head. That is a point of immense importance and one which should never be overlooked.

Now to return to Lord Gladiator. The facts which I have outlined made it obvious that the triumph of his line was not chance. In any case, successive events both inside and outside his line merely followed a pattern similar to that which observers had already noted.

184

21

Breeding for Color

by Miss D. Montague Johnstone

The Romany prefix of Miss D. Montague Johnstone has achieved milestones of quality in the Colored variety as well as produced genetic benefactors in Whites and Color-bred Whites. Her genetic research and experience form the basis for her thoughts presented here.

IT is not difficult to understand how color works—what two colors mated together can or cannot produce—yet it is remarkable how ignorant many breeders still are on this interesting question.

Brindle is the Dominant Color

If a dog* carries the factor for brindle, it will dominate any other colors the dog may carry, and the dog will be brindle in color.

In reverse, if the dog is not brindle (or black-brindle) in color, then, quite obviously, he does not carry the brindle factor. Therefore, if two non-brindles (say two reds, or two fawns, or a red to a tricolor) are mated together, they will produce no brindle or black-brindle puppies, since neither of them carries the factor for brindle.

It is not necessary for both parents to carry the brindle factor; it is sufficient for one parent to carry it.

*The word "dog" covers both sexes as regards color, since in both sexes color behaves exactly alike.

185

Because it is only possible to produce brindle if one or both parents carry the color, brindle is, of all colors, the most easily lost.

Since brindle is the most desired and most popular of all colors, it is essential that all serious breeders of Colored Bull Terriers should aim to retain and preserve this color above all others. This is important.

It is interesting to note that I have seen an odd-colored, almost pale liver-colored bitch with liver nose, who, mated to a Pure White red dog, produced a high percentage of brindle pups. The answer to this one is that either a brindle dog (kept on the place but sworn to have had no part in it) did have a part in the breeding, unknown to the breeder, or that these very rare dilute livers do carry the brindle factor. I am inclined to this latter view, but it must be understood that this is the rarest of rare exceptions that merely prove the rule. I have only seen three or four of these "livers" in nearly thirty years.

White mated to White, Will Produce 100% White litters

This fact is the stumbling block of many breeders, for they do not appear to be able to comprehend it. It does not matter if the two Whites mated are both Color-bred, with or without head marks. It does not matter if they have four rich colored brindle and white parents, they will still only produce Whites, with or without head marks, according to their strain and its tendency to produce head marks or not. The information given above has been known and well proved for many years.

Color-bred Whites

The next important point is the extreme value of the cbw carrying brindle as a mate for the tricolor or black and tan. Later in this chapter I mention that Romany Rough Weather and Romany Rather Lovely had a tricolor sister. She was a very good bitch and if we had known then what we know now, might have become as famous as the other two. Mated to brindles, her color results were always bad. She should have been mated to a cbw-carrying brindle, when she would undoubtedly have given us a high percentage of beautifully marked brindle pups.

The first notable example of that combination is English and American Ch. Romany Remarkable. Her dam was a black and tan (solid) mated to Ch. Romany Reprieved (cbw), known to carry brindle very strongly. The result was an equal percentage of rich brindles and bright reds, well marked.

I have seen several other excellent examples, of which the most interesting are as follows:

Ch. Rickmay Rising Star, all white cbw (by the pws Ch. Ormandy Silveston Starshine, ex cbw Ch. Rickmay Anbanaad), mated to a tricolor

186

bitch, produced a high percentage of rich brindle and white pups. The brindle here managed to come strongly through the sire, with nothing to show for it in the first two generations except a little brindle on Anbanaad's ear! Another interesting example was a tricolored bitch, who, mated first to a rich brindle and white son of the brindle Romany Roast Goose, produced ten pups, and gave the usual bad result: nothing but whites and blacks. Mated a second time to Ch. Romany Repeat Performance (cbw carrying brindle strongly) the same bitch produced eleven pups, five of which were beautifully marked brindles, the remainder being white.

The cbw-carrying brindle is therefore without doubt exactly what is required as a mate for tricolor or black and tan and gives the very best color result.

While on the question of Color-bred Whites, it is worth mentioning again that all such are genetically Colored Bull Terriers and when bred to Colored mates, act as if they actually showed their color. Many of them do show color, of course, as they have head marks. **According to the color of the head mark, so will they act when bred to Colored mates.** Thus, if a cbw carries a brindle head mark, he will act as a brindle; if red, as a red (in which case, of course, he will not produce brindles to a Colored bitch unless she is brindle, because he will act like a red who cannot produce brindle alone).

The all white cbw also carries color (see perfect example of Ch. Rickmay Rising Star, given previously) but the difficulty with them is that one cannot be sure what color they are until tested, which means mating them to a Colored but non-brindle mate. If he gets brindles to such a mate, then he carries brindle.

Needless to say, the cbw who carries brindle is of greater breeding value to breeders of Coloreds than is the cbw who does not. For the breeder of Whites, it does not matter, since whatever color they may carry, they will still produce only white litters from white mates.

Solids

For the show ring we much prefer and breed for the beautifully marked dog—nice white blaze, white chest and feet, as being very showy and attractive in appearance, and drawing attention to profile and head. Dogs so marked, however, will always throw a percentage of white pups if mated to anything except a solid color. Since breeders of Colored Bull Terriers want colored pups, the solid colored dog is of very great breeding value, although he is at a disadvantage in the show ring with no white to show him off.

A dog that is "solid for color" can almost always be recognized on sight. There is very rarely any need to test him out. He can be any color, brindle, black-brindle, red, fawn, or black and tan. He will have very little or no white on face, and very little or none on chest or legs. Such a dog or bitch will never sire or whelp a white puppy, no matter what he or she is mated to, and this includes Pure White Bull Terriers.

Some dogs can carry quite a lot of white on the chest and still be solid for color. Romany Rivet and Contango Cobblestone are two such examples, but neither had a white blaze. Ch. Romany Rhinestone had not only a white chest, but also white on his face and legs; yet, he never sired a white puppy. In my opinion, this was because he was really very nearly one of the rare "livers." But not quite, since he never sired a brindle puppy to a non-brindle mate. His son, Ch. Romany Roman, was another solid for color, but he was expected to be since he had no blaze and very little white elsewhere.

These "solid" dogs and bitches are the ones to breed from above all others when a breeder feels the strain is getting too many white or badly marked pups. For this purpose they are of immense value.

To conclude, here is a list of the colors that appear in the Bull Terrier breed:

Brindle, and Brindle and White. All shades, from very dark, through reddish, to golden and silver.

Black-Brindle, and Black-Brindle and White. Here the dog is black, with or without white markings, and carries on his cheeks, inside of front legs and on thighs, definite brindle color, varying in shade as above.

Red Smut, or Red Smut and White. The body is red, with or without white markings, and the mask and eyebrows shaded in black, the tail also usually being dark.

Fawn Smut, or Fawn Smut and White. Similar to the reds, except that the body color is fawn.

Clear Red and White. Similar to the *red smut and white,* but without the black mask and shadings.

Clear Fawn and White. Similar to the *fawn smut and white,* but without the black mask and shadings. (For breeding purposes the *smuts* are usually more valuable than the *clears*, being stronger for color.)

Tricolor. Black, with tan or red points on cheeks, eyebrows, inside of front legs and on thighs. White on face, chest, and feet.

Black and Tan. As above, but with no white blaze, and very little white elsewhere, a "solid" color.

I have put these *tricolors* and *black and tans* last, but in actual fact, now that we know what they can do when mated to cbw carrying brindle, they are of greater breeding value than the *clear reds* and *fawns,* and probably as valuable as the *smuts.* They are not, however, so popular in the show ring. Although, a good dog can never be a bad color, they are not to me, and to many others, so typical in appearance, and a good one has to be a little better than a rival to look as good.

When Different Colors are Mated

It must be remembered always that although we can say what two colors together can and cannot produce, it depends enormously on the individuals mated as to what they **do** produce. They will not produce what they are unable to produce, but they can quite often disappoint by not producing what they are able to produce, which is probably what you particularly wanted from them. This is because some dogs and bitches are weak, where others are strong in their ability to produce the brindle factor, whether directly through themselves or their mates.

It is possible, for instance, to have two brindle and white bitches carrying behind them the same proportion of brindle blood. When these are mated to the same dog, whatever his color, one bitch may always give an excellent percentage of brindles while the other may fail to do so.

It is also a fact that the same pair can be mated on two occasions and give entirely different color results in the two resulting litters. The percentage of brindles in one litter may be excellent, and in the other very poor. This shows very clearly that one can never forecast a result.

Brindle and White to Brindle and White: A fairly equal proportion of all colors, including white, can be expected. (This mating is not one of our favorites, unless at least two of the grandparents are White, as a concentration of brindle is inclined to lose type. It is also inclined to produce rather a high percentage of black-brindles, who are not as popular as the true brindles, although, personally, I greatly like a well-marked one.)

Solid Brindle to Brindle and White: As above, but with a higher percentage of true brindles and no whites. The same remark regarding type is applicable here.

Brindle and White to Red and White, or to Fawn and White, or to Red Smut, or to Fawn Smut: Usually the best combinations, giving good shades of all colors, including whites. Particularly good if a smut is used to a brindle and white, or solid brindle to a red and white or fawn and white, whether smut or clear.

Tricolor, or Black and Tan: Mated to Color-bred White carrying brindle, expect a good percentage of brindles, with bright reds, and (with the tricolor, not with the black and tan) Whites. Colors always tend to be bright when they get a strong dose of black and white blood.

I have never seen a warm color produced from two cold colors, and I doubt if it is possible, though I do not consider that I have enough evidence to say it definitely is not possible.

We have mated silver brindle to fawns on many occasions, the result has always been silvers, fawns, and whites, never warm shades of brindle, or reds. A brilliant shade of red can always be achieved by mating red to white for several generations, though it is not recommended, as obviously the brindle factor is lost.

Note: With an understanding of the "how" and "why" of breeding Coloreds, the history of the Variety illustrates what Miss Montague Johnstone has learned from many years experience. Much of the following material appeared in an early Handbook of The Golden State Bull Terrier Club, *with the understanding that it would be available for* The Complete Bull Terrier.

The modern Colored Bull Terrier has evolved from the blending of the Pure White Bull Terrier (with White ancestors going back as far as 1860) and the Staffordshire. The three chief pioneers were Mr. Tunmer, who started blending Staffordshires with Whites around 1907 and remained interested until the early 1930's, Mr. E. A. "Sher" Lyon and Mrs. V. Ellis. Mrs. Ellis is really responsible for my start in Coloreds. I saw her in the show ring with two red and whites (one of them the important dam, Red Binge) when I had just returned from a last term at school, and remarked on them to Mr. A. J. Harrison, then secretary of the Bull Terrier Club and most kind and helpful. He told me to leave them alone and stick to Whites. Being perverse, I bet him I'd breed a Colored champion in ten years, and went straight off, that day in the late fall of 1927, to see Mr. Lyon. From him I bought my first Colored. She was six months old, dark brindle, very light in bone and quite flat-sided. Her head was much more like a Fox Terrier's than like the modern Bull Terrier's, with rose ears, and she had a poor coat. To her credit, she had a lovely little black eye, a perfect mouth, and was the gamest thing on four legs. Her name was Sher Fustian, and directly down from her, by using the best of the White blood without losing the color, emerged Ch. Romany Rhinestone in April 1936. I had won my bet!

The object then, was to attempt to improve heads, which as we think of them today, just did not exist in the Coloreds and generally to get bone and substance.

Mrs. Ellis, who continually mated Whites to her red and whites, was far more advanced than Mr. Lyon in these respects. However, it is to him,

Eng. Ch. Romany Rhine Wine, by Ch. Romany Rhinegold ex Ch. Romany Refreshed.

above all, that we owe the preservation of brindle in those early days. Mrs. Ellis had lost this color, but she did get substance, and in Young Woodley had a good headed dog who did well in 1929. In 1930 she bred the outstanding red and white, Hunting Blondi. He won two Challenge Certificates and two Reserve Challenge Certificates, and would undoubtedly have been the first red champion but for his death at 18 months of age, without having sired a litter. He was by The Sheik of Chartham (pws) ex Little Bella (red), a very great bitch, and a unique and brilliant forecast of years to come.

The honor of first Colored champion goes to Mr. Dockerill's Ch. Lady Winifred, who won her title in 1931. Brindle and white, by Typical Jim (pws), chiefly Roscolyn blood, ex Princess Ida (br), Gladiator and Sher blood. She carried more than 50% White blood and was outstanding in her day. She was bred, but nothing outstanding came down from her.

Another famous dog of this day was Mrs. Symes' brindle dog, Nelston Cotton, by Caliph Cotton (pws) ex Brindle Reel (Sher blood). Rarely if ever beaten for best Colored, he was very widely used at stud, and his blood is behind almost every Colored pedigree today.

Those were the great names at that time. The general type of the Coloreds was still so far behind the Whites that they could not be compared with them. How then, was this improved?

Ch. Beshelson Bayshuck (pws) (Ch. Sure Thing ex Fair Charmer of Exford) in my opinion was the fount of greatness. Ch. Hades Cavalier (pws) (Ch. Hampstead White Hot ex Ardua Phoebe) proved to be of equal importance. Bayshuck was whelped in 1928, Cavalier a little earlier.

Bayshuck gave most, I think, for bone and substance. Cavalier was probably the strongest influence for heads. Mated to Ch. Debonair of Brum (pws) (Ch. Hades Cavalier ex Treviso) Bayshuck produced the famous litter brothers Ch. Ringfire of Blighty and Rubislaw. In 1936, by mating Romany Red Rufus (red) [Romany Radium (br) ex Merely Mary Ann (pws litter sister of Ch. Black Coffee) by Bayshuck] to Romany Retrospect (br) [Romany Radium ex Cylva Cynthia (pws) (Ch. Ringfire of Blighty) by Bayshuck] I got Ch. Romany Rhinestone (red). Bayshuck was doubled through his two sons, and Hades Cavalier appears four times, as he is also doubled behind Romany Radium.

If we call Bayshuck and Hades Cavalier the two "headstones," we can call Rhinestone the first "milestone." In him, we have a concentration of the two "headstones," plus a doubled dose of the original and much improved Colored blood from Sher Fustian through her son, Romany Ringer (br). Ringer, mated to the challenge certificate winning Shelford Sweet Surprise (pws) (Ch. Devil of Doore), produced Romany Rondeau (br), the dam of Romany Radium. Rhinestone, of course, was the result of mating halfbrother and sister, both by Romany Radium.

192

This doubling of the Colored line strengthened the actual color factor. Romany Radium had one unbroken line of brindle for ten generations. This concentration of color proved Rhinestone "whole for color": that is, he never sired a white puppy out of any Colored or Pure White bred bitches, nor did his son, Ch. Romany Roman (br).

Ch. Romany Rhinestone, a light red and white, was as sensational in his day as Hunting Blondi was in his. He had a tremendous head, very powerful and completely filled, a beautifully placed eye, and very good feet. His bone was almost unbelievable for those days.

It is interesting to note that two years later (in 1938) Mr. Oppenheimer doubled Rubislaw by mating his Ch. Cedran White Queen (by Rubislaw) to Ch. Krackton Kavalier (also by Rubislaw) to get his great Ch. Ormandy's Mr. McGuffin. McGuffin also had his immense bone, and just as Rhinestone is the source of great bone in modern Coloreds, so Mr. McGuffin is the source in the modern Whites. This proved beyond doubt, I think, that Bayshuck is the original source of bone.

Rhinestone only sired one champion, Ch. Romany Roman ex a good brindle by Ch. Gardenia Guardsman. Roman's career at stud was blighted by the war, and he is chiefly of interest as being behind the lovely Ch. Charm of Coyney and her sister Romany Rendezvous, who won really well at the small wartime shows, and produced Romany Rateing, who sired a lot of winners.

It was from his bitches that great things came from Rhinestone. Two litter sisters are of the greatest importance. Rhinestone ex the lovely brindle and white Ch. Jane of Petworth (Old Jimmy's Double (br) ex Kowhai Chita (pws)) produced Stronghold Lollypop (tricolor) and Stronghold Jeanette (black-brindle).

Lollypop, mated to Borderland Sea Fever (br) became the granddam of a top class brindle bitch, Blanmerle Sea Poppy (br). Sea Poppy, mated to Brendon Branch (pws by Ch. Radium Brigadier), produced a very good litter containing three or four winners, the most important of which were Blanmerle Beau (br) and Blanmerle Barque (br). Many of the best of the present day winners are descended from these two.

Blanmerle Barque is in the female line behind Ch. Romany Rhinegold, Ch. Romany Rhine Maiden, Ch. Romany Rhine Wine and Ch. Ormandy's Limpsfield Winston. Thus, Blanmerle Sea Poppy, Blanmerle Barque, Limpsfield Conk, Limpsfield Fifinella, who, mated to Ch. Romany Rather Likely (br) (by Ch. Ormandy's Young Lochinvar, pws, ex Romany Rather Lovely), produced the two outstanding litter brothers, Ch. Romany Rhinegold and Winston, bred by Mrs. M. Molesworth, whose long-standing prefix of "Limpsfield" is much in evidence here.

Blanmerle Beau is chiefly important through his brindle daughter Blanmerle Bowline (ex Coyney Dainty, by Ch. Ormandy's Mr. McGuffin,

193

pws); Bowline, mated to Ch. Romany Reliance, produced two sisters, Ogbourne Impressive (br) and Blanmerle Bettina (br). Impressive, mated to Ch. Ormandy's Kertrim Bosun (pws), produced the Color-bred White Ch. Contango Dimmick Commodore, and Bettina, mated to Ch. The Sphinx (cbw), produced the Color-bred White Ch. Beech House Snow Vision. Snow Vision, mated to Ch. Romany Rite (by Ch. Romany Rather Likely ex Raydium Belinda) produced Ch. Romany Repeat Performance, winner of the Ormandy Jug for 1955, owned by Mr. and Mrs. James W. Longley, Maryland. All three, Snow Vision, Repeat Performance, and Commodore, carry brindle, although Snow Vision is the only one to advertise the fact with a brindle head mark.

The other sister, Stronghold Jeanette, went to Mrs. "Contango" Schuster, who mated her to a good red, Coulan of Lueuch, and got a brindle bitch called Contango Courtesy. I suggested to Mrs. Schuster that she mate her to Bulak Blackshirt, a good son of the great headed Ch. Gardenia (pws) and she got the key dog Contango Consul (br). Mrs. Schuster then mated Consul back to his own grandmother, Jeanette, and got Contango Cobblestone (br), who had a remarkable head but was undershot.

When Cobblestone was about a year old, I had a magnificent-headed red and white in Northorpe Nonpareil sent down from the North for mating to Ch. Romany Roman. When I saw her, I wired for her owner's permission to use Cobblestone, and got it. Nonpareil was by Old Lane Snow Drift (by Ch. Raydium Brigadier) ex Vintania (by Ch. Velhurst Vindicator). As soon as I was able to do so, I bought these lovely red and white bitches, but was so hampered by the prevailing war conditions that I was unable to do justice to either of them, though Nonpareil did produce a lovely brindle and white bitch to Romany Rambler. We sent her to Ireland and so lost her, but she made a great name for herself over there.

Nonpareil's litter to Cobblestone produced the key bitch Romany Rivet (black-brindle) and another most beautiful red and white bitch that Mrs. Schuster bought and most sadly lost through illness.

Though of entirely different types, both Rivet and her sister would have won their full titles but for the war. Rivet was the cobby type. Her sister was a great big one like her dam.

Rivet, mated to Ormandy Sunny Day (pws) (Ormandy's Mr. McRumpus ex Maginot) produced the *second milestone in Ch. Romany Reliance* (bk-br). In the same litter was Romany Radar (br), who took the reserve challenge certificate behind his brother at the first big postwar show, and Romany Resolve, an Irish champion, a black-brindle bitch and perhaps the best bitch I've ever seen. I lost her with hardpad (distemper) at just under a year. Radar also died young as a result of hardpad. He is

194

chiefly of interest as being behind English and American Ch. Romany Remarkable.

Ch. Romany Reliance sired six champions, two dogs: Ch. Romany Rough Weather (br) and Ch. Rickmay Retort (bk-br); and four bitches, Ch. Blanmerle Brindi (br) sister to Ogbourne Impressive and Blanmerle Bettina, Ch. Rougemont Demoisell (bk-br), Ch. Kowhai Rose Revived (br) and Ch. Bliss of Upend (bk-br). Besides these he sired a multitude of winners. Almost every bitch in the country visited him and to almost every bitch he sired a winner. Many people wondered why I had ever parted with him.

During the war, when I could only keep the bare bloodlines going, and those only because good friends took them in for me, I bred very few litters indeed and had to decide which to keep while they were still very young. But for the kindness of Mrs. "Monkery" Holmes, who took Rivet to live with her and whelped her for me, that litter might never have been bred. I had no home of my own at that time.

When the litter was twelve weeks old, I selected the bitch mentioned above, and Radar, who at that age was much the better of the two brothers, and who was the one Mr. Jennings wanted. I would not part with him and sold him Reliance as being the next best of the dog pups. I saw Reliance again at about seven months and still preferred Radar. Then, between seven months and ten months, Reliance produced the most terrific fill-up and downface. He had a head which will perhaps never be surpassed, though there are some who prefer that of his son, Rough Weather. In addition to the outstanding head, Reliance had tremendous bone, beautiful front and feet, and a really wonderful eye. He also had faults: straight stifles and a body that lacked shape. As a sire, he proved most potent, stamping his stock again and again with heads that left the Whites behind, and which twenty years before would only have existed in a breeder's dream. He also reproduced his faults, so, about 1946, we had to look for something else besides heads. We'd got them, fixed and breeding true. Now we had to get shape: good stifles and hocks, sound action, and a better layback of shoulder.

Onto the stage then, as our *third milestone,* comes an elegant red lady in the person of Marle Hill Miniver, by Still Water (br) ex Betty of Thistlewood (tri). She was Miss Williams' pet bitch, and no thought of stardom ever entered her head when Miss Williams joined me immediately after the war with this birthday present she had received a couple of years earlier. Marle Hill Miniver had a long clean head, with nice high eye placement, but without downface. She was light in bone and rather on the leg, but she had something the others hadn't—beautifully laid back shoulders, a most shapely body and good stifles and hocks. She covered the ground at any speed, smoothly and with grace. She was, in fact, the perfect complement to Reliance. Mated to Reliance in December 1946, Marle Hill Miniver produced four pups, one of which was lost. The three reared became Ch. Romany Rough Weather, Romany Rather Lovely (both rich brindle and white) and Romany Rough and Tumble (tri). The last named had several nice litters but persisted in reproducing almost 100% blacks.

The other two in the litter made history.

Rather Lovely had one litter only, to Ch. Ormandy's Young Lochinvar (pws) (Monkery's Banner ex Tom's of Ormandy (pws)) whelped in January 1949, and consisting of three brindle and white dogs, one black-brindle dog, and three white bitches, one of which was selected for rearing.

The white bitch, Romany Runner Duck, had one litter to Ch. Romany Rich Reward, which included Romany Runner Beau (cbw), challenge certificate winner at Windsor in 1952. The three brindle dogs became Ch. Romany Rather Likely, Romany Roast Goose, and Romany Rolling Spitfire. Spitfire was sold up north, where he sired a number of winners and did well in the ring until he injured a leg and became permanently unsound. The other two remained with us.

Rather Likely sired three champions: the brindle bitch, Ch. Romany Rite, ex Radium Belinda (pws), and two brothers, Ch. Romany Rhinegold and Ch. Ormandy's Limpsfield Winston. Rather Likely was also the sire of the key bitch Romany Rest Cure (fawn) ex Marle Hill Miniver.

Rest Cure had proved herself one of the greatest dams ever. In her first litter, to Reliance, she produced the brindle dog Romany Representative, exported to Italy, now an international champion in Italy, Switzerland, and France, and good enough to have sailed through to his title in this country. In her next, to Ch. Romany Rich Reward, Rest Cure produced Ch. Romany Refreshed, Romany Restored (both silver brindles), African Ch. Romany Rhodesian, and Romany Refresher (U.S.A.).

Romany Roast Goose, sire of many winners, produced two outstanding litters. The first was from Romany Rising Tide (cbw) (Rough Weather ex Romany Rainstorm). This litter included Ch. Romany Reprieved (U.S.A.), Rising Tempo (br), and Rising Flame (red). Reprieved sired English and American Ch. Romany Remarkable. Rising Tempo won one challenge certificate and, before being sold, sired Ch. Vestex Vain Lady (red) from his first bitch. Rising Flame has won many major awards in the north. The second outstanding litter by Romany Roast Goose was from Romany Ridge (br) (Rough Weather ex Raydium Roxanna). This litter included American Ch. Romany Ritual, first Colored Bull Terrier ever to go Best in Show, all breeds, in the U.S.A. (she won four such awards), and Romany Runic (br), a dog who went straight to the top in Kenya, and also went Best in Show all breeds at Kenya's top yearly event.

196

Rough Weather, like his ancestor Rhinestone, has his greatness chiefly through his daughters, of which two are champions—Highville Lassie (br) and Romany Right as Rain (cbw). It is from his daughters, more than any other influence, that this kennel has reached the standard so far achieved. We have yet to improve hind action; we still get bad mouths, but when we turn up a faded snapshot of little Sher Fustian, and then go outside and look at Rhinegold and Refreshed and their twin daughters playing in the paddocks, we know that twenty-five years were not wasted.

To sum up, here are the most-important-of-all dogs in the evolution of Colored Bull Terriers: Ch. Beshelson Bayshuck, Ch. Hades Cavalier, Romany Radium, Ch. Romany Rhinestone, Contango Consul, Romany Rivet with her son Ch. Romany Reliance, Marle Hill Miniver with her son and daughter, Ch. Romany Rough Weather and Romany Rather Lovely, and her most important ancestors, Velhurst Viking, Ch. Velhurst Vindicator, Ch. Raydium Brigadier, Ch. Ormandy's Dancing Time (whose influence is very marked through her grandson Ch. Romany Rich Reward), and Ch. Romany Rather Likely, through his son Ch. Romany Rhinegold. His other son, Ch. Ormandy's Limpsfield Winston, who has so influenced the modern Color-bred Whites, will probably appear later behind Colored winners.

It has given me very great pleasure to note that during the last few years, the Colored Bull Terriers have really been making friends in America. I hope they make many more. I hope that one day, not too long delayed, they may be considered as they are in England, one breed with their White brothers, and be judged together in the same ring.

Mex. Ch. Justeph High Flyer, a brindle male who stands 13¾ inches and weighs 31 pounds.

22

The Miniature
Bull Terrier

by Donly Chorn

SIZE within Bull Terrier litters has always varied enormously. Enterprising breeders took the smaller dogs, probably added a
pinch of Fox or Jack Russell Terrier for more consistency of size, and
created the Miniature Bull Terrier. The Kennel Club in Great Britain
allowed interbreeding between Standards and Miniatures until January
1988. This has improved the type and substance of the Minis so the better
ones look like scaled-down versions of the Standard Bull Terrier.

The written standard against which Miniatures are judged no longer
specifies weight but states that Miniatures should be 10 to 14 inches (at the
withers) in height. Dogs over or under the limits are to be faulted according
to how much they vary from the standard. The typier Minis today are often
slightly over the 14 inches because of interbreeding. Most Minis weight
between 15 and 30 lbs. The official standard calls for a dog that is "strongly
built, muscular, symmetrical and active, with a keen, determined
expression, full of fire and courageous, even temperament and amenable to
discipline." The dog should move with easy strides and a typical jaunty air,
fore and hind legs on a parallel plane, with good flexion and drive. The
head should be long, strong, and deep, egg-shaped and completely filled

with a gently curving profile ending in the tip of the nose bent downwards. The underjaw should be strong. The eyes should be small, dark, obliquely placed, triangular and sunken. The ears should be small, thin, and stiff and set closely together. The teeth should be sound, strong, regular, and meet in a level or scissors bite. The neck should be long, arched clean but muscular, tapering from shoulders to head. The chest should be broad and deep. The body should be rounded with good ribspring, a short back, and a slight arch over the loin. The shoulders should be muscular but not heavy, well laid-back with no dip at the withers. The legs out to be big-boned, but not coarse. Forelegs are straight with elbows turning neither in nor out; pasterns strong and upright. Hindlegs should be parallel viewed from the rear with muscular thighs, well let-down hocks, and a well-bent stifle. Feet should be round, compact, and arched. The tail ought to be short, horizontal, and set low. It is thick at the base and tapers to a fine point. The coat is to be short, flat, harsh and fit tightly. Color for Whites should be pure white, with or without head markings. In Coloreds, any color, which should predominate over white. Deviations from the standard should be considered a fault, serious in the degree of departure from the standard. The complete standard is available from the MBTCA.

Miniatures and even Toy Bull Terriers were shown in the U.S. until the 1920s when a decrease in numbers caused the American Kennel Club to drop classes for them. In the 1960s, Minis were imported into the U.S. and the AKC accepted them into the miscellaneous class in 1963—where they remain. There were never large numbers of Minis and the restricted gene pool held them back. The Miniature Bull Terrier Club of America (MBTCA), formed in 1966, became gradually less active until the 1980s when it was reorganized and picked up momentum with the new importations of quality stock from Great Britain. Today there is renewed interest in Miniatures from people who value a small version of the Bull Terrier. They are again competing at AKC shows. The MBTCA held its first match in 1985 and its first Specialty in 1986. The MBTCA must, in the near future, decide if it wants the Miniature to be accepted as a separate breed or as a variety by the AKC. This affects not only how they will be shown but whether or not interbreeding will be allowed. Until full AKC recognition, Minis are eligible for an indefinite listing privilege and are granted ILP numbers from the AKC.

Like the Standards, Miniatures differ greatly in temperament from one individual to another. Some are mellow, easy-going couch dogs; others are energetic bundles of intensity. They typically are active, smart, people-oriented dogs. Great companions for people of all ages, they seem to have a built-in sense of humor. Their unpredictable antics are immensely entertaining and their athletic ability appealing. Sturdy dogs, they have few

Mex. Ch. Justeph Country Man, a White male who stands 13½ inches and weighs 30 pounds, an example of a 1980s' breeding.

Darby Fairs Firecracker. At six months this brindle male puppy weighs 20 pounds and stands 12½ inches at the shoulder.

Eng. Ch. Solway Navigation Surprise, height 13¾", weight 22 lbs.

Eng. Ch. Fury of Upend, whelped 1951.

Ch. Oldlane Highburn Selby, whelped 1952.

Eng. Ch. Navigation Billy Boy, whelped 1954. Winner of six Certificates, including Crufts 1955 and 1956.

health problems and live about 10 to 12 years. They are comfort loving, clownish, mischievous, stubborn, curious, and intense. Some are good obedience prospects; others great hunters. Many are good watchdogs; most are confirmed lapdogs. They are very individual in their likes and dislikes. Some get along with everything; some are aggressive towards other animals.

Miniatures require special and very responsible people. Potential owners must be tolerant of energetic, destructive puppies that need to be supervised closely in the house, exercised on lead or in a fenced area, and crated or confined to a safe place when not under supervision. Strong dogs for their size, they need to be handled firmly.

Good breeders try to match the dog to the people and their situation. Fortunately, Minis vary so much in personality that the right dog can almost always be found for the person as long as temperament is uppermost in importance to the future owner. The Bull Terrier Club of America sells (for a small fee) an excellent pamphlet called *Buying and Rearing a Bull Terrier*. This candidly details the good points and bad of Bull Terriers and what to expect. Future Mini owners would be well advised to invest in a copy.

Miniatures can make great pets, are fun to show in obedience or in conformation (an easy way to get started since there is seldom much competition in Miscellaneous class), and a real challenge to breed. No one should try to raise Minis without realizing the time, effort, expense, and occasional heartbreak that go into the undertaking. Miniatures should become increasingly popular and need more breeders who are responsible and concerned with the welfare of the dogs. There is definitely a place for the pocket edition Bull Terrier!

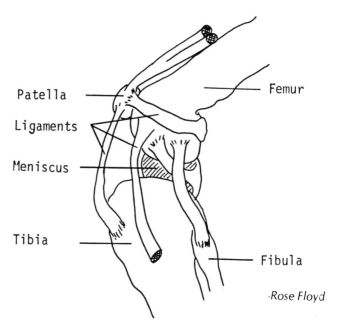

Patella

Ligaments

Meniscus

Tibia

Femur

Fibula

·Rose Floyd

The Stifle Joint (reprinted from *The Dog Owner's Home Veterinary Handbook*).

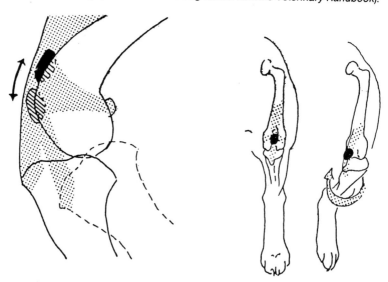

Luxating Patellas (below) are not uncommon, whether through injury or heredity.

23

Genetic Diseases
in Bull Terriers

by W. E. Mackay-Smith

Prepared and edited with the kind assistance of
Donald F. Patterson, D.V.M., D.Sc.,
Chief, Section of Medical Genetics, University of Pennsylvania

T HE rapid development of the Bull Terrier breed in this country in the last ten years has begun to show its effects. Breeders have achieved excellent results with several line-breeding programs, producing high quality individuals from a number of lines, and also broadening the base of good quality breeding animals. While the genetic pool is being concentrated in these several lines, yielding more high quality show animals, it is also beginning to produce more health problems from the mostly recessive or "hidden" genetic diseases which Bull Terriers are heir to. Line-breeding, as we can see, is a mixed blessing for the breed. On the one hand we produce higher quality individual animals, on the other we increase the risk and occurrence of genetic disease.

For the sake of discussion we will divide this article into three categories of genetic problems. The first, or Class I, is a group of congenital problems which have been described and studied in other breeds by researchers who have published material on the results of their research. Class II deals with problems which are observed to be inherited. That is, they have a definite familial association, but the actual mode of inheritance has not been demonstrated through published research. Class III is a group of disorders to which certain families seem predisposed but which seem less specific and more random in occurrence than Class II, and which also seem to have environmental factors.

All of the diseases included in this article are ones which have been either observed by the author or reported to the author as having occurred in Bull Terriers. The purpose of this catalog is NOT to point fingers at the various lines in which the diseases occur, nor to unnecessarily alarm the fancy. It is rather to encourage owners of both stud dogs and brood bitches to IDENTIFY POTENTIAL DANGERS AND ORGANIZE THEIR BREEDING PROGRAMS TO MINIMIZE THE CHANCE OF DISEASE IN THE OFFSPRING.

Class I

There are only three diseases occurring in Bull Terriers in which enough genetic research has been done to identify the actual mode of inheritance. These are Cryptorchidism, Hip Dysplasia, and Zinc Metabolism Abnormality.

Cryptorchidism is a condition whereby one or both testicles are not normally descended into the scrotum.

Checking the little dog puppies to make sure they have "two of everything" becomes an automatic process in the life of the experienced breeder. This is sufficient testimony to the already existing concern over this painless but reproductively important problem. Sometimes the testicles are difficult to feel, especially if the young puppy struggles during examination or stands on his hind legs, both of which often have the effect of drawing the prepuberal testicles back up above the scrotum. Less-than-obvious testicles in young puppies are always a matter for concern, but this should not be certified unless the dog has either no testicles or only one testicle in the scrotum after puberty (at about six months of age). There have been cases reported of testicles descending after this age, one of which occurred in a show dog who had had a "falsie" implanted in the empty side of the scrotum. During his early show career he confounded a judge who distinctly palpated three testicles in the scrotum! The missing testicle had descended after the implant was completed and the owner was certainly sadder but wiser.

If the dog only has one testicle descended, the second one might go up and down between the abdomen and scrotum like a yo-yo (this phenomenon, however, is very rare and most cases which have been reported are due to inaccurate observations), or it might gradually descend and finally decide to stay down.

Cryptorchidism is not an uncomfortable condition for the dog, but can be a problem as the undescended testicle(s) tend to become malignant later on in life. If both testicles are undescended the dog will be unable to sire puppies as the sperm cannot survive the higher temperature inside the dog's body. Retention of the testicles does not, however, prevent the production of male hormones, so that affected dogs still develop all the secondary masculine characteristics. Veterinarians advise castration for cryptorchid dogs in most instances.

This condition is thought to be recessive and can obviously occur only in males although a bitch must also be a carrier of the recessive gene to produce cryptorchid puppies.

Hip Dysplasia is a malformation of the hip joint that does not allow the head of the femur (thigh bone) to sit solidly in the acetabulum (cup) of the hip. It was so rarely mentioned when I first came into the breed in the late sixties that I was extremely surprised to be told by a fellow novice that she had bought a puppy which had turned out to have hip dysplasia so badly that it was put to sleep. I filed away this information and never heard of another case for twelve years, during which time I assumed Bull Terriers to be free from this genetic problem. Imagine my surprise and horror when a puppy bred by a relative newcomer in the breed was brought to us at four months severely crippled with hip dysplasia! Both its sire and dam were instantly examined and it turned out that the mother of the puppy actually had the disease and, oddly enough, she was a direct female line descendant of the litter sister of the dysplastic dog which was reported in 1969!

Hip dysplasia is still relatively rare in Bull Terriers, but it produces pain and suffering in affected animals. In this condition the hip joints of the growing dog do not develop properly and varying degrees of lameness and arthritis result. There is some evidence that rapid growth in heavy puppies exaggerates the effects of the dysplasia.

A puppy or adult with severe hip dysplasia will usually spend a great deal of time lying down, and will be weak and wobbly in the hindquarters when it gets up. Severely affected animals will also tend to "hop" with their hind legs together and stand with a slightly roached and painful attitude. If dysplasia is suspected, the diagnosis should be confirmed by palpation and X-ray of the hips.

The condition is thought to be *polygenic* in its transmission, meaning that the total number of contributing genes are not known and their combinations are variable and not easily predicted. It has been shown that animals which actually have moderate to severe hip dysplasia are much more likely to produce dysplastic offspring, even if the other parent is apparently unaffected. On the other hand, two parents which are dysplasia free (O.F.A. clear) can produce a dysplastic puppy if the right combination of various genes occurs when the two are mated. For this reason animals which demonstrate even a mild degree of hip dysplasia (as determined by X-ray examination) should be eliminated as breeding prospects. They should not even be bred to animals which are O.F.A. clear of dysplasia.

The disease can be strictly controlled if breeders are alert to the possibility of its appearance. If it appears, we must move quickly to identify the ancestral source of the disease in the affected animal and eliminate all affected animals from that line from any breeding program.

Zinc-Metabolism Defect is the failure of the animal to metabolize zinc and affects both immunity and growth. When I first started breeding Bull Terriers, we would occasionally have a litter normally whelped, seemingly happily settled in with "Mum" when suddenly, for no particular reason, a puppy would lose interest in nursing and die, usually at between two and four days of age. I agonized over these puppies and finally, several years later, had another one going down hill when the wife of a veterinarian friend kindly offered to take the puppy and hand-raise it. She saved the puppy by tube-feeding and constant nursing, but it remained small compared to its littermates, although it was fairly active and feisty. Its ears cme up at about four weeks of age and we named it "Mighty Mouse." "Mouse" had a terrific head, and I thought that although he was small, I might really have something. By about four months of age he was obviously developing very strangely; quite cow-hocked and splay-footed. A month later he started to develop scabs between his toes which eventually covered his entire body. The University could find no underlying reason for his abnormality at the time and we had him "put to sleep," as we were unable to control the massive skin infection which he had developed. Several years later I saw another of these puppies, about four months old, and the following year, two more. These last two were taken in to the new genetic disease department at The University of Pennsylvania School of Veterinary Medicine, and their problem was diagnosed as a defect in zinc-metabolism, a disease previously reported in cattle but never reported in dogs.

I personally think that this defect has been present in the breed for some time, but prior to the last few years, the technology for keeping weak puppies alive was not generally available, and the affected puppies just died shortly after birth.

According to current research, the mode of inheritance is thought to be a simple recessive, which means that two outwardly normal parents can produce some affected offspring. Any parents which produce affected

208

puppies can then be identified as carriers. Once these genetic carriers are identified, the influence of affected puppies can be reduced by simply not mating one carrier to another carrier.

Class II

These are the genetic diseases which are inherited, but the actual mode of inheritance has not been discovered by genetic researchers. Included in this category are Luxating Patellas, Pyloric Dysfunction, Atopy and Deafness.

Luxating Patellas or "slipping patellas," is due to a malformation in the groove in the thigh bone (femur) in which the knee cap (patella) is seated. This problem seems to be on the increase in our breed, due probably to more intensive linebreeding which breeders are employing in their programs. As in all genetic diseases, animals which actually have this condition are much more likely to pass it on to their puppies, although the exact mode of inheritance and probability of occurrence has not yet been demonstrated. An interested breeder who has made a study of the problem in his own line feels that it is probably recessive. If this is so, when bred, two animals having the condition should produce only affected puppies. Other advice on the subject indicates a *polygenic* mode of inheritance, which also means that normal parents could transmit the disease without having it themselves.

During normal movement the patella, in combination with its groove and ligaments, stabilizes and protects the joint from excessive rotation. The malformation enables the patella to slip off to the side, which causes lameness. This is often first noticed as being the result of some violent motion of the hind leg such as a sudden turn or landing after jumping off a high place. The conformation of the hind leg is not always indicative of whether or not slipping stifles are present. Some very straight-stifled dogs have very tight patellas which do not slip, and some animals with well-bent stifles have luxating patellas.

If the patella is loose and becomes displaced often, painful lameness and arthritis can result. High doses of Vitamin C and restricted exercise have been reported to have ameliorating effects on the disease, but in severe cases orthopedic surgery can be done to provide comfort for the dog. This surgery is complex and painful. Recovery is slow and difficult for our heavy, active breed. Obviously it is better to prevent patella luxation by careful breeding.

Pyloric Dysfunction is an involuntary spasm of the (pyloric) valve through which food passes from the stomach to the intestine during the digestive process.

We acquired a lovely bitch several years ago who, suddenly, at the age of eight months, began to throw up a frothy vomit when she became excited. We changed her diet, had barium studies of her stomach by X-ray, and changed her kennel location and routine, all to no avail. As she got older she got worse, and finally, at a year and a half, she could not walk a hundred yards without prostrating herself and retching—always producing the frothy, mucousy vomit.

On consultation with another breeder who had encountered several of these over a period of time, I discovered that these affected animals are often observed to have certain symptoms as puppies. When they are first put on solid food they will sometimes, an hour or two after feeding, become quite rigid and obviously uncomfortable. Other affected animals will simply throw up their food with quite a lot of force, which is known as "projectile vomiting" and is classically linked with a disease called "pyloric stenosis." These puppies often always develop the symptoms of frothy vomit somewhere around seven to ten months of age.

I also discovered that the condition seemed to be controllable by the use of the same drugs which are used to control epilepsy. The bitch in question was taken to the University of Pennsylvania and the drugs were used with excellent effect.

Further questioning revealed that the litter brother of the affected bitch had the same problem and had been "put to sleep." While it is possible that these were isolated incidents due to virus or diet, the fact that they occurred in animals which were geographically widely separated but closely related suggests some sort of a rare genetic combination. There have since been reports of this condition in succeeding generations of Bull Terriers. It is hoped that this problem will not become more widespread in the breed. Like all hereditary defects, it should be recognized as such, and animals which display the symptoms should be highly suspect as breeding prospects.

Atopy or skin allergy is probably the most common problem with Bull Terriers in this country, especially evident in hot climates and areas with biting insects such as fleas and mosquitoes. Any Bull Terrier owner is aware of the reaction of their dog to an insect bite, which varies from a small red welt at the site of the bite to a generalized eczema out of all proportion to the original bite. Allergy to fleas is probably the most common problem, and some dogs are so allergic that one flea bite will cause a severe and generalized skin reaction. This reaction is accomplished by unbearable itching, inflammation of the skin, loss of hair, and often a secondary infection which causes serious weeping and raw, open sores.

As in human allergy, atopy has been shown to be inherited in dogs, although it is probably a combination of genetic factors which produces the atopic dog. For this reason, dogs which demonstrate a high degree of allergic response to insects or grasses should not be mated to animals with a similar problem. Desensitizing injections can be given to affected animals once the allergy is identified. This treatment can bring relief from the itching and eczema. The treatment does not, however, affect the probability that the animal will reproduce this problem in its offspring, and a frankly allergic Bull Terrier should be used for breeding only with great circumspection.

Deafness is perhaps the genetic disease of longest standing in the breed. It is hard to trace the problem, as deaf dogs are usually born of normal parents. It seems to be associated with lack of skin pigmentation, as it occurs mostly in breeds with white hair and white skin color. General awareness of the possibility of deafness occuring in any litter, testing of puppies and older animals before they are bred, and observation of the tendencies of any given animal or strain to produce hereditary deafness are all indicated in order to control the condition. Deaf animals absolutely should not be bred from, and normal animals from strains or families which have produced deafness in recent generations should not be mated to other animals with the same familial tendencies. If they are mated, great care should be taken to identify deaf offspring before they are unwittingly sold. Minor degrees of hearing loss occur in some dogs and cannot be detected without special equipment available to veterinary neurologists. The total elimination of hereditary deafness would require that such partially deaf dogs be identified.

Entropion or ingrowing eyelid is a hereditary defect which is endemic in Chow Chows and which has been reported in Bull Terriers. The eyelid is deformed in a way which forces the lashes to grow in toward the eye which scratches the surface of the eye producing painful ulcers and eventually blinding the dog.

The mode of inheritance has not been demonstrated for this condition, however it is listed in the literature as a genetic disorder, which indicates that dogs which are born with this acutely painful defect are genetically positive for the defect, and therefore, they absolutely should not be bred.

Behavioral Abnormalities are the compulsive behaviors reported in Bull Terriers passed on genetically through successive generations, just as differences in behavioral characteristics have been shown to be genetically determined. The mode of inheritance is thought to be *polygenic,* that is, a combination of genes which, when it occurs, produces a particular type of compulsive behavior. In Bull Terriers these behaviors include tail-chasing, thigh-sucking and fear-biting.

No one likes to think that they have produced a neurotic dog, but all of the above conditions represent neurotic or compulsive behaviors which

211

seem to have a family relationship. As in most neurotic behaviors, environment does play an important part, but the fact that some animals react to isolation, excitement or confinement with these set patterns of behavior and others do not, indicates an inherited tendency to these behaviors. I have noticed, for instance, that one family we have bred comes up with a spinner, or tail-chaser every now and then, even though only one of the tail-chasers was ever actually used for breeding about ten years ago. The behavior is brought on initially by excitement, when the puppy will start spinning in circles, snapping at its tail. Confinement and boredom will often produce the same effect in these dogs, and, if left to its own devices, the dog will soon seek out a corner somewhere and spend hours circling there, seemingly mesmerized by the motion. Tail-chasing can be controlled in many cases if caught early enough. "Bitter Apple" (a nasty tasting preparation) put on the tail, combined with a severe reproach for spinning can modify the behavior if the animal is corrected consistently. The environment must be adjusted as well, to avoid situations such as crate confinement, isolation or excitement which initially start the dog in the spinning behavior.

Thigh-sucking is a term used to describe compulsive licking behavior directed at some part of the body, usually an area of the flank or thigh. All dogs lick themselves occasionally, usually in the area of a skin sore of some kind, but thigh-sucking is not connected with a lesion. It is a compulsive behavior which seems to have a soothing effect on the dog, as thumb-sucking does in children. This also seems to occur in animals who are anxious or stressed by confinement or neglect.

Fear-biting is a catch-all expression for dogs which become suddenly agitated and bite the nearest person whether or not that person is the cause of the agitation. In some cases the cause is readily apparent; an aggressive "other" dog or a child on a bicycle, for instance, will send the dog into hysterical behavior and it will bite any person or dog within reach. In some cases, however, the cause is a complete mystery; the dog will be lying quietly and suddenly attack without any visible provocation. There is a comparable problem in Cocker Spaniels which is simply termed "rage," and is thought to be passed on through families from one generation to the next.

In Bull Terriers, fear-biting can occur in isolated cases, but certain families seem to produce a higher percentage of reported cases than others, especially when close linebreeding and inbreeding is used. It is best, therefore, in all matters of breeding research, to check thoroughly into the behavioral tendencies of the ancestors and close relatives of the animals being mated. Families which have a low tolerance to stress, exhibited by lapses into compulsive behavior, should be linebred with only the greatest discretion and willingness to cull all affected animals from the breeding program.

Class III

I have included several conditions in this category which have not, as yet, been reported officially in the veterinary literature, but which have been observed by breeders to have definite familial tendencies. These are laryngospasm, interdigital cysts, and demodectic mange.

Laryngospasm results from the combination of excitement and pressure on the throat causing such difficulty breathing that the dog may fall unconscious from lack of oxygen.

Some years ago, I was watching the judging at the Bronx K.C. show in March, when suddenly a Bull Terrier collapsed and fell unconscious. Once unconscious, he began to breathe, although somewhat spasmodically, and soon revived. The owner volunteered the information that whenever the dog was on a lead he would wheeze and cough if the collar exerted any pressure on his throat. I saw one other case of this several years later which was a bitch who used to turn quite blue in the mouth and gasp when she was in the show ring on a snug lead, and who once fell unconscious when being tightly held during mating. She was, I believe, closely related to the dog I had seen several years before. Since then I have been made aware of three more cases, all within the last year, two of them littermates, and the third with a strikingly similar pedigree to the other two. Although this is, strictly speaking, not definite proof that laryngospasm is a genetic abnormality, it seems safe to assume that animals who have a predisposition to this problem should have their mates carefully selected to avoid doubling up on it. If they are severely affected, that is, if they fall unconscious due to severe spasm of the larynx when the stimuli of excitement and point pressure are present, it is debatable whether they should be used for breeding at all.

Interdigital Cysts are sore, hard lumps in the skin webbing between the toes which the dog may lick incessantly.

Our first Bull Terrier was plagued by interdigital cysts from the age of a year and a half. Gentle squeezing of these areas would elicit a pained response, and no amount of antibiotic therapy seemed to alleviate the condition. Prednisolone, a cortisone-type drug, seemed to give him relief, but as soon as we took him off the drug, the cysts reappeared. When he was about six years old, he began to break out in oozing sores on his hocks and legs, and he was diagnosed by a specialist in skin disorders as suffering from *"atopy,"* or skin allergy. He was tested, under what was, at that time, an experimental program, to find what he was allergic to. Some types of grasses and the weed "lamb's quarter" turned out to be the culprits. He was given a series of injections which were extremely effective in desensitizing him, and his skin cleared up within months. Miraculously, his interdigital cysts regressed also, and with seasonal "boosters" of the desensitizing injections, he never had any more trouble.

During this period, I discovered that several long-time breeders thought interdigital cysts to be a hereditary problem, and one breeder had even pinpointed the dog from whom it was thought to be inherited.

The condition actually seems very closely related to generalized skin allergy, or *"atopy"* which is an inherited condition (see discussion under Class II). The fact that Bull Terriers seem to be seasonally affected with interdigital cysts, coinciding with being outdoors and in contact with growing grasses and weeds; the fact that cortisone, an anti-inflammatory drug often used to control allergic reactions, is effective in treating the symptoms of this condition; and the fact that desensitizing for allergy coincidentally produced remission of the interdigital cysts, all seem to connect this condition with other genetically transmitted allergies in the Bull Terrier.

Demodectic Mange may occur if the puppy is exposed to an overwhelming infestation of mites, or, if for some reason the health of the puppy suffers and the immune system momentarily lags, mites can multiply very rapidly in the hair follicles and cause the hair to fall out leaving bare spots. This usually happens between four and sixteen months of age.

Susceptibility to Demodectic Mange is perhaps the most difficult disorder to describe, as the mode of inheritance is totally unknown. All dogs apparently harbor the mites which climb from the mother on to the nursing puppies in early infancy and nest in the hair follicles. This mite population is usually kept under control in some way by the puppy's immune system. Normally, even if the mites become active, the immune system recovers and reduces the mite population on the skin and the hair grows back. However, in five percent of cases where the bare patches occur (usually on the head, face or forelegs) the animal's immune system cannot regain control over the mites, the hair loss continues and a secondary bacterial infection invades the weakened skin. Sometimes this bacterial infection is totally resistant to therapy, the immune system proves totally inadequate, and the dog is overwhelmed by an incurable infection. Needless to say, this is a problem which no breeder wants to have any part in perpetuating, but it is difficult to deal with genetically as no one seems to be sure whether it is one or both parents involved, if it is inherited, why only five percent of the affected animals develop complications, and exactly what stressing factors precipitate the disease. However, a bitch who has produced a litter of mangey puppies, any of which have been unable to overcome the infestation and subsequently have become infected should be suspect as a breeding animal for future litters.

214

There are other disorders, possibly genetically transmitted, which have been reported in Bull Terriers, such as persistent pupillary membrane, ulnar epiphysitis, thyroid deficiency, tibial osteodystrophy, juvenile kidney failure, umbilical hernia and dry-eye (KCS). These, however, have not been reported often enough to enable us to form an opinion as to their hereditary nature, or their danger to the breed. The diseases which have been discussed in this article are those which should be of concern to those interested in the genetic integrity of the breed. By observation and indentification, careful record keeping and circumspection when planning matings, especially of a closely linebred or inbred nature, these hereditary problems can be controlled for the benefit of Bull Terriers everywhere.

Eng./Am. Ch. Abraxas Achilles, perhaps one of the greatest Bull Terriers ever bred. Exported to America for Ralph Bowles. Winner of the 1972 Regent Trophy.

Fall

216

24

English Imports

SINCE the early 1970s, many significant Bull Terriers have been imported from England. I feel that the people who have imported them could perhaps best explain why the animals were imported and in fact answer the question: "What do we hope for when we import from England?"

Iceni: Bob and Lynne Myall

Am./Can. Ch. Monkery's Buckskin

"We visited several kennels in England in 1975 but were most impressed by Mrs. Holmes' friendly openness plus Moonride, Sea Shanty and Minx, all of whom were stabled in her kennel at that time. We asked her to find us a Specialty winning young dog for which we were willing to wait. Eighteen months later, up popped Buckskin and we bought him having seen his sixteen-week photograph.

"Phyllis Holmes was one of the first to use Jackadandy (about the same time that Mrs. Schuster promoted Come On Jack) and I think this point in itself says something about the 'eye' that these two ladies had.

"It's interesting to conjecture about what would have transpired if Buckskin had stayed in England. Would Jackadandy have reigned supreme for so long? Undoubtedly Buckskin was also enormously prepotent as witnessed by his eighty or so American champions from a wide range of litters.

217

Ch. Pyreril's Milky Way

Am./Can. Ch. Monkery's Buckskin

218

"Among his accomplishments was Stud Dog of the Year—All-Breeds in 1983 with thirty-two champions."

Ch. Pyreril's Milky Way

"I saw Milky Way as a youngster of ten weeks and was wowed by her bone, substance and beautiful head. She had little difficulty becoming a champion or gaining her ROM. Another big plus for her was the combination of Monkery and Ormandy/Souperlative blood which is a well-proven combination for success. We have followed this strategem religiously for the last ten years. Milky Way produced both Micklefell and Spellbinder who won extensively at the Silverwood '86 Weekend."

Peter DeFlesco

Am./Eng. Ch. Catrana Eyeopener of Aricon

"Bred by Peter Parkinson, 'Dominic' was sired by Eng. Ch. Eyeshiner of Aricon ex Eng. Ch. Kenstaff Shirley.

"Various breeders, both English and American, had expressed their admiration of this dog to such a degree that my curiosity made me want to know more. After a trip to England and seeing him in the flesh, he was everything I had expected: sweet temperament, good bone structure, conformation, expression (that wonderful penetrating look) and exceptional muzzle power. Carrying these credentials I thought he would do our breed in the United States some good. To my family and me, 'Dominic' has been a wonderful experience. There is not a day that goes by that my admiration for him diminishes."

Dane and Evelin Jackson (Li'l Jack)

Ch. Jacktar of Kearby, ROM

"As a son of Ch. Souperlative Jackadandy of Ormandy, England's top sire, and linebred to Ch. Jobrulu Jacqueminot, we thought he could be used to Ch. Souperlative Special of Ormandy ROM and Ch. Monkery's Buckskin ROM daughters and granddaughters as well as other imported bitches of similar pedigrees needing make and shape. 'Winston's' virtues include his excellent temperament, balance, exceptional breed type, short back and very good topline."

Norma and Gordon Smith (Magor)

Am./Can. Ch. Maerdy Magdalene, ROM

"Magdalene was a first class bitch and as well made as they come,

Eng./Am. Ch. Catrana Eyeopener of Aricon ROM

Eng./Am. Ch. Aricon's Chief Eye Shy ROM, grandsire of Eng./Am. Ch. Catrana Eyeopener of Aricon.

Ch. Ghabar Midnight Son ROM, grandson of Eng./Am. Ch. Catrana Eyeopener of Aricon.

Bancoup Evan's Girl

Ch. Jacktar of Kearby ROM

Can./Am. Ch. Maerdy Magdalene ROM

having a perfect front and wonderful body with great rib spring. Her head was very strong and filled. She also had wonderfully strong, well-developed hindquarters. A real gem, she passed many of these outstanding qualities on to her great son, Can./Am. Ch. Magor the Marquis, ROM."

W. E. Mackay-Smith (Banbury)

Ch. Kashdowd Bounce, ROM

"In December of 1966 we bought our first Bull Terrier from Mabel Smith. He was a charming white dog which we named 'Brick.' In 1967 we decided he needed a wife. Mabel was on her way to England in August of 1967 and while there, she contracted with George and Audrey Jarrett and Mrs. Higgs to send us a white bitch puppy from a litter just whelped.

"Bounce grew up on the farm with the Jack Russells, the odd hound, the Catahoulas, the horses and our children. The following summer we went with Mrs. Smith to a match show at the Colkets'. Cecil Mann was judging. She won Best in Match and a large ceramic bowl, which is still one of my most treasured possessions. Bill Colket, Oliver Ford and Cecil encouraged us to show her that Fall.

"Bounce was a tremendous success in the ring and subsequently as a brood bitch. It was through Bounce and Alva Rosenberg that we met Raymond Oppenheimer and Eva Weatherill, who became our mentors until Raymond's death in 1984. It was also through Bounce that we learned all the basics of breeding good Bull Terriers. She had six litters over the course of seven years and her influence on the Banbury line remains strong to this day."

Ch. Souperlative Silver Spoon, ROM

"In 1973 the Banbury Kennel was pretty well established, with the littermates Buttercup and Briar (by Ch. Targyt Silver Bob of Langville ex Charity Cyclamen, by Ormandy Souperlative Bar Sinister) having been Silverwood winner and runnerup in '71 and the good Silver Bob—Ch. Kashdowd Bounce daughter, Ch. Banbury Bountiful, doing some winning as well. Having used Silver Bob rather extensively, and his son Briar also, we were running into problems with fronts and mouths. 'Trooper Duffy,' by Killer Joe, had been used to advantage with Buttercup, but we found ourselves in need of a dog with a good front and shoulder and a good mouth. Eva Weatherill was breeding her Frosty (Eng. Ch. Monkery's Mr. Frosty of Ormandy) daughter, Souperlative Kaybella, to Eng. Ch. Ormandy Archangel, and offered me a dog puppy from the litter. Eva and Raymond had decided to keep one of the three dog puppies who was named Sunstar, as he had a very good head (and actually his front and

Ch. Kashdowd Bounce ROM

Ch. Souperlative Silver Spoon ROM

Ch. Souperlative Special of Ormandy ROM

Ch. Souperlative Seqouiah Sequin ROM

mouth were not his strong points). I was given my pick of the other two, Beauregard and Silver Spoon. Of the two, Silver Spoon had the better shoulder and front, and the safer mouth, plus an enchanting temperament, so I chose him. Beauregard (nicknamed 'Moe') became Raymond Oppenheimer's house pet and lived happily at White Waltham Place for many years. Silver Spoon ('Louie,' named for Raymond's uncle) came to the U.S.A. and became the essential link in the Banbury breeding program. He produced beautiful, quality puppies, very well-made, mostly with good mouths and with fabulous temperaments. 'Louie' himself was a gentleman through and through, and taught me the value of temperament in our breed."

Ch. Souperlative Special of Ormandy, ROM

"In January of 1977, I was on one of my frequent and customary pilgrimages to 'the source,' the Ormandy-Souperlative Kennel in England and we were sitting down to tea at Eva's house. There was discussion between Raymond and Eva about some nine-week-old puppies, and suddenly Eva disappeared and reappeared with the most magnificent dog puppy I had ever seen. His head was unbelievable. His bone and substance were amazing and his temperament so kind that he was called 'Smoochie.' We all marvelled, and then he was whisked back to the kennel. In the Spring of '77, I wrote to Raymond that my use of Louie had resulted in very good fronts and mouths, but I was losing head power and substance. At that point, Smoochie had teethed, undershot, and his ears would not stay up as he was allergic to the tape and it couldn't be left on more than two or three days before he scratched it off. I was offered Smoochie, and of course, took advantage of the offer. He was named Souperlative Special of Ormandy because he was so 'special,' and he went on in this country to produce an extraordinary percentage of Specialty winners, including the leading Colored sire of all time, Ch. Banbury Benson of Bedrock, ROM."

Ch. Souperlative Seqouiah Sequin, ROM

"In January of 1977, a litter was born by Maestro out of Ch. Souperlative Dancing Star (by Souperlative Sunstar) from which Eva had selected a bitch puppy for me. I had fallen on evil times the Fall before, losing two of my best bitches (reproductively speaking), Buttercup and Bouquet, who both had to be spayed, one with pyometra and the other with a ruptured uterus. My third bitch, Blaze of Glory, was also suffering from a peculiar complaint, thought to be cystic ovaries, and the fourth bitch in the kennel, Bounce, was ten years old. The bitch which Eva had picked out was Ch. Souperlative Seqouiah Sequin, bred by John and Gay Branch. In the

Can./Am. Ch. Abraxas Armonit ROM

Ch. Abraxas Apex ROM

summer of 1977, Eva came to visit me and brought both 'Special' and 'Sequin' with her. This had the effect of reviving the kennel as Special produced Benson and Sequin, by then co-owned with Maggie Burns, was bred to Ch. Van Don's Silver Chancellor and produced Barnstormer. The progeny of these two dogs have been admirably suited to each other, both physically and in the ability to maintain the wonderful temperaments which Silver Spoon introduced us to so many years ago."

Bill and Cheryl Edwards

Ch. Abraxas Armonit, ROM

"I brought Arthur over because I felt in Canada we needed more bone and substance. I wanted a dog like that with a good temperament. Tom Horner told me that 'Violet never kept a bad dog' so I went to Violet Drummond-Dick for a good one. We got what we wanted.

"Along with being named Canada's top terrier, Arthur has managed to accumulate thirty-seven ROM points. We feel it is always good for the breed when a dog can win in both the Specialty ring and the all-breed ring."

Dave Merriam (Broadside)

Ch. Souperlative Verdict of Broadside, ROM

"I was visiting Raymond at the time that Mrs. Priest brought in a litter for Eva and Raymond to look at. This was about the time that Raymond announced that they would not be raising any more dogs to show. A giant battle ensued between Eva and Raymond and fortunately for the breed, Eva prevailed. The pups were left that day at Ormandy: the great Jim, Ra and Geof. It was an opportune time to make a pitch for a promising ten-week-old puppy dog. Eva ran Geof on and personally brought him to California at about five months when she came over for a holiday."

Ralph and Mary Bowles

Eng./Am. Ch. Abraxas Achilles, ROM

"Achilles came to the U.S.A. because he simply was the best Bull Terrier I had ever seen. My opinion was supported by Raymond Oppenheimer, who wrote in *The Bulletin,* 'This is a wholly exceptional animal, indeed in my book the best I ever saw in the ring.' In addition, he was well-bred, sired by Eng. Ch. Ormandy Archangel out of Eng. Ch. Abraxas Athenia."

Ch. Harper's Hawkeye of Phidgity

"I imported Hawkeye because he was loaded with virtue, had almost

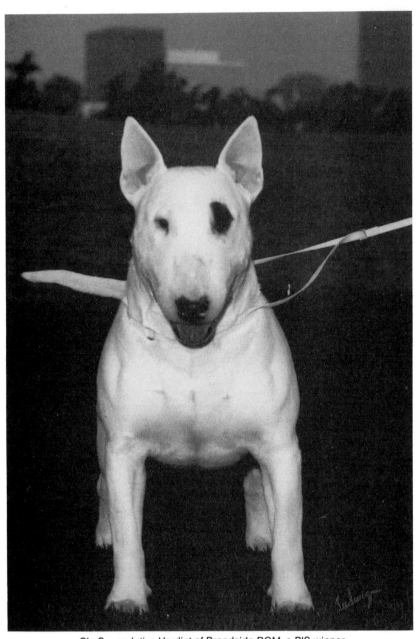

Ch. Souperlative Verdict of Broadside ROM, a BIS winner.

Ch. Agate's Bronzino

Ch. Harper's Hawkeye of Phidgity

Ch. Abraxas Archibald ROM

Eng./Am. Ch. Rambling Rose of Foyri ROM

no faults, was very typey and Eng. Ch. Romany River Pirate's son. He was a heavyweight dog with good bone, an excellent head, good mouth, perfect balance and moved well both ways. He was exactly what the breeders of Coloreds in the U.S.A. needed. He is behind almost every Bull Terrier that Drue King has bred. He is in the pedigree of three of the last seven Silverwood Winners and two of the last seven Runners-Up."

Ch. Agate's Bronzino

"This dog could be the greatest loss to the breed—ever. I imported him because he was a Ch. Abraxas Ace of Aces son, and I could visualize the linebreeding that could take place. Think of Ch. Midnight Melody, Ch. Molyha Snip Snap Snorum, Nocturne and Ch. Aces Dynamite Galore, to mention the most prominent Ace of Aces daughters in the U.S.A. already. Bronzino was a different type from his father, as he was short, compact and had excellent bone. His head was phenomenal and his bite perfect. He was a far better dog than his sire and was about twenty years ahead of his time. Unfortunately, he had insufficient sperm and sired only one litter."

Bob Thomas-Trebor

Ch. Abraxas Archibald, ROM

"After viewing the trophy shows in January, 1977, it was very obvious that Eng. Ch. Badlesmere Bonapart of Souperlative was going to be a very important stud force. Bonaparte was to sire six important sons, Eng. Chs. Jobrulu Jacobinia, Jobulu Jacqueminot, Charlesdon Commander, Hardra's Prince Charming, Eng./Am. Ch. Abraxas Apex, and Am. Ch. Abraxas Archibald, ROM. Archibald never finished his Eng. Ch. as he was imported just after winning his second C.C. Archibald had a perfect mouth, good bone, gunbarrel straight front and a *superb* expression. He was a natural cross into the Achilles and Silverspoon line already in this country, as he was *very* linebred to Mr. Frosty. Jason produced fourteen AKC Champions and 5 ROM Champions, numerous Specialty winners and a Silverwood runner-up. 'Jason' was invited to the 1977 Ormandy Jug for Dogs.

Eng./Am. Ch. Aricons Chief Eye Shy, ROM

"'Billy' is probably the finest all-around Terrier I've ever seen. Superbly filled and turned head, beautifully made, tremendous eye and expression. Absolutely glorious temperament, gentle as a lamb, never angry with any animal, superb with puppies, other males and small children alike, yet very showy and animated in the ring; a very rare

233

combination indeed. I saw Billy for the first time as a young dog (less than a year old) in January, 1981, and I thought that he was sensational. In August, 1981, I judged the Northern Provincial Bull Terrier Club Show of Warrington and put up a six-month-old dog at his very first show, Bulivar Battlestar (later an English Champion). I found out after the show that he was by Billy (Eye Shy) and commented to Raymond Oppenheimer that if that puppy was any indication, Eye Shy was going to be an important stud dog. After the show, Raymond received a call from Eric Stanley who wondered if Raymond was interested in buying Eye Shy. Raymond explained that at his age and deteriorating health, he could not purchase any young dog but thought he knew of an interested party. Hanging up, Raymond returned to dinner and told me of the call. I thought about for 30 seconds, called Eric and completed the purchase. As I felt strongly that Billy should be allowed to compete in the Major Trophies, I left him in England to stand at stud. He won the Ormandy Jug for Dogs in March of 1982. In eleven English litters, Billy produced eight English Champions, an absolutely phenomenal percentage. His descendants have truly been dominant in England since 1982, winning Regent Trophies, Ormandy Jugs, Sandawanas Trophies, and Stud Dog Trophies right and left. One of the most prepotent sires in the breed, Billy was also B.O.B. at four U.S. Specialties."

Eng./Am. Ch. Jobrulu Savior Faire, ROM

"I was in England in December 1983 to judge the Ladies Kennel Association Championship Show. I had gone to the Kenway's with the idea of acquiring a young (ten weeks old) brindle/white dog puppy by Knight Valiant (which I did), but I was very taken by his all-white brother. I asked Joan and Brian to sell me both dogs and they did. I chose to leave both of them there for showing and potential breeding.

"The white dog teethed beautifully and looked more promising as the days passed. We decided to name him Jobrulu Superstar of Trebor and entered him under Raymond Oppenheimer as a six month old at Bath Championship Show. Raymond's increasingly poor health forced him to withdraw at the last minute. Thomas won his first C.C. at this show under the substitute judge, Albert Harwood. He won his second C.C. at his second show three weeks later at the Three Counties Championship Show under George Couzens. He was retired for six months to await his one year birthday (English Kennel Club Rules do not allow a Champion under one year of age). During this retirement, the Kennel Club rejected his name and we re-submitted him as Jobrulu Savior Faire. Thomas finished his English title shortly after he came out of 'retirement.'

"Sired by Eng. Ch. Moatvale Knight Valiant ex Jobrulu Tangerine (by

234

Ch. Woodrow Arabis, litter brother to Ch. Woodrow Carrissa. This dog had the most extraordinary head this author has ever seen. It seems to be prepotent in the line.

Ch. Woodrow Carrissa ROM

Eng./Am. Ch. Jobrulu Savior Faire ROM

Eng./Am. Ch. Bulivar Real McCoy ROM

236

Bifray's Magician.

Ch. Brummagem the Brigand.

237

Jacobinia), Thomas has heavy bone, a very good eye, short back and a very well-turned, powerful head coupled with a perfect mouth. He has proven to be an excellent sire from very few litters to date, with three invitees for the 1986 Trophy Shows and a Best Puppy in Show at the Bull Terrier Club Championship Show in October of 1986. His first U.S. progeny are still too young to be shown. Thomas was invited to the 1985 Regent Trophy and 1985 Ormandy Jug for Dogs."

Eng./Am. Ch. Bulivar Real McCoy, ROM

"Sam, a black brindle/white, is by Eng. Ch. Bulivar Battlestar (by Eye Shy) ex Bulivar Bardott (by Eng. Ch. Cousin Charlie of Hollyfir). I saw Sam at the 1984 Regent Trophy and Ormandy Jug for Dogs and felt he was the best coloured male that had been shown in England since Eng. Ch. Romany River Pirate. I asked Mrs. Mitchell, Sam's breeder/owner, to give me first right of refusal on him if she ever sold him and she agreed. Approximately five months later, she decided to sell him. I could still have him, if I were still interested and would match a price she had been offered. I agreed to purchase him, as I felt strongly that he was going to be a fantastic sire and be a tremendous influence on the breed's future.

"Sam was incredibly well made, with a very good head, a perfect mouth and several generations of good mouths behind him. His father, Battlestar, had been the most like his sire of all Eye Shy's champion sons and Sam was incredibly like Billy in head, style and temperament.

"At the time that I bought him, I had not seen any of his get. In the 1985 Trophies, his son, Eng. Ch. Burundi Black, became the first tri-colour English Champion, the first Coloured male to win the Regent Trophy and the first Bull Terrier to win the Regent Trophy, the Ormandy Jug for Dogs and the Sandawana Trophy (as the top Coloured shown in the previous year). In the 1986 Trophy shows, his daughter, Eng. Ch. Geham Godiva, won the Regent Trophy and the Ormandy Jug for Bitches. Sam, himself, won the Jackadandy Trophy and the Monkery Stud Dog Trophy as the Top Bull Terrier Stud Dog of 1986. He was also first Runner-up in the Dog World (England) newspaper as the Top Terrier Stud Dog of 1986. At the Bull Terrier Club Championship Show in October of 1986, the Dog C.C. Winner, the Reserve Dog C.C. Winner and the Reserve Bitch C.C. Winner were all sired by Sam."

David and Anna Harris

"The key dog in our line is Ch. Brummagem the Brigand, a cobby solid brindle son of Eng. Ch. Romany River Pirate out of a daughter of Eng./S.A. Ch. Curraneye Independence. The Brigand was prepotent for

Ch. Bandetta of Brummagem ROM

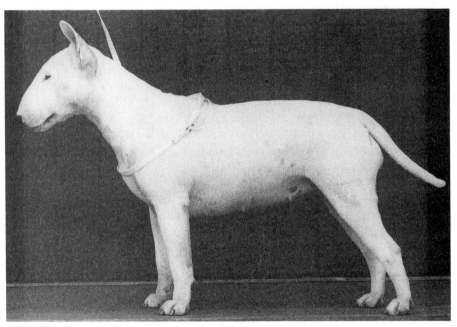

Ch. Jaquenetta of Brummagem ROM

Ch. Monkery Sea Link figures prominently in pedigrees of Colored Specialty winners of the 1980s, either by being Sea Shanty's and Sea Boots' sire, or as grandfather of Ch. Banbury Boothia ROM, top-producing Colored bitch of all time.

Eng./Am. Ch. Monkery's Meltdown Sea Shanty ROM. One of the greatest Colored dogs ever imported, he figures prominently in many of today's very best dogs.

Ch. Monkery Sea Boots ROM, outstanding show dog of the late 1970s
with multiple Best in Show honors,
handled by owner Carl Pew.

Ch. Ragged Hills Backstroker, bred by Peggy Arnaud, a 1980 Specialty winner and
son of Eng./Am. Ch. Monkery's Meltdown Sea Shanty.

Eng./Am. Ch. Kearby's Merry Dancer ROM

Int./Dutch Ch. Polytelis Silver Convention

242

his superb breed type. A great showman, he endowed his progeny with his wonderful character and temperament.

"Ch. Jacquenetta of Brummagem, ROM, a white granddaughter of the Brigand, comes from a wonderful female line. The Brigand was mated to a bitch sired by Eng. Ch. Ionem Corvette out of a half sister to Winkie Mackay-Smith's Ch. Kashdowd Bounce. From this came the top class brindle, Mischief of Brummagem, who, mated to Jackadandy, produced Jaquenetta.

"Jaquenetta has proved to be a key dam, with four ROM champions coming from two litters. A number of outstanding grandchildren are now making their mark on the breed, among these is Ch. Brummagem Bacarole, ROM, Runner-Up and Best Colored in the 1985 Silverwood."

Jim and Maggie Burns—"Iffinest"

Eng./Am. Ch. Kearby's Merry Dancer, ROM

"On the night of her second bid for the Regent Trophy, having been runner-up to the Regent Trophy and Ormandy Jug the previous year, the Burns wisely scooped her up when it was known she was for sale. A bitch of intense quality, often one had to 'really look' at her to realize that she was more than feminine. Her great bone has come through over and over in her children as has her superb temperament, perfect mouth and nearly perfect front. She quickly earned her championship and ROM at Specialty shows.

"When bred to Buckskin, she produced a good bitch, Iffinest Iceni Nick of Time, who was sold to the Myalls. When bred to Int. Ch. Polytelis Silver Convention, she produced Iffinest Pirouette, shown and owned by Kay Marshall, and a Canadian star, Iffinest Northern Dancer. The Combination also showed Silver Convention's ability to throw good profiles with excellent dentition, a superb temperament and the best hind movement again and again."

Ch. Jobrulu Moss Campion

"Ch. Jobrulu Moss Campion was purchased by Jim and Maggie Burns a year and a half after Maggie saw him in the 1978 competition for the Regent Trophy and Ormandy Jugs. Judge Mrs. Holmes reported that had a reserve award existed, she'd have given it to Moss Campion.

"The dog's showmanship was outstanding. He never disappointed his owners. He is the ultimately typey dog with an exceptional temperament. Both of these traits plus good bone and a scissors bite have been passed on through to his great-grandchildren. His topline has never faltered even today at age twelve and the great strength of head is still there. Although very lightly used, here and in England, he has produced remarkably well."

243

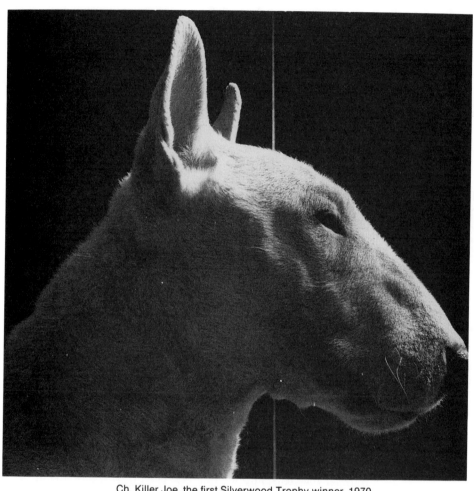

Ch. Killer Joe, the first Silverwood Trophy winner, 1970.

25

The Silverwood
Competition

THE Bull Terrier in America has changed dramatically in the last fifteen years. A new wave of breeders has elevated the breed to new heights. The single most significant event in this progress has been the Silverwood Trophy Competition. Through its legacy one can learn the history of these recent years.

Origin of the Competition and its Awards

Hope and Bill Colket conceived the idea of holding a major trophy show for American-bred Bull Terriers late in the 1960s. Encouraged by Raymond Oppenheimer, the event came into existence in 1970 after the tragic deaths of the Colkets. The competition is modelled along the lines of the Regent Trophy show in England and is recognized by the American Kennel Club as a fun match, thereby open to Bull Terrier Club of America members only. Over the years, although the rules and numbers of judges have varied as have the actual trophies awarded, the basis for the competition has remained essentially the same.

The top award is the Silverwood Trophy. It is a carved wood White Bull Terrier crafted by Mr. Harris, a fine English carver. It was presented to the Bull Terrier Club of America by the Bull Terrier Club (England) in memory of Hope and Bill Colket, whose prefix was Silverwood.

Can./Am. Ch. Banbury Bergerac ROM,
Silverwood winner, 1974.

Can./Am. Ch. Paupen's Mr. Wiggins, Silverwood winner, 1973.

Ch. Sunburst Solar System, Silverwood
winner, 1972. *Schreiber*

Ch. Banbury Charity Buttercup, Silverwood winner, 1971.

The award for Best of Opposite Sex was also presented to the Bull Terrier Club of America by the Bull Terrier Club. It is a Nymphenburg porcelain figure of a White Bull Terrier and is the Regent Trophy replica won by Eng. Ch. Raydium Brigadier in 1937 and willed to the Bull Terrier Club by his owner, Gladys Adlam. At the beginning of World War II, Mrs. Adlam exported Brigadier to the United States to Jessie Bennett's Coolyn Hill kennels. Thus, the Raydium Brigadier Trophy is awarded in memory of Gladys Adlam and Jessie Bennett.

The BTCA, in 1970 only, awarded a trophy for Reserve to best in each variety, but this award was discontinued.

Beginning in 1972, the BTCA awarded a trophy to the runner-up to the Silverwood Trophy winner. This award was dedicated to the memory of Lavender Lovell in 1973 and has since been known as the Lovell Trophy. It is a Royal Doulton porcelain figure of a Colored Bull Terrier dog *and* a Royal Copenhagen porcelain figure of a White Bull Terrier bitch.

Beginning in 1977, the BTCA has awarded the breeder(s) of the Silverwood Trophy winner with the Ch. Bramblemere Gay Carolynda Trophy in memory of George C. Pinque.

Additionally, the BTCA gives awards to first and reserve in each of the four classes, as well as to the Best of Opposite Variety to the Silverwood Trophy winner.

Purpose of the Competition

The purpose of the Silverwood Trophy competition is to provide a forum by which all Bull Terrier fanciers can learn to effectively evaluate their individual breeding programs in the context of the breed as a whole. Such a forum is only as useful as those who participate. Fortunately, many people in the United States have taken advantage of this fantastic opportunity and as a result have elevated the quality of the breed to very high levels. More importantly, it has served as a successful arena to exchange ideas and share experiences.

The breed is at a turning point now. More than ever before, all of the collective knowledge of all of the breeders must be brought together and shared. Only then will the Silverwood continue to serve as the tool for progress.

Rules Governing the Silverwood Competition

The Silverwood Competition is for *American Bred* Bull Terriers. *American Bred* is defined as animals whelped on the North American Continent, Hawaii, or offshore islands and resulting from a breeding which took place in one of these same locations with both sire and dam present.

Ch. Banbury Brass Tack of Maldon, CD,
Silverwood winner, 1975.

Schreiber

Am./Can. Ch. Magor the Marquis ROM, Silverwood winner, 1976.

Ch. St. Francis Gypsy Rover ROM, Silverwood winner, 1977.

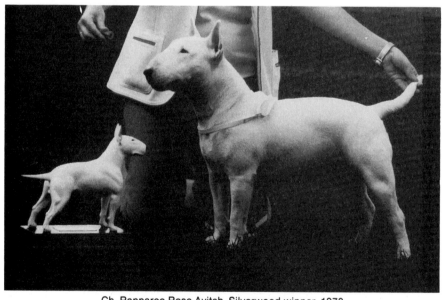

Ch. Rapparee Rose Avitch, Silverwood winner, 1978.

There will be awards for both Best and Runner-up to Best in *each sex* of *each variety for a total of eight winners. These eight winners will compete for:*

Best American Bred Bull Terrier—the **Silverwood Trophy,** presented by the Bull Terrier Club (England), to be held for one year.

Breeder of the Best American Bred Bull Terrier—the **Ch. Bramblemere Gay Carolynda Trophy,** presented by the Bull Terrier Club of America in memory of George C. Pinque, to be held for one year.

Runner-up to Best American Bred Bull Terrier—the **Lovell Trophy,** presented by the Bull Terrier Club of America in memory of Lavender Lovell, to be held for one year.

Best of Opposite Sex to Best American Bred Bull Terrier—the **Raydium Brigadier Trophy,** presented by the Bull Terrier Club (England) in memory of Gladys M. Adlam and Jessie Bennett, to be held for one year.

Best of Opposite Variety—presented by the Bull Terrier Club of America.

Eligibility—For American Bred Bull Terriers ONLY; the following shall be eligible to enter the competition if owned or co-owned by a member in good standing of the Bull Terrier Club of America.

Bull Terrier which has completed the requirements for a U.S.A. or Canadian championship prior to entry closing date.

A BOV, BOS, WD, RWD, WB, RWB (with major) at a 3 point ROM show.

A BOV or BOS (with major) at a 2 point ROM show.

Runner-up or BOS from a previous Silverwood.

Any Bull Terrier may receive a Special Invitation from the BTCA Board of Directors to enter the competition. Requests for an invitation must be in writing for consideration by the Board. They must include: a picture of the animal, a two-generation pedigree (may be hand written in draft form) and a brief summary of any show record. Requests must be filed with the BTCA Show Chairman along with the entry form and fees, prior to entry closing date.

Judges Selection—Three Silverwood judges will be selected by the BTCA Board after hearing recommendations from the Judges' Selection Committee.

Ch. Magor Mint Julep of Trebor ROM,
Silverwood winner, 1980.

Ch. Peterbuilt, Silverwood winner, 1981.

252

Ch. Ann Dee's Red Adair, Silverwood winner, 1979.

Ch. Westbrook Wild One ROM, Silverwood winner, 1982.

The Board of Directors will select the three Silverwood judges in executive session so that there can be discussion of qualifications, etc. without discomfort to those being considered or their friends. If a Board member is being considered, then that member will also leave. As a systematic and unbiased way of determining class assignments, the Board will assign the reference numbers 1, 2, and 3 to the selected judges.

An officiating judge shall not own, co-own, or exhibit any entry at that Silverwood. An exhibitor may not exhibit under a judge who bred the entry, owned the entry within the past 12 months, or who has handled the entry more than twice during the past 12 months. Any other possible conflict of interest should be brought to the attention of the Show Chairman for referral to the Board. The BTCA Board will determine wheter, in fact, a conflict exists and will then rule accordingly. Any Board ruling will be FINAL.

Judging Procedure—The Silverwood Competition is judged by a panel of three judges. Procedures are designed so that two judges must agree on any of the top placements or trophy awards in the competition.

Classes—There will be four: White Dogs, White Bitches, Colored Dogs and Colored Bitches. After entries have been received, the Show Chairman will make assignments based on class size and the reference numbers assigned to the judges. Judges #1 and #2 will judge the two largest classes. Judges #3 and #1 will do the third class and Judges #3 and #2 the fourth. If classes happen to be equal in number, then Whites and/or Bitches will be assigned first. Judges #1 and #2 will award the major trophies. In each case the unassigned judge will serve as referee if needed.

Class Judging—Each judge will examine each entry and then both will stand together while each entry is moved. When this preliminary judging is completed, each judge will submit on their card the numbers of up to four entries which they wish to re-examine in the final round of competition for best and reserve in class. The number four is a maximum, each judge will list *only* entries which in their opinion are at the pinnacle of breed development, and in which they are truly interested for one of the top placements!! Judges will be aware that a great deal of significance is attached to participation in the final round and *only the very top entrants should be so rewarded.* This selection process will result in a minimum of two and a maximum of eight entries which will return to the ring for final judging. With all class entrants in the ring, the steward will combine numbers from the judges' cards and read in ascending order the entry numbers which will return for final judging.

Final Round Judging—Best and reserve of each class will be awarded

254

Ch. Banbury Briar ROM, Raydium
Brigadier Trophy, 1971.

Ch. Banbury Barnstormer ROM, Silverwood winner, 1984.

first. Then the four winners will be judged together in the ring for the Silverwood Trophy. The judging order will be: a) Silverwood Trophy, b) Lovell Trophy, c) Brigadier Trophy, d) Best of Opposite Variety. (After the Silverwood Trophy winner is chosen, the Reserve Dog or Bitch to the winner in the classes will enter the ring to compete for Runner-up).

Conferring—There will be no prohibition of conferral between the judges. If the judges *wish* to confer, they may do so at their own discretion. At no time during the judging of a class will either of the judges in that class converse with the referee of that class.

Referee—If the two assigned judges disagree between two entrants for a class or trophy placement, then the referee will enter the ring, judge *those two* entrants, and render a decision which will break the tie. If the tie was for the class win, then one entry is class winner and the other is automatically reserve.

Silverwood Trophy Winners

1970 Ch. Killer Joe (dw)
(Ch. Kracton Robin of Wentwood ex Holcroft Kowhai Lottie)
Breeder: Peggy Arnaud
Owners: Peggy and Michael Arnaud
1971 Banbury Charity Buttercup (bw)
(Eng./Am. Ch. Targyt Silver Bob of Langville ex Charity Cyclamen)
Breeder-Owner: W. E. Mackay-Smith
1972 Sunburst Solar System (bw)
(Can./Am. Ch. Tantrum's Trad Lad ex Can. Ch. Iella Desdamona)
Breeders: Mr. and Mrs. Gary J. Travers
Owners: Mr. and Mrs. Len Spicer
1973 Can. Ch. Paupen's Mr. Wiggins (dw)
(Can./Am. Ch. Maerdy Moonstone ex Romany Rock Rose)
Breeder: Joseph J. Cowan
Owners: Paul and Penny Maier
1974 Banbury Bergerac (dw)
(Eng./Am. Ch. Targyt Silver Bob of Langville ex Ch. Harper's Hemstitch)
Breeder: Ken Neuman
Owner: Philip D. Hyde
1975 Ch. Banbury Brass Tack of Maldon (dw)
(Ch. Banbury Briar ex Banbury Butterfly)
Breeders: Mr. and Mrs. Thomas Griswold
Owners: W. E. Mackay-Smith and Dr. and Mrs. John Blumberg
1976 Magor the Marquis (dwb)
(Eng./Am. Ch. Abraxas Achilles ex Can./Am. Ch. Maerdy Magdalene)
Breeders-Owners: Gordon and Norma Smith

Ch. Shavin's Queen of Hearts ROM, Silverwood Trophy, 1985.

Ch. Westbrook Windborne ROM, Silverwood winner, 1983.

257

Ch. Carling's Goodness Gracious, Brigadier Trophy, 1973.

Ch. Banbury Backchat, Brigadier Trophy, 1976.

1977 Ch. St. Francis Gypsy Rover (dwb)
(Eng./Am. Ch. Abraxas Achilles ex Silverwood Swan Song)
Breeder: Frank Foley
Owners: Frank Foley and Bill Shipley
1978 Ch. Rapparee Rose Avitch (bwb)
(Ch. Rapparee Ragna ex Rapparee Rebecca)
Breeder: Michael Shames
Owners: Steve Ringler and Paula Shames
1979 Ch. Ann Dee's Red Adair (drw)
(Am./Can. Ch. Paupen's Mr. Wiggins ex Hollyfir's Coppernob)
Breeder: George Schreiber
Owners: Elaine Bernard and R. Angus
1980 Magor Mint Julep of Trebor (bw)
(Can./Am. Ch. Magor The Marquis ex Magor Merrilee)
Breeders: Norma Smith and Robert K. Thomas
Owners: Norma Smith and Donna Medders
1981 Ch. Peterbuilt (dw)
(Can./Am. Ch. Monkery's Buckskin ex Ch. Binkstone Duchess Daphne)
Breeders: R. and L. Papineau
Owner: Arthur Cleff
1982 Ch. Westbrook Wild One (dwb)
(Ch. Ragged Hills Lady Killer II ex Ch. Westbrook Wit's End)
Breeder: Drue King
Owners: Drue King and Merry Hobbins
1983 Ch. Westbrook Windborne (bbw)
(Ch. Westbrook Wild Thing ex Ch. Westbrook Windsong)
Breeder-Owner: Drue King
1984 Ch. Banbury Barnstormer (dw)
(Can./Am. Ch. Van Don's Silver Chancellor ex Ch. Souperlative Seqouiah Sequin)
Breeders: Margaret Burns and W. E. Mackay-Smith
Owners: M. P. and W. E. Mackay-Smith
1985 Ch. Shavin's Queen of Hearts (bw)
(Ch. Brobar Minder ex Ch. Shavin's Brandy Bonkers)
Breeders: Roland and Patricia Edwards
Owners: Roland and Patricia Edwards and Linda Lethin
1986 Rambunctious Sea Spray (bwb)
(Ch. Iffinest Local Hero ex Can./Am. Ch. Rambunctious Seabreeze)
Breeder: Kathleen Marshall
Owners: Kathleen Marshall and Ethel and Joseph Vande Vorde

Raydium Brigadier Trophy Winners

1970 Midnight Melody (bbw)
(Ch. Abraxas Ace of Aces ex Snowlady)
Breeder-Owner: Charles A. Fleming

1971 Banbury Briar (dwr)
(Eng./Am. Ch. Targyt Silver Bob of Langville ex Charity Cyclamen)
Breeder-Owner: W. E. Mackay-Smith
1972 Ch. Highland's Big Ben (dbw)
(Ch. Abraxas Ace of Aces ex Ch. Kearby Maxwell's Gold Dust)
Breeders-Owners: Agnes and Forrest Rose
1973 Carling's Goodness Gracious (bw)
(Can./Am. Ch. Tantrum's Trad Lad ex Carling's Roseberry)
Breeders: Ingrid Ackerman and R. Conti
Owners: Ed and Mary Nentwich
1974 Ch. Banbury Butter Rum (bw)
(Ch. Trooper Duffy of Manchester ex Ch. Banbury Charity Buttercup)
Breeder: W. E. Mackay-Smith
Owner: Harvey Shames
1975 Ch. Banbury Bouquet (bwr)
(Aricon's Acetylene of Banbury ex Ch. Kashdowd Bounce)
Breeder-Owner: W. E. Mackay-Smith
1976 Ch. Banbury Backchat (bw)
(Ch. Banbury Briar ex Ch. Kashdowd Bounce)
Breeder: W. E. Mackay-Smith
Owners: W. E. Mackay-Smith and Margaret Burns
1977 Carling's Copprehead (brw)
(Ch. Rapparee Ragna ex Sugarhill's Lady in Satin)
Breeder: Charles Cuccullo
Owner: Ingrid Ackerman
1978 Camelot's Zyphel Excalibur (dwb)
(Eng./Am. Ch. Abraxas Achilles ex Camelot's General Patton)
Breeder: Joseph M. Jayson
Owners: Mike and Carol Zylka
1979 Ch. Cannoro Claret (bwb)
(Eng./Am. Ch. Foyri Electrify ex Banbury Bobbin)
Breeder: Bernard E. McCann
Owners: Jay and Mary Remer
1980 Ch. Ragged Hills Backstroker (dbb)
(Eng./Am. Ch. Monkery's Meltdown Sea Shanty ex Ch. Ragged Hills
Aurora)
Breeder: Peggy Arnaud
Owner: David Phillips
1981 Ch. Oyster Bay's Lady Sadie (bw)
(Can./Am. Ch. Monkery's Buckskin ex Oyster Bay's Lady April)
Breeders: E. L. and Carol A. Oppelt
Owners: Greg and Luana Sender
1982 Ch. Banbury Bow's Heart of Bedrock (bwr)
(Ch. Souperlative Special of Ormandy ex Ch. Banbury Boothia)
Breeders-Owners: Jay and Mary Remer and W. E. Mackay-Smith

Ch. Camelot's Zyphel Excalibur, Brigadier and Lovell Trophies, 1978.

Ch. Carling's Copprehead ROM, Brigadier and Lovell Trophies, 1977.

Ch. Oyster Bay's Lady Sadie ROM, Lovell Trophy, 1981.

Ch. Cannoro Claret ROM, Brigadier and Lovell Trophies, 1979.

Ch. Chadwell Chamaco ROM, Lovell Trophy, 1976.

Ch. Banbury Bow's Heart of Bedrock ROM, Brigadier and Lovell Trophies, 1982.

1983 Ch. Banbury Barnstormer (dw)
      (Can./Am. Ch. Van Don's Silver Chancellor ex Ch. Souperlative Seqouiah
      Sequin)
      Breeders: W. E. Mackay-Smith and Margaret Burns
      Owners: M. P. and W. E. Mackay-Smith
1984 Shavin's Queen of Hearts (bw)
      (Ch. Brobar Minder ex Ch. Shavin's Brandy Bonkers)
      Breeders-Owners: Roland and Patricia Edwards
1985 Shadowood Mighty Sting (dw)
      (Ch. Jobrulu Corydalis ex Ch. Trebor Secondhand Rose)
      Breeder: Sharon Whalen
      Owners: Sharon Whalen and Mark and Lisa Anderson
1986 Am./Can. Ch. Iceni Micklefell (dbw)
      (Am./Can. Ch. Bulwark's Iceni Just William ex Am./Can. Ch. Pyreril's
      Milky Way)
      Breeder: Robert Myall
      Owners: Dr. and Mrs. Robert Myall

Lovell Trophy Winners

1972 Ch. Molyha Snip Snap Snorum (bbw)
      (Ch. Abraxas Ace of Aces ex Ch. Huntress of Molyha)
      Breeder-Owner: Halina Molyneux
1973 Ch. Banbury Borealis (dw)
      (Ch. Banbury Briar ex Souperlative Meteor)
      Breeder: Mabel Smith
      Owners: Allan and Marie Gerst
1974 Ch. Banbury Butter Rum (bw)
      (Ch. Trooper Duffy of Manchester ex Banbury Charity Buttercup)
      Breeder: W. E. Mackay-Smith
      Owner: Harvey Shames
1975 Ch. Banbury Bouquet (bwb)
      (Aricon's Acetylene of Banbury ex Ch. Kashdowd Bounce)
      Breeder-Owner: W. E. Mackay-Smith
1976 Can. Ch. Chadwell Chamaco (dwb)
      (Ch. Banbury Briar ex Can./Am. Ch. Sunburst Solar System)
      Breeders-Owners: Mr. and Mrs. Len Spicer
1977 Carling's Copprehead (brw)
      (Ch. Rapparee Ragna ex Sugarhill's Lady in Satin)
      Breeder: Charles Cuccullo
      Owner: Ingrid Ackerman
1978 Camelot's Zyphel Excalibur (dwb)
      (Eng./Am. Ch. Abraxas Achilles ex Camelot's General Patton)
      Breeder: Joseph M. Jayson
      Owners: Mike and Carol Zylka

Ch. Bulwark's Iceni Just William ROM, Lovell Trophy, 1984.

Ch. Huntsman's No Jemima ROM, Lovell Trophy, 1983.

265

1979 Ch. Cannoro Claret (bwb)
      (Eng./Am. Ch. Foyri Electrify ex Banbury Bobbin)
      Breeder: Bernard L. McCann
      Owners: Jay and Mary Remer
1980 Binkstone's Buckskin Maggie (bw)
      (Can./Am. Ch. Monkery's Buckskin ex Gilavon Glisse)
      Breeders: G. and J. Binks
      Owners: Dr. Robert Myall and Anne Hamilton
1981 Ch. Oyster Bay's Lady Sadie (bw)
      (Can./Am. Ch. Monkery's Buckskin ex Oyster Bay's Lady April)
      Breeders: E. L. and Carol A. Oppelt
      Owners: Greg and Luana Sender
1982 Ch. Banbury Bow's Heart of Bedrock (bwr)
      (Ch. Souperlative Special of Ormandy ex Ch. Banbury Boothia)
      Breeders-Owners: Jay and Mary Remer and W. E. Mackay-Smith
1983 Huntsman's No Jemima (bwb)
      (Ch. Westbrook Wild Thing ex Huntsman's Bonisa Bululu)
      Breeder: Herb Joffee
      Owners: Liz Grano and Marge Naughton
1984 Can./Am. Ch. Bulwark's Iceni Just William (dbw)
      (Can./Am. Ch. Monkery's Buckskin ex Kyra's Sweet Briar Buttress)
      Breeder: P. Michael Hodsman, P.C.
      Owners: Robert and Lynne Myall
1985 Ch. Brummagem Barcarole (bbw)
      (Ch. Cinema the Omen of Westbrook ex Brummagem White Sands)
      Breeders: David Harris and Linda Lee Chmiel
      Owners: David and Anna Harris
1986 Am./Can. Ch. Iceni Micklefell (dbw)
      (Am./Can. Ch. Bulwark's Iceni Just William ex Am./Can. Ch. Pyreril's
      Milky Way)
      Breeder: Robert Myall
      Owners: Dr. and Mrs. Robert Myall

26

New Champions— The Recognition of Merit Award

$\mathbf{F}$ROM 1970 to the present there has been an emormous number of Bull Terrier champions. Many are very good dogs, but certainly not all of them. In order to identify those dogs who are a cut above, the Bull Terrier Club of America devised a system engineered by Ralph Bowles and called the Recognition of Merit Award. Although the system was set up in 1980, Mr. Bowles tabulated which Bull Terriers would be recipients of the designation retroactive to 1970.

Bull Terrier fanciers have voiced a need for recognizing the breeding potential of dogs by a means stronger than breed wins and group placements tabulated by all-breed scoring systems. Because Specialty and Supported shows usually are judged by breeders or specialists, dogs likely to advance the breed generally win. The Merit Award fosters this high quality competition and recognizes the virtues of Specialty and Supported show winners.

To receive this award, a Bull Terrier must accumulate seven points at Specialty and Supported shows. The total of seven points must include at least one three-point award (BOV or BOS at a Specialty, or Best Dog or

Eng./Am. Ch. Targyt Silver Bob of Langville, Regent Trophy and Ormandy Dog Jug winner. In the United States, he earned his championship in four shows and although not himself a ROM, he figures prominently in the pedigrees of many ROM titleholders.

Ch. Belle Terre's Patience ROM, 1970, daughter of
1970 Silverwood winner, Ch. Killer Joe.

Ch. Banbury Bountiful ROM, 1971.

269

Bitch, both varieties, at the Silverwood or Runner-up to the Silverwood Winner).

At a Specialty show, BOV and BOS earns three points with WD and WB worth two points. Supported shows earn two points for BOV and BOS and one point for WD and WB. Silverwood earns the Best Dog and Best Bitch, both varieties, three points and two points to Runner-up Dog and Bitch, both varieties. Three points will be earned by Runner-up to the Silverwood Winner if the Runner-up did not earn three points by being Best Dog or Best Bitch, both varieties.

In order for a given dog to receive points at either a Specialty or Supported Show, there must be a major, as defined by AKC rules, in the class in which a dog competes. However, if there is not a major in the class in which said dog competes but the dog is placed over the opposite sex where there is a major, the points will be awarded to both dogs. This also applies to BOW where applicable.

The BTCA may have two Specialty Shows and an unlimited number of Supported Shows. Each Regional Club and the two Canadian Clubs may have one Specialty Show and one Supported Show. Regional Clubs not eligible to hold a Specialty Show may have two Supported Shows. Some Regional Clubs may support more than one or two shows during a year. In this event, the Regional Club must designate to the BTCA Board of Directors in advance which show or shows will earn ROM points.

If a Regional Club is not eligible to hold a Specialty Show and wants one of its Supported Shows to be designated as a Specialty Show, the club must apply to the BTCA Board of Directors for permission. Permission will be granted only if the Regional Club applies in advance of the show being held and the show is being judged by a breeder or specialist. At least 40 Bull Terriers must be shown for the show to have Specialty status.

The Merit Awards are tabulated and administered by the Bull Terrier Club of America. The system gives recognition to those dogs and bitches which consistently win under specialist judges, and helps to form a solid basis for the breed's progress in North America.

Bull Terrier Club of America Recognition of Merit Awards

1970
Ch. Belle Terre's Patience
Ch. Kashdowd Bounce
Ch. Killer Joe

1971
Ch. Banbury Bountiful
Ch. Banbury Briar
Ch. Carling's Minnie the Masher

Eng./Am. Ch. Comanche of Upend
Ch. Harper's Hemstitch
Ch. Highland's Big Ben
Ch. His Nibs of Brobar
Can./Am. Ch. Tantrum's Trad Lad
Ch. Turney's Nocturne
Ch. Valkyrie Ventura

Ch. Arundela Cardinal ROM, 1973.

Can./Am. Ch. Tantrum's Trad Lad, ROM, 1971.

Ch. Ann Dee's Fire Chief Zodiac
ROM, 1979.

Ch. Griffwood's Jurisprudence ROM, 1975.

Ch. Beefeater Black Magic ROM, 1979.

Ch. Iceni Penny Lane of Beefeater ROM, 1983, sired by Ch. Beefeater Black Magic
ROM.

273

Ch. Carling's Charisma ROM, 1979.

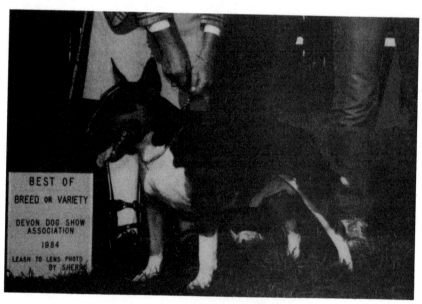

Ch. Banbury Sargent Major ROM, 1984.

274

Ch. Banbury Benjamin of Bedrock ROM, 1980.

Ch. Banbury Burlesque of Bedrock ROM, 1980.

275

Ch. Futura's Kidd Jabba ROM, 1984. He is a grandson of both Silver Chancellor and Arabis, a significant blending.

Can./Am. Ch. Van Don's Silver Chancellor ROM, 1981, sire of Ch. Banbury Barnstormer ROM.

Ch. Westbrook Whiz-Bang ROM, 1982.

Ch. Westbrook Wit's End ROM, 1979.

1972

Ch. Ali Baba of High Knolls
Ch. Banbury Charity Buttercup
Ch. Belle Terre's Sampson
Ch. Carnelian's Beloved Rogue
Ch. Lavender's Robin Hood
Can./Am. Ch. Maerdy Magdalene
Ch. Midnight Melody
Ch. Sunburst Solar System

1973

Eng./Am. Ch. Abraxas Achilles
Ch. Arundela Cardinal
Ch. Banbury Beret
Ch. Banbury Borealis
Ch. Banbury Butter Rum
Ch. Carling's Marauder
Ch. Molyha Snip Snap Snorum
Can./Am. Ch. Paupens Mr. Wiggins
Can./Am. Ch. Regina of Colostaurus

1974

Can./Am. Ch. Banbury Bouquet
Ch. Dreadnaught's Top Deck
Ch. Highland's Bashful Dwarf
Ch. Souperlative Iceberg

1975

Ch. Banbury Brass Tack
  of Maldon, CD
Ch. Canterbury's Dover Delight
Ch. Canterbury's Taste of Honey
Ch. Embassy Girl of Phidgity
Ch. Griffwood's Jurisprudence
Ch. Harper's Haversack
Ch. Humphries
Ch. La Mirada's Wheel of Fortune
Ch. Lenster's Wild Magic
Ch. Monkery Sea Boots

1976

Ch. Banbury Backchat
Can./Am. Ch. Bymarket Gunmetal
  Grenadier
Ch. Carling's Goodness Gracious
Ch. Chadwell Chamaco
Ch. Lady Ann-Dee's Julie
Can./Am. Ch. Magor the Marquis
Ch. Senator of Lenster

Ch. Souperlative Silver Spoon
Ch. Sunburst Sea Siren
Ch. Tenacious Chadwell Kelly Gay

1977

Ch. Abraxas Archibald
Ch. Banbury Bachelor's Button
Ch. Broadside Music Maker
Ch. Carling's Copprehead
Eng./Am. Ch. Monkery's Meltdown
  Sea Shanty
Ch. Signature's Black Bart
Ch. Souperlative Seqouiah Sequin
Ch. Souperlative Verdict of Broadside
Ch. St. Francis Gypsy Rover

1978

Ch. Abraxas Ardeur
Ch. Ann-Dee's Red Adair
Ch. Banbury Blaze of Glory
Ch. Banbury Boothia
Can./Am. Ch. Camelot's Zyphel
  Excalibur
Ch. Cerberus Cinnamon
Can./Am. Ch. The Duke of
  Goodwood
Ch. Grandopera Hansel of Raeybrand
Ch. Montara's Morning Light
Ch. Primate's Piranha Air Major
Ch. Ragged Hill's Witchcraft
Ch. Rapparee Rose Avitch
Ch. Souperlative Special of Ormandy

1979

Ch. Abraxas Abbey Rose
Eng./Am. Ch. Abraxas Apex
Ch. Ann-Dee's Fire Chief Zodiac
Ch. Ann-Dee's Vinegar Joe
Ch. Aricon's Archemedes of Foyri
Ch. Banbury Iffinest Och Aye
Ch. Beefeater Black Magic
Ch. Bow Bell's Leeward Sea Wench
Ch. Bulland's Mountain Star
Ch. Cannoro Claret
Ch. Carling's Charisma
Eng./Am. Ch. Jobrulu Hosta
Ch. Kearby's Salvationist
Ch. La Mirada's Sweet Bells

Eng./Am. Ch. Jobrulu Hosta, ROM 1979.

Ch. Grandopera Hansel of Raeybrand, ROM 1978.

279

Ch. Banbury Briar, ROM 1971.

Ch. Banbury Beret, ROM 1973.

280

Ch. Banbury Borealis, ROM, son of Ch. Banbury Briar, ROM. Borealis won Specialties in 1973 and 1975.

Ch. Abraxas Abbey Rose, ROM 1979.

Ch. Catrana Sandra Bella, ROM 1985.

Ch. Atilla's Iffinest Moss Royal, ROM 1981.

Ch. Essex Evita of Rapparee, ROM 1982.

Ch. Pyreril's Bodeciar, ROM 1984.

Can./Am. Ch. Magor the Marquis, ROM 1976, also the Silverwood Trophy winner that year.

... of Bedrock

...enson of Bedrock

...nbury Burlesque of Bedrock

Ch. Canterbury's Queen of Hartz

Ch. Haslemere Restless Fire

Ch. Ragged Hill's Backstroker

Ch. Rambling Rose of Foyri

Ch. Rapparee Banbury Sweet Sixteen

1981

Ch. Ann-Dee's Star Buck

Ch. Jacktar of Kearby

Ch. Peterbuilt

Ch. Terriwood's Peppermint

Ch. Van Don's Silver Chancellor

Ch. Atilla's Iffinest Moss Royal

Ch. Dress Circle Red Hot Flame

Ch. Jacquenetta of Brummagem

Ch. Magor Mint Julep of Trebor

Ch. Oyster Bay's Lady Sadie

Ch. Rambunctious Lickety Split

Ch. Westbrook Windborne

1982

Ch. Ann-Dee's Billy Budd

Ch. Aricon Chief Eye Shy

Ch. Banbury Barnstormer

Ch. Brigadore Barron of Bedrock

Ch. Brighton's Murphy of Grandview

Ch. Magor Midas Touch

Ch. Terriwood's Merrimac

Ch. Trebor Troubador

Ch. Westbrook Wild One

Ch. Wyndham's Sir Cedric The Bear

Ch. Banbury Bow's Heart of Bedrock

Ch. Bandetta of Brummagem

Ch. Bonney's Ms. Lillian

Ch. Brobar Showpiece

Ch. Brummagem Genuine Risk

Ch. Essex Evita of Rapparee

Ch. Kearby's Merry Dancer

Ch. Pyreril's Milky Way

Ch. Westbrook Whiz-Bang

1983

Ch. Banbury Briared

Ch. Bulwark's Iceni Just William

Ch. Casanova's Crusader of
   Headstrong

Ch. Catrana Eyeopener of Aricon

Ch. Cinema the Omen of Westbrook

Ch. Cinema The Whiz of Westbrook

Ch. Domino Repete of Cedarcroft

Ch. Dress Circle Flash Gordon

Ch. Headstrongs Heritage

Ch. Iceni's Pilgrim of Med O Lyn

Ch. Iceni Son of Corduroy

Ch. Stewart's Nutmeg

Ch. Westbrook Wishful Thinking

Ch. Banbury Bendetta of Bedrock

Ch. Banbury Brassy Lass

Ch. Feisty Cock Robyn

Ch. Huntsman's No Jemima

Ch. Iceni Penny Lane of Beefeater

Ch. Iceni Rhapsody of Med O Lyn

Ch. Kuon Kalypso

Ch. Lady Ann-Dee's Red Teddy Bear

Ch. Rapparee Rainbow Tour

Ch. Terron's Tallahassee Lassie

Ch. Zodiac Star Attraction

1984

Ch. Abraxas Armonit

Ch. Banbury Bellringer

Ch. Banbury Sargent Major

Ch. Futura's Kidd Jabba

Ch. Iffinest Amadeus

Ch. Iffinest Local Hero

Ch. Jocko's Jack Frost

Ch. Meregis Pot Black of Abraxas

Ch. Nautilus Monsoon Moonray

Ch. Sheetz' Pooder of Penzance

Ch. Vicvin Shadowood Eyewitness

Ch. Westbrook White Hot

Ch. Action's Leading Lady

Ch. Autum's Amor

Ch. Bullock's Brown Sugar

Ch. Jocko's Almond Bark

Ch. Banbury Bachelor's Button, ROM 1977.

Ch. Sylabull Sailin' Shoes ROM, 1984.

Ch. Agate's Bohemian Girl, ROM 1980.

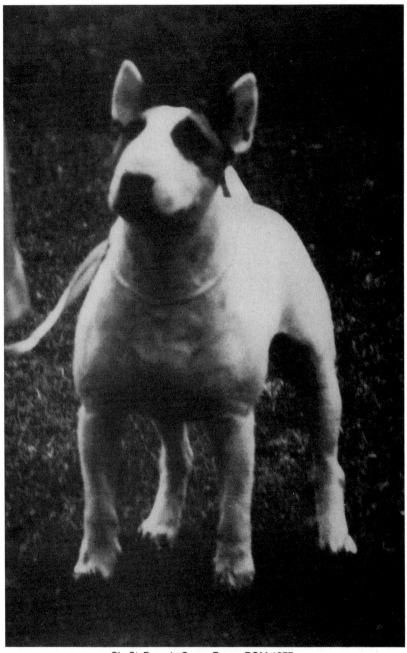

Ch. St. Francis Gypsy Rover, ROM 1977.

Ch. Jocko's Silver Show Off
Ch. Jolly's Toot Toot Tootsie
Ch. Pyreril's Bodicear
Ch. Shavin's Queen of Hearts
Ch. Sylabull Sailin' Shoes
Ch. Zodiac Starlet II

1985

Ch. Booksale Beau Brummel
Ch. Bonney's Repossed
Ch. Chelsea Knight of the Condor
Ch. Fastnet of Iffinest
Ch. Ghabar Midnight Son
Ch. Headstrong's Bullyrock Boris
Ch. Iceni Micklefell
Ch. Iffinest Brian Boru
Ch. Jobrulu Corydalis

Ch. Kuon King Cobra of Sussex
Ch. Metry's Warlord Excaliber
Ch. Shadowood's Mighty Sting
Ch. Ann Dee's Headstrong Applause
Ch. Banbury Beguine
Ch. Banbury Bittersweet
Ch. Booksale Action and Drama
Ch. Brummagem Barcarole
Ch. Catrana Sandra Bella
Ch. Durena Kristobel
Ch. Garalee's Emma Lou O'Faze
Ch. Rambunctious Riptide
Ch. Royalbon's Eyecatcher
Ch. Westbrook Walking Song
Ch. Zodiac Jarrogue Prima Donna

Ch. Rapparee Banbury Sweet Sixteen ROM, 1980.